English Landscaping and Literature
1660–1840

EDWARD MALINS

English Landscaping
and Literature

1660-1840

LONDON
OXFORD UNIVERSITY PRESS
NEW YORK TORONTO
1966

Oxford University Press, Ely House, London W.1

GLASGOW NEW YORK TORONTO MELBOURNE WELLINGTON
CAPE TOWN SALISBURY IBADAN NAIROBI LUSAKA ADDIS ABABA
BOMBAY CALCUTTA MADRAS KARACHI LAHORE DACCA
KUALA LUMPUR HONG KONG

Printed in Great Britain by
W. & J. Mackay & Co. Ltd., Fair Row, Chatham

FOR
Francis Warner

Preface

Many books have recently been written about the horticultural and practical aspects of English landscape gardening. This is not another such book, but is an endeavour to trace the direct influence of contemporary writers and artists on the formation of these landscapes. To some extent I have treated the development chronologically, starting with Milton, whose idea of the perfect garden was so different from his monarch's imported French notions; then to Addison in *The Spectator* and Alexander Pope in his 'Moral Essays', both of whom implicitly restate the philosophic theories of Lord Shaftesbury's *Characteristicks*. In political and social terms, these theories outlined a love of reasoned freedom; in landscaping, a belief in the rightness of a moderate Aristotelian improvement of Nature by Art. And this was obviously antithetical to the formalism of Le Nôtre's gardens reflecting the despotism of Louis XIV. Nor did the clipped yew and box of Dutch gardens, introduced by William and Mary, become popular in England. In both French and Dutch examples Nature was disciplined, ruled, and proportioned by Art—an autocratic concept. So the English love of liberty threw down perimeter walls, and formed a Lockeian contract between Art and Nature in which each mutually respected the other.

Fortunately, Alexander Pope was also a painter, and in the creation of his own garden at Twickenham, for which he was nationally famous, he collaborated with William Kent. Similarly, lesser poets, like James Thomson and William Shenstone, came to see created landscape in visual terms; and it was not uncommon for great landowners like Henry Hoare of Stourhead or George Lyttelton of Hagley to be able to draw competently and be sufficient connoisseurs of painting to view landscaping with artists' eyes. Indeed, many young men returning from the Grand Tour brought with them memories of the perfect landscape of the Roman campagna as seen through the eyes of Claude Lorrain or Gaspar Poussin. These they tried to re-create on their own estates in England.

By so doing they were unconsciously reaffirming in practical terms the concepts of Longinus, the first-century Greek philosopher translated by Boileau—'art is perfect just when it seems to be nature, and nature successful when the art underlies it unnoticed'. And when by the middle of the eighteenth century Edmund Burke had analysed, and Mark Akenside had paraphrased in verse, Longinus's distinctions between Sublimity and Beauty—the former in majestic, rough, and dark forms, the latter in colourful, smooth, and cheerful objects—the philosophic and aesthetic background to landscaping was set. Soon after this Hogarth followed with his analysis of the perfect line of Grace which he thought to be serpentine, intricate, varied, and above all, universally observed in nature. So it was easy to translate Hogarth's concept into landscaping terms on ground in which a hatred of straight lines in the French fashion had already been sown.

The most famous landscaper to follow Burke's tenets of the Beautiful was Capability Brown, whose ruthless clearing on a grand scale aroused much criticism. He was not a painter, but treated Nature as a raw goddess whom he thought he could improve by imitating only her best characteristics. In landscape terms, he and his followers believed that the rhythms of paths and vistas, the counterpoint of trees and lawn, the dynamic surprises of buildings and rocks and the modulations of streams and lakes could arouse moods of melancholy, excitement, or calm by which the Man of Taste, if sensitive, might be morally elevated. This associationist concept of the aesthetic and the moral naturally induced much criticism and satire, whether in the letters of Horace Walpole, the plays of Garrick, or the novels of Peacock. In addition, later landscapers like Humphry Repton, in the Brownian tradition lined up against those who thought in more Picturesque terms, deriving from Longinus's idea of Sublimity. The volleys fired were long and bitter, and even Jane Austen took sides by casting her heroines as lovers of the Picturesque like herself and ridiculing the work of Repton.

So we arrive at the final chapter in the flowering of the Picturesque before 1840. But throughout all this, in the background, the soft melancholy music of *sic transit gloria mundi* echoes in the ruins where Nature had once again triumphed over Art, and landscapes disintegrate quicker than buildings. Yet whether our ancestors who landscaped were believers in the Sublimity of the Picturesque or the Beauty of a Brownian landscape, they had a genius for respecting the Spirit of the Place, inspired by a unique succession of writers, artists, and gardeners. They created the corpus of what Sir Kenneth Clark has described as one of the finest contributions to the arts of Europe, and in so doing changed the face of much of England for the better. Its fate today is tragic.

I should especially like to thank Mr. A. H. Buck, Professor Sir Anthony Blunt, Professor Walter Kaiser, Miss Ann Sutherland, Miss S. Tucker, Dr. Francis Warner, and Mr. Kenneth Woodbridge for their scholarly advice so generously given; and I am most grateful to Mr. James Lees-Milne for his comments on my script. I am also indebted to Mr. J. Shum Cox, Librarian of Bristol University, and to Mr. John Farrell, Assistant Librarian, for their constant and unsparing help in finding material; likewise to the Librarian of the Guildhall Library and the staffs of the Bath and Bristol Reference Libraries. I am grateful for the help of Mr. T. S. Wragg, Keeper of the Chatsworth Collection; Mrs. Francis Bacon of Chippenham Park, Ely; Dr. F. S. Grimwood, Warden of Moor Park College; Commander E. S. Satterthwaite, Secretary of the Garrick Club; Dr. Peter Murray and Mr. Michael Rinehart, Witt Librarians of the Courtauld Institute of Art; and to Dr. John Malins and Mr. Jeremy Jessel as well as students of the Bath Academy of Art for their practical assistance on more than one occasion. I have also been fortunate in having at my disposal the photographic skill of Mr. Richard Morling and Mr. Alan Hamilton. I am moreover indebted to Mrs. Francis Nott for her tireless and efficient work in proofreading. Finally, I am under an obligation to the owners of the many houses I have visited, who, with their staffs, have so often given me useful information not to be found in books.

Contents

Plates

French Influence Criticized

*. . . the most pleasant of all outward pastimes is . . .
to walk amongst orchards, gardens, bowers, mounts,
and arbours, artificiall wildernesses, green thickets,
arches, groves, lawns, rivulets, fountains and such
like pleasant places.*

ROBERT BURTON, *Anatomy of Melancholy*

MILTON was said by Horace Walpole to have been the
poetic inspiration of English landscape gardening. He based
this premise on passages in 'Paradise Lost' describing the
Garden of Eden. This scene as delineated by Milton lacked any of
the regular plan or formal features of a seventeenth-century garden,
possessing instead a wild variety of terrain, a natural freedom, light
and shadow, open fields, and contrasting views. So Walpole found
these characteristics synonymous with those of the romantic gardens of his own day at Stourhead and Hagley.

> Of *Eden*, where delicious Paradise,
> Now nearer, Crowns with her enclosure green,
> As with a rural mound the champain head
> Of a steep wilderness, whose hairie sides
> With thicket overgrown, grottesque and wilde,
> Access deni'd; and over head up grew
> Insuperable highth of loftiest shade,
> Cedar, and Pine, and Firr, and branching Palm,
> A Silvan Scene, and as the ranks ascend
> Shade above shade a woodie Theatre
> Of stateliest view.[1]

[1] 'Paradise Lost', Book IV, lines 132–42.

And in a later passage Milton shows that it is not Art but Nature which is predominant.

> Flours worthy of Paradise which not nice Art
> In Beds and curious Knots, but Nature boon
> Powrd forth profuse on Hill and Dale and Plaine,
> Both where the morning Sun first warmly smote
> The open field, and where the unpierc't shade
> Imbround the noontide Bowrs: Thus was this place,
> A happy rural seat of various view;[1]

At first sight it seems that Milton manifested exceptional vision in thus describing the Garden, for he can never have known such a scene. Yet Walpole, and Stephen Switzer the royal gardener before him, must have forgotten that Tasso in his 'Gerusalemme liberata' (1575) had portrayed a garden in terms even more suitable as a starting-point for the conception of English landscaping in Walpole's time. In the garden of Armida, Art is more specifically concealed by Nature; and there are silver lakes, crystal streams, cool vales, sunny hills, groves, caves and grottoes as well as the flowers, fruits and green of Milton's scenery. John Hoole (1743) translates it as

> Art show'd her utmost power, but art conceal'd
> With greater charms the pleas'd attention held.
> It seem'd as nature play'd a sportive part
> And strove to mock the mimic works of art.[2]

Nevertheless, the typical garden in Milton's time was that shown in the prints of another book he read, *L'Adamo* (1617),[3] a sacred drama by the Florentine Giovanni Ardieni. Many of the characters and much of the action in the development of the same theme—the Fall of Man—is similar to 'Paradise Lost'. There are, for example, God the Father, Michael and his Angels; Satan, Lucifer, and Beelzebub; Adam and Eve, the Serpent, Death, and, in addition, the

---

[1] ibid., lines 242–8.

[2] *L'Arte che tutto fa, nulla si scopre.*
  Stimi (si misto il culto e col negletto)
  Sol naturali, e gli ornamenti, e i siti.
  Di Natura arte par, che per diletto
  L'imitatrice sua scherzando imiti.

[3] Voltaire, in his *Essai sur la Poésie Épique* (1726), Chap. IX, says that Milton saw *L'Adamo* at Milan in his youth.

Seven Deadly Sins, who dance with the Devil at one point. To compare the vaudeville of *L'Adamo* with the epic tragedy of 'Paradise Lost' is impossible, so great is Milton's conversion of absurdity to sublimity. And the Garden of Eden is one example of this. Ardieni's Adamo is appropriately surrounded by 'clipt hedges, square parterres, strait walks, trees uniformly lopt, regular knots and carpets of flowers, groves nodding at groves, marble fountains and water-works'.[1] Milton's Adam needed a less confined environment as the child of a God who could not be presumed to have created a garden made with the obvious trappings of Man.

But for Charles II's wisdom in preventing the more fanatical Cavaliers from taking revenge on Milton as one of Cromwell's 'murderous crew', he would never have written 'Paradise Lost'.[2] Charles also acted wisely on realizing that the countryside had been almost denuded of trees by the Tudors, and had suffered in the Civil War, so causing a serious shortage of hard wood for the Navy. He therefore encouraged John Evelyn to write *Sylva* (1664) in the hope that instructions in planting, propagating, and pruning of trees would help to provide timber and improve the landscape. Those who read his book may have wished to find out more of forestry, or of recent botanical and horticultural discoveries, or just to enjoy the improvement of their estates. Evelyn's wide knowledge was presented with reassured clarity and urbanity, yet spiced with quaint anecdotes, such as one in which he speculated on the wood used for the Cross. He was the most widely read man of his age, and seems to have been at home in discussions on forestry, science, architecture, the visual arts, and literature. Therefore the book was immediately popular and went through many editions, until 1786, when it was finally edited by Dr. Hunter, F.R.S., with as many notes as text. Evelyn was right in thinking that his book would encourage planting, for the figure has been reliably put at nearly a million new trees, though planting was a rare habit then as now.

Men seldom plant trees till they begin to be wise, that is till they grow old and find by Experience the prudence and necessity of it.

[1] Joseph Warton, *An Essay on the Genius and Writings of Pope* (London, 1772).
[2] His *Defence of the English People* justifying the King's execution particularly enraged them.

E.L.L.–B

When Ulysses, after a ten years' absence, was returned to Troy, and, coming home, found his aged father planting of trees, he asked him why (being now so far advanced in years) he would put himself to the fatigue and planting that which he was never likely to enjoy the fruits of? The good old man (taking him for a stranger) gently replied, I plant against my son Ulysses comes home.

Evelyn's *Diary* has constant references to gardens, at home and in Europe; for when on a journey he would stop to examine estates, buildings and works of art, then reveal his careful visual observation in his subsequent comments. In 1644 he visited many French gardens in and around Paris before going on to Italy. One of the most magnificent seems to have been Cardinal Richelieu's estate at Reuil,[1]

a Parterre, having in the middst divers noble brasse statues, perpetualy spouting Water into an ample Bassin . . . a vast enclosure, containing Vineyards, Corne fields, Meadows, Groves whereoff one is of Perennial Greenes; and Walkes of vast lengthes, so accurately kept and cultivated. . . . In one of these Walkes within a square of tall trees, or rather a Grove is a basilisc of copper, which as it is managed by the Fountaniere, casts Water neere 60 foote high, and will of itselfe move so swiftly that it is almost impossible to escape wetting.[2]

And in the other parts were

fountaines that cast Water of an exceeding height; and Piscinas very large in which two of them have Ilands for fowle . . . a large and very rare Grotto of shell-worke, artificialy stuck on, in the shape of Satyres and other wild fansys; In the middle stands a table of Marble, on which a fountaine playes in divers forms of glasses, cupps, crosses, fanns, crownes &c. Then the Fountaniere represented a showre of raine from the topp which was mett with the slender pissers from beneth; at the going out, two extravagant Musqueteeres shot us with a streme of water comming out very fiercely from their musket barrills.

This has all the ingredients of the French Renaissance gardens before the time of André Le Nôtre. The parterre, of geometric shape,

---

[1] E. S. de Beer, ed., *The Diary of John Evelyn* (Oxford, 1955), Vol. 2, p. 109.

[2] See *New and Rare Inventions of Water Works* by Isaac de Caus, tr. John Leak (1659), for details of such water works which were copied at Wilton. Some were very ingenious. For example, the musical barrel organ turned by water, below a statue of a pan-piper, which plays when the sun shines on it.

with its regularly placed fountains; a 'vast enclosure' divided into symmetrical sections, with cross alleys, even the groves having trees planted quincuncially at regular intervals; the grotto—not as we think of it, like a cave, but set in a classical building—looking on to a parterre or terrace; and, after the Italian model at Villa Lante, a water joke, the salvo from 'musqueteers'' barrels; the perimeter of the whole area forming a rectangle or square, as did each of the sections or compartments.

It is the pattern which Charles II would have seen when in exile in France; but just before returning to England he might also have visited the improvements at Vaux-le-Vicomte for Fouquet, or at Chantilly for Condé. These landscapes of André Le Nôtre, precursors of Versailles improvements for Louis XIV, had features which the geometric plan of Richelieu's garden did not possess. The whole conception was more spacious. At Versailles avenues directed the eye from the palace windows in perspectives to vanishing-points meeting the sky; and vast basins of water, with encircling fountains, reflected the palace. Everything contrived to delude Le Roi Soleil and his Court into feeling that they were the centre of the universe, from which a well-ordered life radiated. Nature was artificially directed; water flowed from impossible distances to arched fountain jets that played to untold heights before dropping on accumulated statuary. One such was Latona and her children, who stood 'on the top of a rock in the middle, on the sides of which are the peasants, some half, some totally changed into frogs, all which throw out water at her in great plenty'. Gray typifies the eighteenth-century English attitude to Versailles:

too much of art; all is forced, all is constrained about you; statues and vases sowed everywhere without distinction; sugar loaves and minced-pies of yew; scrawl-work of box, and little squirting jets-d'-eau, besides a sameness in the walks.[1]

In fact, Nature bowed to the monarch's will to make 'a garden for a great child;'[2] and, fortunately, the scale was of a magnificence which Charles was not able to repeat in England for financial reasons. At Versailles 30,000 soldiers were employed to dig the

[1] Thomas Gray to Richard West, 22 May 1739.
[2] Horace Walpole to Richard West, *c.* 15 May 1739.

Grand Canal; 25,000 grown trees were transplanted from Artois alone; 1,400 jets of water flowed from fountains. Buildings were erected and later torn down; one of these being the Chinese Trianon de Porcelaine, completed in faience in 1670 and replaced in 1688. Le Nôtre's layout was not only vaster, but more interesting than the previous one; for although groves and bosquets were still planted in geometric fashion, the alleys radiated from different ronds-points as spokes from wheels, and not at right-angles as previously. At Chantilly miles of radial avenues in goose-foot style still plunge through the forest, ending in focal points of buildings or statuary.

Charles II was quick to copy. The old Renaissance compartments that Evelyn had seen at Reuil in 1644 had become outmoded by Le Nôtre, and as early as June 1662, Evelyn records the new planting at Hampton Court: 'sweet rows of *limee trees,* and the Canalle for water neere perfected . . . a rich and noble fountaine, of Syrens, statues &: . . . but no plenty of Water . . . all these Gardens might be exceedingly improved, as being too narrow for such a Palace.' Even with the money which Charles constantly received from Louis XIV, he was not able to emulate Versailles, and the three-quarter-mile canal at Hampton Court had insufficient water.[1]

Work also started quickly on St. James's Park bordering the Mall, the 'noblest avenue in Europe'.[2] Less than four months after Charles II's return Pepys remarks that he went to see 'how far they had proceeded in the Pell-Mell and in making a river through the park'; and again on 11 October of that year he observes the engine which carried up the water from the Thames into the canal in the Park, at which sight he was 'very much pleased'. Edmund Waller gives a more detailed account.

> For future shade, young trees upon the banks
> Of the new stream appear in even ranks;
> The voice of Orpheus, or Amphion's hand,
> In better order could not make them stand.[3]

That Amphion should make a wall out of trees, rather than stones might be taken to be satirical; but this is a serious, sycophan-

---

[1] E. S. de Beer, ed., op. cit., Vol. 3., p. 324.
[2] Colen Campbell, *Vitruvius Britannicus* (London, 1717), Vol. 1.
[3] 'On St. James's Park, as lately improved by his Majesty'.

tic poem in which Waller praises his monarch and all his actions, however preposterous. So one doubts the accuracy of his details of the beauties of the park, after reading hyperboles of Charles's body of 'shape so lovely', in which 'no private passions does indulgence find'. Waller has to flatter to the full in order that his assiduous praise of Cromwell may be forgotten. Later, his romantic vision of the park and . . .

> the love that shall be made,
> The Lovers walking in that amorous shade,

becomes the wanton lewdness that Rochester, a contemporary, observed in the same spot, 'Nightly now beneath their shade'.[1] Here Charles and his advisers also walked; among them Samuel Pepys, who remarks how this wish to take the air and walk had become a feature of the English life, so, in their parks, there were 'the best walks of gravell in the world, France having none, nor Italy . . . So our business here being ayre, this is the best way, only with a little mixture of statues, or pots, which may be handsome.'[2] From the moment that the French idea reached England it seems to have been interpreted more freely, for René Rapin in the second book of his *Hortorum libri quattuor* (1665), translated by Evelyn in 1673, advises formality even in the park (*nemus*), with trees planted quincuncially, avenues at right-angles, and beeches clipped to make straight walls. There were two great Versailles-type landscapes made in England at this time, the first being at Boughton, Northamptonshire, by Ralph Montague, Ambassador to the French Court. With the aid of Vandertmeulen, a Dutch gardener, and money from dowries of two of the richest women in the kingdom, he laid out over a hundred acres in the pattern of Le Nôtre: branching radial avenues, water in straight geometric canals, endless parterres and a walled perimeter. Nothing now remains but a broken Pegasus in the fields, and traces of elm avenues stretching far into the country. Montague's cousin, Arthur Capell, 2nd Earl of Essex, with the aid of John Rose, the royal gardener whom Charles

[1] John Wilmot, Earl of Rochester, 'A Ramble in St. James's Park'.
[2] H. B. Wheatley, ed., *Diary of Samuel Pepys* (London, 1893). Conversation with Hugh May, the architect, on 22 July 1666.

had sent to France to study Le Nôtre's methods, laid out similar grounds at Cassiobury in Hertfordshire, which were the finest in detail and site in the south of England. Unfortunately, Essex cannot have seen the results of his labours, as he was implicated in the Rye House plot (1683) and died in the Tower. Nothing recognizable remains of his landscape.

The copper engravings of Kip and Knyff, the Dutchmen, show these and many similar estates, of which the Duke of Beaufort's at Badminton, with its twenty radial avenues stretching far into the country is one of the largest in conception, and of a form which, like many of the others, has completely disappeared.[1] In any other country the great dukes would have been known as princes, and although Lord Montague and William Cavendish were not created dukes until William III's time, their improvements were on a princely scale. Charles Cotton writes in 1681 of 'The Wonders of the Peake', of which the seventh and last is the landscape at Chatsworth, started a few years before the rebuilding of the house. The remaining six Wonders are natural features—wells, hills, rocks, or pot-holes.

> A Country so deform'd, the Traveller
> Would swear those parts Nature's Pudenda were.

In similar physical metaphors, 'Peake's Arse, Intestinum Rectum of the Fiend' and 'catarrh' for a stream, and a 'wart' for a hill, he describes the dark horrors of the countryside around Chatsworth, until he is able to spotlight the pure body of the house and gardens,

> Tis now adorned with Fountains and Cascades
> Terass on Terass with their Stair-cases
> Of brave and great contrivance . . .

and

> . . . the sweetest walks the world can show.
> There Wood and Water, Sun and Shade contend,
> Which shall the most delight and most befriend;
> There Grass and Gravel in one path you meet,
> For Ladies Tend'rer and men's harder feet.

> .   .   .   .

[1] 'Divers of the gentlemen cut their trees and hedges to humour his [the Duke's] vistos; and so plant their hills in his lines for compliment': contemporary, unnamed, quoted by David Green in his *Gardener to Queen Anne* (London, 1956), p. 32.

The Groves where curled brows shade ev'ry lake
Do everywhere such waving Landskips make
As Painter's baffl'd Art is far above,
Who waves and leaves could never yet make move.

So, with this conceit, Cotton's panegyric puts the art of land-scaping before that of painting, on account of the additional quality of movement. In his final eulogy of William Cavendish, Cotton anticipates Shaftesbury in stating the requisite moral qualities of the owner of such an estate:

But that which crowns all this, and does impart
A lustre far beyond the Power of Art,
Is the great Owner, He, whose noble mind
For such a Fortune only was designed . . .

Despite hyperbole in describing the awful terrors of the Peak—later belittled by Defoe when on his Tour—Cotton was right in thinking the alterations at Chatsworth were second to none, for its dramatic site, so suited to an Italianate garden, remains unequalled and very English. For although Grillet, who designed the Great Cascade, was an assistant of Le Nôtre, yet the garden was not entirely centred on the house in the French manner, each of the features having to be seen from its own *point de vue*. Leonard Knyff's perspective drawing of September 1699, shows much detail (Plate I). There are signs of the Cascade, without the water temple, approximately where it is now; and also of the Seahorse fountain in the centre of the Great Parterre on the south front. As yet there is no park across the Derwent on the west side. The first Duke of Devonshire must have much appreciated a prospect, for in 1702 he removed a hill which blocked the view down the valley, so that Defoe hardly recognized the terrain when on his tour in 1725:

The mountain was so entirely gone, that having a strict view of the gardens at my first being there, and retaining an idea of them in my mind, I was perfectly confounded at coming there a second time, and not knowing what had been done; for I had lost the hill and found a new country in view which Chatsworth itself had never seen before.[1]

[1] *Tour through the Whole Island of Great Britain* (Everyman edition, London, 1927), Vol. 2, p. 173.

Another steep site, now a field, was at Dyrham, Gloucestershire, on the east side of the house which was, like Chatsworth, designed by Talman. Here the young Dudley Ryder noted a 'steep cascade of 224 steps, the finest in England except for the Duke of Devonshire's'. If Ryder was accurate, there must have been more steps than at Chatsworth; but he was there on an occasion when he was emotionally upset as the worthless woman with whom he was madly in love had slighted him, and he had, on his own admission, retired to the wilderness to weep.[1] The cascade staircase is at the top of Kip's perspective view (Plate II), and the water can be traced as it flows past fountains, through the long canal, under the greenhouse and offices to the basins on the near side of the house. The wilderness where Dudley Ryder and his companions had 'dinner of some cold things . . . upon the grass', is presumably on the extreme left, opposite the house. |

But in France there were critical voices crying from the metaphorical wilderness. The spirit of discipline, rule and proportion, exemplified by Boileau in literature and by Le Nôtre in his embroidered parterres, straight axial sweeps and bosquets in *pattes d'oie*, was not always appreciated even in his own country. In that they failed to deter Le Nôtre, these critics may have cried in vain; but ultimately they hastened the opening of *clairvoyées* to a freer landscape. Charles Dufresny (1648–1724), dramatist and courtier to Louis XIV, prepared naturalistic plans for Versailles, which were refused on the grounds of expense. Pierre Huet (1630–1721), bishop, and tutor to the Dauphin, criticized the work at Versailles as a

factitious parterre, composed of earth brought together to a plan of M. Le Nôtre, having for its whole decoration but a few rows of box, which never distinguish the season by change of colour; surrounded by vast sanded alleys, very compact and very bare; such a parterre forms the delight of polite society.

Ironically, it is the real *jardin anglais* which eventually supersedes the straight alleys of Le Nôtre in France and the rest of Europe. At

[1] Dudley Ryder, *Diary 1715–16*, transcribed and edited by W. Matthews (London, 1939). Switzer, a more knowledgeable and reliable observer, devotes fourteen pages to Dyrham in *Ichnographia*, and had never seen 'So agreeable a place for the sublimest studies'.

the beginning of the eighteenth century the only English feature of
the French garden was a *parterre à l'anglaise* of grass and flower
borders. It was considered by the French to be 'the plainest and
meanest of all', despite the flowers. Le Blond considered the Embroidery Parterre to be the finest. Its composition of box, a little
grass, sand and 'scales beaten off at the Anvil or Iron Filings',
despite elaborate and intricate baroque designs, must have been
most tedious, except when viewed from the windows of the *piano
nobile*. In fact, a freer progression into the rest of the landscape was
soon to come, and can be seen in the two plans of Marly. In 1686,
after Le Nôtre's and Mansart's operations, it has the typical formality of a French garden; but by 1700, the year of Le Nôtre's death,
sinuous paths and a small Chinese domed kiosque appear in the
bosquets of Louvenciennes. On New Year's Day 1700 the festivities
on a grand scale at the Court of Versailles were Chinese. For some
years Jesuit missionaries had been bringing back novel stories of
Chinese life. Louis le Comte, who was in China in 1685, described
'grottos, little artificial eminences . . . and how they transport
thither by pieces whole rocks, which they heap one upon another
without any further design than to imitate Nature'. At the turn of
the century Fr. Attiret published his *Lettres Edificantes et Curieuses*,
with accounts of the two hundred palaces of the Emperor Ch'en
Lung, surrounded by a landscape of like magnificence: a Grand
Canal with lakes, one with a shoreline of five miles and a palace of
over a hundred rooms set on a central rock. Such descriptions must
have impressed even *le grand monarch*.

This apparent freedom in design, and the particular enchant-
ments which it portrayed, rightly came to be associated with both
Chinese and English thought. The first reference in England to
Chinese landscaping is in Sir William Temple's *Upon the Garden of
Epicurus* (1685). After negotiating the Triple Alliance with Holland
and Sweden, which tried to save Europe from French domination,
Temple retired, at the height of his career, and left the Court for
his country house at Sheen, 'hard by Richmond', and after 1680 for
Moor Park, near Farnham, Surrey. For the remaining years of his
life he became the Epicurean philosopher, reading and writing
amongst his vines and fruit trees; even visits from William III,

who wished to persuade him to become Secretary of State, could not lure him away. 'The pleasures of the senses, for a private man, grow a little more choice and refined . . . the most exquisite delights of sense are pursued, in the contrivance and planting of gardens.' So he leads on to the contention that the best Epicurean philosophy combines pleasure with virtue, to make happiness. This was achieved in 'tranquillity of mind' and 'indolence of body', and what better place than a garden? Epicurus had been one of the first to have a garden in Athens (though many Athenians had farms outside), and there he worked and taught.

This was Temple's model, and he eventually describes his 'perfect garden' at Moor Park in Hertfordshire, after which he had named his own. The estate had originally been made by Lucy, Countess of Bedford, the patroness of John Donne; but Temple admits that during his lifetime it had passed 'through several hands that have made great changes'.

It lies on the side of a hill (upon which the house stands) but not very steep . . . the great parlours open into the middle of a terrace gravel-walk that is even with it, and which may be . . . 300 paces long, and broad proportion; the border set with standard laurels, and at large distances, which have the beauty of orange-trees out of flower and fruit: from this walk are three descents by many stone steps, in the middle and at each end, into a very large parterre. This is divided into quarters by gravel-walks, and adorned with two fountains and eight statues in the several quarters.

So far it is of a typical French geometric plan. Below, there were cloisters covered in vines, and from the middle of the parterre were more symmetrically placed steps leading to a grotto in a shady fruit garden, in a 'wilderness'. This might be thought to be an unkempt area, and indeed some have taken that third of Francis Bacon's ideal garden[1] for princes, which he designated 'wilderness', to imply a freedom from formality. But this was not the case. There is an exact description of such an area at Henrietta Maria's house at Wimbledon:[2]

[1] *Essays*, 'Of Gardens' (London, 1902), p. 129.
[2] *Parliamentary Survey of Wimbledon*, Survey No. 72, Record Office, November 1649.

The Wilderness (a work of vast expense to the maker thereof) consists of many young trees, woods, and sprays of a good growth and height, cut and formed into several ovals, squares and angles, very well ordered; in most of the angular points whereof, as also in the centre of every oval, stands one Lime tree or Elm. All the alleys of this wilderness, being in number eighteen, are of gravelled earth, very well ordered and maintained, the whole being compiled with such order and decency, as that it is not one of the least ornaments of the said Manor.

After his description of Moor Park, which could hardly have been more formal in layout, Temple describes a freer method of landscaping, by the Chinese: 'there may be other forms, wholly irregular, that may for ought I know, have more beauty than any others'. He has seen these in some places of 'extraordinary disposition of nature', and he has heard of them in China, where the way of life is quite different from England. He remarks that the Chinese say that a boy can plant avenues of trees in straight lines opposed to one another; but that it requires some imagination in 'contriving figures, where the beauty shall be great and strike the eye, but without any order or disposition of parts, that shall be commonly or easily observed. And when this has been successful, they say the sharawadgi is fine or admirable.'[1] But Temple does not advise anyone to try this difficult task, as twenty to one he will fail; whereas in making a parterre it is not easy to make faults.

In fact, these observations on sharawadgi should not be taken to be his recommendation for greater freedom in English landscaping; and his own grounds at Moor Park were formally Dutch, a style which his wife, Dorothy Osborne, and he may have grown to like when he was Ambassador at the Hague. The Chinese style was for him a curiosity from a civilization very different from our own; and it was certainly not imitated in his own garden. As can be seen in the perspective view (Plate III), the ground slopes westwards from the house to the formal canal, and this area was terraced and laid out as garden by Sir William Temple. There is no sign of sharawadgi, the canal and the Broad Walk bounding the level, symmetrical

[1] For the meaning of the word sharawaggi/sharawadgi, see S. Lang and N. Pevsner, 'Temple and Sharawaggi', *Architectural Review*, December 1949.

parterres and bowling green. The whole garden area, according to Christopher Hussey (*Country Life*, 25 November 1949), was about five acres.

A frequent visitor to Temple's Moor Park was the antiquarian and physician, Sir Thomas Browne (1605–82), whose incantatory metaphysical prose in *The Garden of Cyrus* (1658) so charms the ear.

Nor will the sweetest delight of Gardens afford much comfort in sleep; wherein the dulnesse of that sense shakes hands with delectable odours; and though in the Bed of *Cleopatra*, can hardly with any delight raise up the ghost of a Rose.

Magically, Browne unfolds an endless, curious knowledge: a quincunx, or network plantation is not only an aspect of the planets but, as Coleridge later remarked, 'in bones, optic nerves, in roots of trees, in leaves', and this Browne discusses at length.

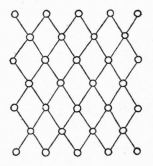

'What looks better than quincunx layout, which is in line whichever way you look?'

The five trees were so set together that 'a regular Angularity and thorough Prospect was left on every side'. Thus, as we can see in Knyff's and Kip's bird's-eye views, did landowners plant, though not perhaps influenced by Sir Thomas Browne as much as by André Le Nôtre; for, in France, not only orchards, but woods, radiations of roads and even houses were quincunxed.

Before coming to England in 1689, William III and Mary had had much experience in landscaping at Het Loo, their favourite royal palace, and unfortunately, Englishmen showed their loyalty not just by harmless planting of orange trees but by rooting up their existing gardens and planting in the Dutch manner. This is what Queen Mary soon did at Hampton Court, her favourite palace in England. First she ordered the lime trees of Charles II (then thirty years old) to be transplanted, and then added more water and fountains near the house. She disliked the sour smell of box, so the scrolls and *bordures* in 'lace patterns'[1] were also dug up, and a wilderness with a labyrinth was put in their place by Henry Wise. Queen Anne parsimoniously neglected the gardens. Thus were landscapes torn apart and replaced by royal personages and their subjects for the next two hundred years, so that today we have few examples left of original designs.

These Dutch gardens of William and Mary resembled the Renaissance garden of pre-Le Nôtre times in that they were divided into one spatial unit which followed another: but the boundaries of these were more often in canals and ditches than in hedges. Their outlines were similarly rectangular and their parterres of scrolled box were after the French fashion. For a hundred years Dutch gardens were still formed in this way, perhaps 'more confined, more covered with trivial ornaments, and more intersected with waters, either stagnant or of which the current is imperceptible'.[2] The divisions of the compartments were often by twenty-foot hedges of thick beech, hornbeam or oak, sometimes tied to frames and sheared. Yew and box were often cut to resemble brick walls, and pyramids were treated in verdure. Even grottoes were artificial and formal, without a naturally grotesque or fantastic appearance, as in Italy. Solar clocks, dials in box and painted hedges with windows, curiously shaved, were additional adornments. William Beckford's account in 1780, when on his way between Amsterdam and Utrecht, shows how little had changed.[3] Along this route were country houses of 'opulent citizens' with 'endless avenues and stiff parterres, scrawled and flourished in patterns like the embroidery of an old maid's work-bag'.

[1] John Gibson, *A Short Account of Several Gardens near London* (London, 1691).
[2] Christian Hirschfeld, *Theorie der Gartenkunst* (Leipzig, 1775).
[3] Jan Van der Groen, *Den nederlandischen Hortenier* (Amsterdam, 1669).

We gain a general idea of landscape layout in the 1690s from that tireless traveller, Celia Fiennes, who visited most of the aristocratic houses up and down the country. Although she was a Whig and in sympathy with contemporary ideas in architecture, she never mentions any form of landscaping other than what appears to have been formal French or Dutch. With the exception of Chatsworth and Wilton, which she describes at length, the same conventional terms are used for twenty or more large estates that she visited: 'rows of trees paled in gravel walks, fine cut hedges, flower-pots on walls, terraces, statues, fountains, basins, grass squares and exact, uniform plots'. Even at Woburn where the gardens were new, and therefore 'fine', she describes no especial features to distinguish them from any of the others. Nor do there appear to be more specific references in the Bedford papers, except that, in 1685, a new plantation was made and walled round with bricks baked locally. For Celia Fiennes there seems to have been little to distinguish the settings of Broadlands, Longford, Burghley, Burton Agnes, Ingestre, Witley Court and others.

In the long run, a greater freedom in landscape design in England was inevitable. The subjugation of Nature by Art, whether in the detail of clipped trees and hedges, or in the basically concentric plan of French gardens, was fundamentally autocratic. It had none of the strong Whig virtues of benevolence, moderation or reason, and it required an extravagant expenditure of money which fortunately the English, and, in particular, their monarchs did not possess. Those majestic levels of the French garden, with a flat perimeter wall, were an additional autocratic feature which was fortunately almost impossible to construct in England; for the average terrain in the south may be said to be more gently hilly than in northern France, giving visual delights which the French never knew. Above all, it was the English rainfall which hastened the development away from French methods. Even with artificial watering, flowers and grass parterres wilt in France, whereas in an English garden they are the chief features; and so the smooth, wide walks of grass provided an opportunity for the English love of exercise, which was unknown to a Frenchman or an Italian.

After the 'sensible Revolution', as Professor Tawney calls it, a scorn of French ways grows, and what Locke meant by freedom, a contract between people and ruler, in landscaping might imply a contract between art and nature, in which each respected the other. Perhaps the greatest exponent of this freedom was Pope, who repeatedly shows his scorn of French ways, in criticism and land-scaping.

> But *Critic Learning* flourish'd most in *France*.
> The *Rules*, a Nation, born to serve, obeys,
> And *Boileau* still in Right of *Horace* sways.
> But *we*, brave *Britons*, *Foreign Laws* despis'd,[1]

Ironic tho' [handwritten annotation]

This was published in 1711, the year of Boileau's death; yet it is strange that in this passage Pope should have chosen Boileau as the exemplar of Horatian sway, for in adopting Horace's idea of 'bliss in retirement' Boileau and Pope had much in common. They both praised unadorned Nature, and both thought that Art should be based on a study of Nature, and both upheld the sway of Reason. How Pope achieved this at Twickenham will be seen in Chapter 2. In the meantime, it was John Vanbrugh, that 'most singular archi-tect', who nailed down the coffins of the French formal gardeners, although their ghosts still walked on the parterres immediate to the house.

By directing Henry Wise, the royal gardener, Vanbrugh planned the landscapes of Blenheim, Castle Howard, Eastbury, and Seaton Delaval; his imagination sweeping away the regular avenues of the French style by moulding the middle and far distances from the houses as Nature directed. As early as 1705, at Castle Howard, he employed Wise to lay out a parterre and then, in the surrounding landscape, formed regular avenues furnished with arches and a crossing. But, on the east side, he preserved Ray Hill, curving his chief walk from the castle round it, despite opposition from Wise, who had wished to clip the wood into a star shape. Vanbrugh then placed a bridge and a pyramid on a hill eccentric to the house. Similarly at Blenheim, again employing Wise for the formal parterre in the vicinity of the house, he treated the surrounding landscape more freely than in any previous example: the shores of the lake to

---

[1] 'An Essay on Criticism', lines 712–15.

the north being left with natural, sinuous banks, rather than being canalized. However, it was Vanbrugh's wish to preserve old Woodstock Manor, one of the existing features of the landscape, which reveals how far he had left Le Nôtre behind in the alleys of Versailles. Le Nôtre would quickly have demolished any object which detracted from his geometric, ordered plans based on the house.

In his *Reasons for Preserving Part of the Old Manor, 11th June, 1709,* Vanbrugh shows how much he appreciated the concept behind a ruin; in this case, the history and romance of Henry II entertaining his fair Rosamond. Also he was strongly conscious of the visual impact of this ruin in the landscape that he wished to make.

'There is perhaps no one thing, which the most Polite part of Mankind have more universally agreed in; than the Vallue they have ever set upon the Remains of distant Times.' He continues to say that Woodstock Manor had not been erected on 'so Noble or justifiable an Occasion as Blenheim itself: but it was raised by one of the Bravest and most warlike of English Kings'. The association may have been inspired by Michael Drayton's

> *Henry* the Second keepeth (with much care)
> Lord *Cliffords* daughter, *Rosamond* the faire;
> And whilst his Sonnes doe *Normandie* invade,
> He forc'd to *France*, with wond'rous cost had made
> A Labyrinth in *Woodstock*, where unseene
> His Love might lodge safe, from his jealous Queene:[1]

And he goes on to explain the labyrinth, which was, in fact, a paved maze of underground arched vaults which eventually led to the open country, where 'if neede be by secret Issues' the fair Rosamond could take the air.

If the 'Historical Argument' fails, then there is much to be said for preserving it on other grounds.

That part of the Park which is seen from the North Front of the New Building, has little Variety of Objects. Nor does the Country beyond it Afford any Vallue. It therefore stands in Need of all the helps that can be given, which are only two; Buildings and Plantations. These rightly dispos'd will indeed supply all the wants of

---

[1] The Argument to 'The Epistle of Rosamond to King Henry the Second'. W. Hebel, ed., *The Works of Michael Drayton* (Oxford, 1932), Vol. 2, p. 133.

I. Chatsworth: Knyff's perspective view, September 1699, from Kip's *Théatre de la Grande Bretagne*, 1716.

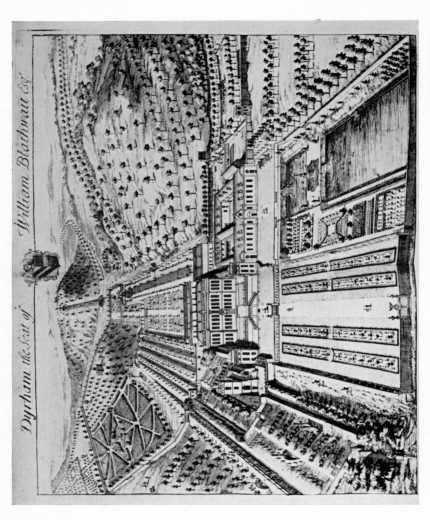

Dyrham _the Seat of_　　　_William Blathwait Esq_

II. Dyrham: Kip's perspective view from Sir Robert Atkyns's _Ancient and Present State of Gloucestershire, 1712_

Nature in that Place. And the Most Agreeable Disposition is to Mix them: in which this Old Manor gives so happy an Occasion for: that were the inclosure filld with Trees (principally Fine Yews and Hollys) Promiscuously set to grow up in a Wild Thicket; so that all the Building left (which is only the Habitable Part and the Chappel) might appear in Two Risings amongst 'em, it would make one of the Most Agreeable Objects that the best of Landskip Painters can invent. And if on the Contrary, this Building is taken away; there then remains nothing but an Irregular, Rugged, Ungovernable Hill.

Despite these cogent arguments for the Picturesque, so movingly stated, he was unsuccessful in his appeal. Unfortunately, the scale on which he conceived Blenheim—one of monumental grandeur befitting the triumphs of an incomparable soldier in whose debt was the whole nation—did not coincide with the ideas of Sarah, Duchess of Marlborough, who from the start had wished for nothing more than a comfortable and convenient house in an unostentatious setting. Furthermore, she showed neither knowledge of nor sympathy with art nor landscaping, so the appeals of Vanbrugh gained nothing but her sarcastic disapproval. After he had roofed over part of the Manor, without consulting her, she accused him of spending the Queen's money on a wretched ruin, and eventually it was torn down and the stones used in the Grand Bridge. Today it is apparent, even after Lancelot Brown's subsequent improvements, how right Vanbrugh was in his wish to preserve the Old Manor ruin; for a sycamore tree, overhanging the water, is a weak substitute for a feature which, when viewed from the house, would have been a focal point of the whole landscape. Even the 'ridiculous bridge' and the Triumphal Gate do not compensate for the lack of buildings.

But perhaps that is better than being overdressed, which has been the fate of Stowe landscape. Here the problem for Vanbrugh was simpler, as the view from the garden front of the house is virtually the only axis of importance. The first extant plan is not earlier than 1739, so it is impossible to assign exactly the authorship of the landscape, but Laurence Whistler makes out a convincing case for Vanbrugh's work, with Bridgeman as assistant.[1] He cites the freedom of style in the Octagon Lake, and the wandering paths,

---

[1] *Sir John Vanbrugh, Architect and Dramatist* (London, 1938).

joining, without formal pattern, fields, woodland, and temples. By 1739 Kent had added many buildings, columns and statues to Vanbrugh's Ionic Rotonda, the Boycott Pavilions and the Temple of Bacchus.

Vanbrugh's landscape work, so full of imagination and freedom, flowered in the philosophic climate at the beginning of the eighteenth century. Much of this was warmed by the benevolent Whig sunshine of Ashley Cooper, 3rd Earl of Shaftesbury (1671–1713), whose essential trust in man's goodness, and whose belief in the certain rightness of passion before reason helped to penetrate the chilled air of Locke's cold reasoning. For Shaftesbury, Taste and Morals harmonized to make the perfect man; and Taste was the product of correct feelings or 'the polite imagination'. This is the future philosophic direction of the century, away from the world of the undervalued imagination of Locke; though his reasonableness lives on in Addison and Thomson. But they also have the compassionate and benevolent sympathy of Shaftesbury, as well as his measured Enthusiasm. It is repeated by Pope in his 'Essay on Man', and again in 'Men's actions can never proceed immediately from Reason: the Passions are to the Mind as the Winds to a Ship'.[1]

In a startling passage Shaftesbury, using the form of Platonic dialogues, takes the idea a step further, for he shows his preference and even Enthusiasm for Nature which has a 'genuine order'. Even 'rude *Rocks*, the mossy *Caverns*, the irregular unwrought *Grottos*, and broken *Falls* of Waters, with all the horrid[2] Graces of the *Wilderness* itself, as representing Nature more, will be the more engaging, and appear with a Magnificence beyond the formal mockery of princely Gardens'.[3] Assuming that 'horrid graces' means nothing more than rough graces and the wilderness to be well ordered, all these features might be included in part of a princely garden. Later he outlines certain features of these princely gardens, showing his preference for ordered wildness. But more important to him is harmony to the eye of 'various shapes and colours agreeably mixed and ranged in lines intercrossing without confusion, and fortunately co-incident',

---

[1] *The Spectator*, No. 408.
[2] For the meaning of 'horrid' see p. 143, n. 2.
[3] *Characteristicks*, Vol. II (1732), The Moralists, Part 3, p. 231.

and still more important is the mind of the Prince, for which he expresses concern lest it might not be answerable in harmony and order. For this purpose he suggests that statues be placed here and there, of 'virtue, fortitude and temperance; hero's-busts, philosopher's heads; with suitable mottos and inscriptions; . . . with all those symmetrys which silently express a reigning order, peace, harmony and beauty!' In placing Man first and Nature's harmony and order as a means to his attaining Virtue, Shaftesbury states one of the themes which were constantly repeated throughout the century. Unfortunately, his 'swelled' style, his 'inflated finical rhapsodies'[1] did not achieve a popularity for the *Characteristicks* as great as that of Sir William Temple's conversational prose.

The most widely influential writing of the time was undoubtedly from Addison, who from the age of 27, for five years travelled in Europe (1699–1704). His reactions to Italy are unfortunately those of an antiquarian and historian rather than an artist, for he writes of Roman remains rather than of contemporary painters. Amphitheatres, baths, grottoes, catacombs, rotundas, bridges, and paved highways are described in detail, as are ancient coins, medals, and statuary. His comments on the scenery at the Alban lake, the Capuchin garden at Albano and the view from the Medici villa are no more than any intelligent traveller with his eyes open would have made. But contemporary painting did not interest him, nor, it seems, did contemporary events, for he left Rome just before the Holy Week celebrations, which were 'the most august and affecting ceremony which is known among men'.[2]

While in France he met the aged Boileau, who talked on literature 'incomparably well', and much of the 'majestic simplicity' of Addison's work in *The Spectator* may have been influenced by his admiration of Boileau's writings. There were hundreds of short-lived journals during the first quarter of the century, but the 555 copies of *The Spectator*, published from 1 March 1711 to 6 December 1712 alone reached a country-wide public, possibly about 10,000 at the finish. The declared purpose of the paper, in the words of

---

[1] Charles Lamb, *The Essays of Elia*, 'The Genteel Style in Writing' (Everyman edition, London, 1906), p. 233.

[2] Lord Macaulay, *Literary Essays*, 'The Life and Writings of Addison' (London, 1852), Vol. 3, p. 450.

Richard Steele, the co-editor, was 'to enter into the Passions of Mankind, and to correct those depraved sentiments that give birth to all those little Extravagances which appear in their outward dress and Behaviour'. For, as Steele said in Number 6, to follow the dictates of passion and humour is 'going into a road that is both endless and intricate'. Nature and reason should also be pursued, for then 'the passage is delightful and what we aim at easily attainable'.

The essays cover a variety of subjects without being repetitious or tedious, and this applies to their comments on landscape. In Number 37, Addison sets the theme in describing the garden of a lady whom Sir Roger de Coverley often visited. Nature and Reason go hand in hand:

> there are rocks shaped into artificial grottoes covered with wood-bines and jessamines . . . the woods are cut into shady walks . . . the springs are made to run among pebbles . . . collected into a beautiful lake that is inhabited by a couple of swans

and which empties itself 'by a little rivulet which runs through a green meadow'.[1] The works of nature are 'more delightful than artificial shows';[2] but even better is a landscape in which the works of Nature resemble those of Art; and, conversely, in a well-laid-out prospect, a work of art rises in value as it resembles nature. This is a restatement of Longinus, 'For art is perfect just when it seems to be nature, and nature successful when the art underlies it unnoticed.' To be unnoticed it has to be organic and not artificial. The state which Thomas Browne describes in *Religio Medici* (1643), 'Now Nature is not at variance with Art, nor Art with Nature', is another repetition of the theme.

It is at this point in the essay that Addison mentions the freer landscapes of the Chinese, who laugh at the plantations of Europe that are laid out by rule and line. He hints at sharawadgi in saying they 'have a word for it', but he does not mention it. In England, he says, the 'marks of the scissors upon every plant and bush' compare unfavourably with the more natural landscape. He would rather an 'orchard in flower' than 'the labyrinths of a finished parterre'. In

---

[1] 12 April 1711.   [2] No. 414, 25 June 1712.

fact, he makes his preferences clear in describing his own garden,[1] with flowers of 10,000 different colours, planted irregularly, and in which 'the blackbirds' music' is more worth than cherries. Unfortunately we have no specific evidence that his garden at Bilton, near Rugby, was planted in this way. He later praises the royal gardeners, George London and Henry Wise, for their preserving, in work at Kensington Palace, the 'beautiful wildness of nature, without affecting the nicer elegancies of art'. In summing up, he joins Temple and Shaftesbury in echoing Epicurus's 'laudable satisfaction' in this 'innocent delight' which should bring with it 'a virtuous habit of mind'.

An anonymous description of landscaping in *The Spectator*, Number 425, of 8 July 1712 bears a resemblance to Le Nôtre's pattern, and the contemporary work of Wise at Melbourne in Derbyshire, or of Lord Burlington at Chiswick. Despite the yews and the water, there is nothing Dutch in it, and much of it is French still:

twelve stone steps to a large square divided into four grass plots, in each of which is a statue of white marble . . . separated from a large parterre by a low wall . . . through iron gates to a long broad walk of the finest turf, set on each side with tall yews, and on either bordered by a canal, which on the right divides the walk from a wilderness parted into variety of alleys and arbours, and on the left from a kind of amphitheatre, which is the receptacle of a great number of oranges and myrtles.

The campaign against the Dutch theme is carried on in *The Guardian*, Steele's successor to *The Spectator*. Was Pope thinking of the ridiculous topiary work at Levens Hall—the umbrellas, mushrooms and chessmen which clutter the area round the house—when he concocted his satirical Catalogue of Greens, as if at a sale of trees that had been tonsured into whimsical shapes?[2]

ADAM and EVE in Yew; ADAM a little shatter'd by the fall of the Tree of Knowledge in the Great Storm; EVE and the Serpent very flourishing.

The Tower of BABEL, not yet finished.

---

[1] No. 477, 6 September 1712.   [2] *The Guardian*, No. 173, 29 September 1713.

St. GEORGE in Box; his Arm scarce long enough, but will be in a Condition to stick the Dragon by next APRIL.

A GREEN DRAGON of the same, with a Tail of Ground Ivy for the present.

N.B. THESE TWO NOT TO BE SOLD SEPARATELY.

EDWARD the BLACK PRINCE in Cypress.[1]

A LAURUSTINE Bear in Blossom, with a Juniper Hunter in Berries.

A pair of Giants, STUNTED, to be sold cheap.

A Queen ELIZABETH in Myrtle,[2] which was very forward, but Miscarried by being too near a Savine.[3]

An Old Maid of Honour in Wormwood.

A topping[4] BEN JOHNSON in Lawrel.

Divers eminent Modern Poets in Bays, somewhat blighted, to be disposed of a Pennyworth.

A Quickset Hog, shot up into a Porcupine, by its being forgot a Week in rainy Weather.

A Lavender Pigg with Sage[5] growing in his Belly.

NOAH'S ARK in Holly; standing on the Mount;[6] the ribs a little damaged for want of Water.

A Pair of MAIDENHEADS in Firr, in great forwardness.[7]

In thus ridiculing topiary[8] work, and extolling a freer landscape, Pope set the way for the development of that very English contribution to the art of landscaping, in which Art serves Nature, while Nature improves Art, in a mutual and reasonable freedom. By a

---

[1] Associated with funeral black.

[2] The symbol for lovers in Elizabethan poetry.

[3] Savin: a coniferous shrub of the genus Juniperus. Its oil is a powerful irritant.

[4] Topping: fine or noble. A word condemned by Samuel Johnson as 'low'.

[5] A reminder of cooking.

[6] Mount: a play on words implying either Mount Ararat or the artificial hill often a feature of formal gardens.

[7] On a fir tree the male flowers are a long way from the fruit, so Pope may be thinking of uncontaminated virginity.

[8] In Roman times, *topiarius*, the pleacher, shaped evergreens and also managed trailing plants.

fortunate coincidence, the imaginations of young Englishmen were further stimulated by what they saw in art and landscape in Italy, and many of them viewed the contemporary artistic scene with greater perception than Addison had shown. In fact, the next few years brought to fruition that especial English landscape, inspired by painters and justified by writers, which we now take so much for granted.

Kent, Burlington, Pope and Friends

. . . all must be adapted to the Genius *and* Use *of
the Place, and the Beauties not forced into it, but
resulting from it . . .*
ALEXANDER POPE, Argument to 'Moral Essays IV'

AT the same time as Shaftesbury and Addison were theoretic-
ally urging a greater freedom in the landscape, practical
advice came from the royal gardener, Stephen Switzer. His
Ichnographia Rustica is the ideal book of its kind, written by a gardener
who has endless horticultural knowledge, but who can also see a
landscape as an artist, and his craft as an historian. The first volume
is largely concerned with the history of planting and gardening,
from the Creation to the eighteenth century, and in the latter part
he criticizes his immediate predecessors for their 'medley of Clipt
Plants, Embroidery etc.'. Although he seems to have some knowledge of contemporary French gardening, he had never been abroad,
nor does he mention Le Nôtre. But he had read John James's
translation of Le Blond's *The Theory and Practice of Gardening* (1712)
on which he based his disapproval of French methods, with the
exception of Le Blond's ingenious method of preserving both the
view and a fence for cattle—'thorough viewes with concealed
ditches called Ah! Ah! which surprise and make one call, Ah! Ah!'
Switzer could also see the results of foreign influence in Charles II's
large semicircle at Hampton Court; in the replanting of St. James's
Park; and in Queen Mary's Great Garden by the river, in the Dutch
manner, 'too thick with box'.

Switzer's ideal must have been realized at Castle Howard, where

Henry Wise was constrained upon by Lord Carlisle to leave Ray Hill—an incomparable wood on the side of a hill—rather than hew it into a star to suit an overall design. There is, in these recommendations of Switzer, a very eighteenth-century emphasis on moderation. Firstly, *in utile dulci*, in which both pleasure and profit should be considered, avoiding the extravagances of French methods that were unconcerned with cultivation. Secondly there should be *ingentia rura*, the Grand Manner as opposed to the clipped plants in the various compartments of French and Dutch gardens. And above all, a prospect is essential from the house—'the adjacent country should be laid open to the view', and the eye should not be imprisoned by walls or other obstructions. One should not have to look at a series of straight lines converging on ronds-points, but at 'the extensive charms of nature and the voluminous tracts of pleasant country', which should be absorbed into the garden by means of gravel paths and grass, vistas, statuary and perspectives. His third tenet is *simplex Munditiis* of Horace, a noble elegance and decency in the several corresponding parts of the garden.

> In Wit, as Nature, what affects our Hearts
> Is not th' Exactness of peculiar Parts;
> 'Tis not a *Lip*, or *Eye*, we Beauty call,
> But the joint Force and full *Result* of *all*.[1]

One of his finest characteristics, which distinguishes him from many other more famous landscapers, is his horror at the felling of many a 'Noble Oak or sometimes whole lines of these and other umbragious Trees, fell'd to humour the regular and delusive schemes of some Paper Engineers'. One would as soon fire one's house, he says, as cut down such noble trees, for it is the work of many years and ages to grow them again.

The second and third volumes of *Ichnographia* are largely concerned with improvement of soil, action of air and water on vegetation, raising of forest trees, improvements in husbandry, and surveying with a theodolite.

In summarizing, he insists that landscape designs must submit to Nature, rather than make Nature submit to them. Where there

[1] 'An Essay on Criticism', lines 243–6.

was a wood, as at Castle Howard, he would plan paths through it, rather than formalize its perimeter. Even so, his plans for gardens near the house have a certain formality and intrinsic geometricality, similar to his contemporary, Vanbrugh; but there are variety and a balanced proportion of parts. He strongly advises landowners against wall building—an unnecessary expense for a boundary which may limit a prospect. Gravel or sand walks should run through the entire estate, even through cornfields! 'The careless loose tresses of Nature offer more to the imagination than the most delicate Pyramid.' But he realizes, as Vanbrugh did, that the house itself needs to have a terrace of parterre around it, for it looks mean if it is surrounded by a flat lawn.

In direct ideological descent from Switzer was William Kent (1684–1748), the Yorkshire painter, who in 1716 was sent to Rome to study by 'some gentlemen of the country' [county]. There he met Richard Boyle, 3rd Lord Burlington (1695–1753), and this was the start of a lifelong artistic partnership in designing houses, interiors, furniture, and landscapes. Kent's letters, with their extraordinary spelling and grammar, indicate a lack of formal education in his early years: but he must have made up for this empirically by being brought to maturity by the son of Lord Burlington, 'The Apollo of the Arts', whose Palladian light radiated through his coterie in Italy and at home. In later years, the Signior, as Pope called Kent, on account of his smattering of Italian phrases in his writing and conversation,[1] was at home among artists at the St. Luke's Club, treated as an equal by the nobility and the friend of literary men.

Before he returned from Italy in 1719, Lord Burlington had employed Charles Bridgeman, the royal gardener, at his villa at Chiswick. If Eastbury and Stowe were typical of Bridgeman's 'phlegmatic' work, then Chiswick must have been formal and symmetrical also. Although Bridgeman had been known to use the French idea of a sunk fence[2] to allow an uninterrupted view to the

[1] For example, a *disgratzia* when his horse was lamed, or a *purgatzioni* to cure a cold!

[2] John James, *The Theory and Practice of Gardening* (London, 1712). 'The end of this Terass is terminated by . . . an Ah, Ah, with a dry ditch at the foot of it.'

park, his gardens were designed after Le Nôtre's pattern. Not until his work at Rousham does William Kent leap this ha-ha 'and see all Nature as a garden'. At Chiswick he retained some of the formal features of Bridgeman. Among these was a main avenue, four hundred feet long, with radially disposed subsidiary avenues, flanked by close-set trees clipped into walls, and leading to the View of Cain and Abel, the Birdcage, and the Grand Temple. There was also a semicircular exedra of myrtle, in whose niches were antique statues of Cicero, Pompey, and Caesar, filched from Hadrian's Villa at Tivoli. In contemporary engravings one can see that Kent's canal has slightly sinuous banks, in 'French curves', yet its main direction is in a straight line from point to point. There is no real serpentining as appeared in later treatment of lakes, and even the rococo paths in the wilderness were not a new idea, for they are included in Israel Silvestre's plan of the Petit Parc at Versailles, dated 1698. Kent was still working at Chiswick in 1738, but before that the Burlington group had begun to turn against the formality of Bridgeman. In 1736 Thomas Coke, 1st Earl of Leicester, who employed Kent to build Holkham (writing as Lord Lovell), refers to some

damned dull walks at Jo: Windhams those unpictoresk those cold & insipid strait walks wch make the signior sick, to think that they, wch even Mr Pope himself could not by description enliven should be the scenes of such a romantick passion makes me mad.

Two years later, work was still going on at Chiswick under Kent's direction. In September 1738 he tells Lord Burlington that the Cascade will soon be started, and in November he declares that the bridge with the 'Piedastals for the Lyons' at its approach has been completed.

Chiswick is now a public park, with the inevitable asphalt roads beloved by boys who illegally ride their bicycles through the dusk. It deserves, but does not receive, the care bestowed on a national monument, so it is heartening to see that the Ionic Temple is being restored to its elegant beauty after years of neglect. Perhaps the Archimedean screw will be renewed and once again force the waters over the cascade. 'This deep desert solitude' still has more memories of the Burlingtonians than the Victorians, and, maybe, one of the large cedars is that very tree under which 'the said William Kent' would 'solace himself with Syllabubs,[1] Damsels and other Benefits of Nature'.[2]

At Rousham, General Dormer's house in Oxfordshire, Kent again had to remake an earlier layout of Bridgeman's. This time he obliterated all traces of a rectangular garden with terraces on the north side of the house, and made a landscape with no formal avenues, clipped hedges or pleached alleys, by laying out the adjacent country open to the view from an idealized natural setting, in the true Switzer manner. This site has not suffered from subsequent landscapers and still retains an Albano enchantment. A steep concave slope drops down to the winding Cherwell, which is on its way to join mother Isis. The vistas are bordered by woods which enter as wing screens, and are ornamented by ponds, cascades, statues, a Praeternestum, and a serpentine rill. In the contemporary plan, the key-point is the Praeneste[3] or seven-arched portico, with its formal terrace walk above it, from which the surrounding country lies opened. How admirably Kent's conception has come to life can be seen by comparing his original drawing of Venus's Vale with the present view from the Great Pond. Horace Walpole thought that it was Kent's greatest achievement, with its 'Gothic buildings, Arcade from ancient baths, temples, old bridges, Palladian do.; river, slender stream winding in a stone channel through 'grass walks in wood; cascades over grown with ivy; grove of Venus of Medici; the whole, sweet'. And he also thought that 'the opening and retiring of Venus's Vale' may have been modelled on 'Mr. Pope's'. It still enchants, despite uncouth buildings on the skyline in addition to Kent's pinnacled Eye-Catcher. Christopher Hussey rightly describes it as that rarity, 'an organic yet disciplined design,

---

[1] 'Sillabub: a frothy food to be slapped or slubbered up by milking the cow into a vessel containing wine or spirits, spice, etc.'—Wedgwood, *Dictionary of English Etymology* (London, 1859–65).

[2] George Sherburn, ed., *Correspondence of Alexander Pope* (Oxford, 1956), Vol. 4, p. 323: Mock Petition (1741?) to ask Lord Burlington to leave a certain tree standing; written by Pope and signed by Lady Burlington, her two daughters, and four other men friends.

[3] Praenest (Palestrina), one of the most ancient towns of Latium, on a steep hill about twenty miles from Rome. Cool and healthy in summer heat, hence *frigidum Praeneste* in Horace.

applying order loosely yet lucidly to a slice in English country, and, in effect, crystallising Nature'.[1]

Horace Walpole's assumption that Kent and Pope consulted in planning both Rousham and Twickenham is based on visual observation of their work. That they saw each other often there is no doubt. In November 1736 Pope writes to Lord Burlington that he meets the Signior frequently, and is going to him 'in good earnest' to learn what he can and as often as he can. In the same letter in which Kent mentions the work on the cascade at Chiswick, he says that he has called on Pope, who was 'going upon new works in his gardens' that he (Kent) had designed there. And in the same year Kent writes to Lord Burlington that he has seen Pope once only in two months—evidently an exceptional absence for the 'suff'ring trio', as Kent, Pope, and Bolingbroke were called. A quotation from part of the letter will indicate both the intimacy of his relationship with Pope and the originality of his unusual style:

—I had not seen Pope but once this two months before last sunday morning & he came to town the night before the next morning he came before I was up it had raind all night & rain'd when he came I would not get up & sent him away to disturb some body else—he came back and sayd could meet with nobody, I got drest & went with him to Richarsons & had great diversion he shew'd three picturs of Lord Baulingbrok one for himself for Pope, another Pope in a mourning gown with a strange view of the garden to shew the obelisk as in memory to his mothers Death, the alligory seem'd odde to me, but after I found, its to be in the next letters as I suppose some of the witt that was write to Londesbrough[2] will be in print—the son of Richardson[3] & Pope agree'd that popes head was Titziannesco, the old long Glow worm sayd whe have done our best . . .[4]

This is a style which suits gossip, and, in particular, one inimitable fragment in January, 1739,

---

[1] Introduction to Margaret Jourdain, *The Work of William Kent* (London, 1948).

[2] Lanesborough, Lord Burlington's favourite Yorkshire seat.

[3] A portrait of Pope, attributed to Richardson, hangs in the National Portrait Gallery. Another, of the poet and his dog, Bounce, of undoubted attribution, remains where it was originally placed by Lyttelton, above the fireplace in the library at Hagley.

[4] William Kent to Lord Burlington, 28 November 1738.

Pope is very busy, last night came to me about eight a clock in liquor & would have More wine, which I gave him, you may tell Mr Bethell he's very sorry, so am I he's not well, but he lays it all his not takeing a cup of red . . .

Kent followed Bridgeman again, at Lord Cobham's Stowe. As the eighteenth century progressed this was to become one of the show gardens of Europe—on a monumental, four-hundred-acre scale, befitting the wealth of its owner. As usual, Kent cleared away formal gardens and parterres around the house, cut out broad vistas to temples and made the lakes sinuous. Vanbrugh, Gibbs, and Kent in turn designed some of the forty temples, buildings, monuments, statues, arches or bridges that 'enriched' the landscape, as Horace Walpole later remarked. His and others' reactions to this magnificent landscaping will be discovered in a subsequent chapter. While Bridgeman and Kent were working there, Pope visited Lord Cobham from 1725 to 1735 nearly every summer.

They had known each other for many years, and, after Kent had returned with Lord Burlington from Rome, Pope was making his garden at Twickenham, farther up the river from Chiswick. In 1720[1] he had written to Charles Jervas of 'many Draughts, Elevations, Profiles, Perspectives etc. of every Palace and garden propos'd, intended and happily raised, by the strength of that Faculty wherein all great Genius's excel, Imagination', and he enclosed the plans. A few weeks earlier he had described Twickenham as delightful, 'so very airy, and yet so warm, that you will think yourself in a sort of heaven, where the prospect is boundless'.[2] Very quickly his trees 'like new acquaintance brought happily together' were growing nearer each day, and his Tuscan porticoes and Ionic pilasters were attracting the curiosity of those passing in boats. Pope's gardener must have been as skilled as others at that time in planting large trees. It was then not an unusual state of affairs for Lord Dacre to write that he had 'planted above 200 elms, the least of them twenty feet high, and many of them thirty'.[3] Although Pope had only about

---

[1] Alexander Pope to Charles Jervas, dated later by Pope as 12 December 1718. See *The Correspondence of Alexander Pope*, ed. George Sherburn, (Oxford, 1956), Vol. II, p. 23.

[2] Alexander Pope to William Broome, 31 December 1719.

[3] Lord Dacre to S. Miller, from Belhus, January 1748.

five acres at his disposal, that had 'not ten sticks in it when he took over', after eleven years' improvement, spending annually as much as £5,000, he had managed to introduce an orangery, a garden-house, a grove, an obelisk in memory of his mother, a bowling-green, a shell-temple, a vineyard, and a grotto with a spring.

From the *Plan of Mr. Pope's Garden by his Gardener, John Serle* (1745),[1] one can see what pains he had taken to perfect the grotto (Plate IV). His friends from all over the world sent him specimens of rocks and fossils, and he spent years in constructing this beautiful *cabinet de curiosités*. The materials used, and the places from which they came, are romantic and exciting: German spar; yellow mundic; flint, crusted, pellucid and shot round a globe of copper; Cornish diamonds; lead ore; kullan or wild ore; sparry marble; pieces of lava from Vesuvius; spar shot into prisms; fossils; gold ore from the Peruvian mines; silver ore from Mexico; petrified wood; Brazil pebbles; large lumps of amethyst; coral and petrified moss; two stones from the Giant's Causeway; and a fine piece of uncommon petrification from Okey Hole.[2]

Mrs. Thrale once said that Samuel Johnson hated to hear of 'prospects and views and laying out of ground and taste in garden-ing', so it was unfortunate that Johnson should ever have paid a visit to Pope's house, for he saw only the utilitarian side of the grotto:[3]

. . . being under the necessity of making a subterraneous passage to a garden on the other side of the road, he adorned it with fossil bodies, and dignified it with the title of a grotto; a place of silence and retreat, from which he endeavoured to persuade his friends and himself that cares and passions could be excluded.

A grotto is not often the wish or pleasure of an Englishman, who has more frequent need to solicit than exclude the sun; but Pope's excavation was requisite as an entrance to his garden, and, as some men try to be proud of their defects, he extracted an ornament from

---

[1] His old and faithful friend, whom he remembered in his will, and mentioned in the opening line of the 'Epistle to Dr. Arbuthnot'. He was employed by Ralph Allen at Bath after Pope's death.

[2] This was a large stalagmite from Wookey Hole caves in Somerset, where the stump can still be seen.

[3] *Lives of the English Poets.* 2. Alexander Pope (Everyman edition, London, 1946), p. 172.

an inconvenience, and vanity produced a grotto where necessity enforced a passage.

Fortunately, these magnificent antithetical strictures on *furor rusticus* were delivered after Pope's death, or they might have spoilt his pleasure. In June 1725 he writes happily to his friend, Edward Blount, of the enjoyment he has in his garden, and the delights of the grotto's camera obscura, that eighteenth-century cinema.

I have put the last Hand to my works of this kind, in happily finishing the subterranean Way and Grotto; I there found a Spring of the clearest Water, which falls in a perpetual Rill, that echoes thro' the Cavern day and night. From the river *Thames*, you see thro' my Arch up a Walk of the Wilderness to a kind of open Temple, wholly compos'd of Shells in the Rustic Manner; and from that distance under the Temple you look thro' a sloping Arcade of Trees, and see the Sails on the River passing suddenly and vanishing, as thro' a Perspective Glass. When you shut the Doors of this Grotto, it becomes on the instant, from a luminous Room, a *Camera obscura*; on the Walls of which all objects of the River, Hills, Woods, and Boats, are forming a moving Picture in their visible Radiations: And when you have a mind to light it up, it affords a very different Scene: it is finished with Shells interspersed with Pieces of Looking-glass in angular forms; and in the Cieling is a Star of the same Material, at which when a Lamp (of an orbicular Figure of thin Alabaster) is hung in the Middle, a thousand pointed Rays glitter and are reflected over the Place.
There are connected to this Grotto by a narrower Passage two Porches; one toward the River, of smooth Stones, full of light and open; the other toward the Garden, shadow'd with trees, rough with Shells, Flints; and Iron Ore. The Bottom is paved with simple Pebble, as is also the adjoining Walk up the Wilderness to the Temple, in the natural Taste, agreeing not ill with the little dripping Murmur, and the Aquatic Idea of the whole Place. It wants nothing to compleat it but a good Statue with an Inscription, like that beautiful antique one which you know I am so fond of,

> *Hujus Nympha loci, sacri, custodia fontis,*
> *Dormio, dum blandae sentio murmur aquae.*
> *Parce meum, quisquis tangis cava marmora somnum*
> *Rumpere, seu bibas, sive lavere, tace.*

III. Moor Park, Farnham: perspective view of Sir William Temple's house and garden, c. 1690.

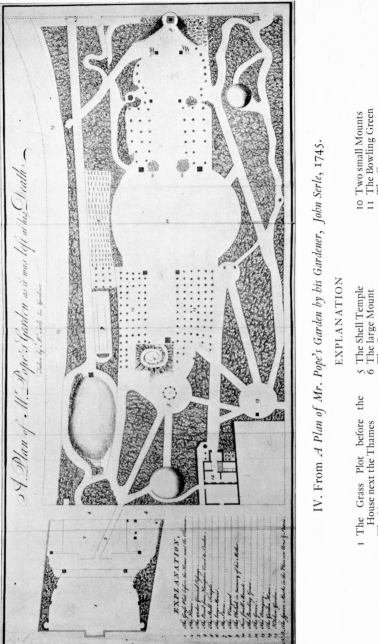

IV. From *A Plan of Mr. Pope's Garden* by his Gardener, *John Serle*, 1745.

EXPLANATION

1 The Grass Plot before the House next the Thames
2 The House
3 The under Ground Passage
4 The Road from Hampton Court to London
5 The Shell Temple
6 The large Mount
7 The Stoves
8 The Vineyard
9 The Obelisk in memory of his Mother
10 Two small Mounts
11 The Bowling Green
12 The Grove
13 The Orangery
14 The Garden House
15 Kitchen Garden

> Nymph of the Grot, these sacred Springs I keep,
> And to the Murmur of these Waters sleep;
> Ah, spare my slumbers, gently tread the Cave!
> And drink in silence, or in silence lave!

You'll think I have been very Poetical in this Description, but it is pretty near the Truth. I wish you were here to bear Testimony how little it owes to Art, either the Place itself, or the Image I give of it.

This transmutation of the visual image into poetical terms was also felt by Horace Walpole, who, after a visit, thought that

the passing through the gloom from the grotto to the opening day, and the retiring and again assembling shades, the dusky groves, the larger lawn, and the solemnity of the termination at the cypresses that lead up to his mother's tomb, are managed with exquisite judgement.

Pope saw it as no vain creation, but as a place in which only those with noble thoughts should rest, for

> Unpolish'd Gemms no Ray on Pride bestow,
> And latent Metals innocently glow![1]

A place, therefore, in which an ideal community of patriot friends could receive inspiration; a symbol, as much as Yeats's Tower, of the nourishment of reason and imagination.

> There, my Retreat the best Companions grace,
> Chiefs, out of War, and Statesmen, out of Place.
> There, *St John* mingles with my friendly Bowl,
> The Feast of Reason and the Flow of Soul:
> And He, whose Lightning pierc'd th' *Iberian* Lines,
> Now, forms my Quincunx, and now ranks my Vines,
> Or tames the Genius of the stubborn Plain,
> Almost as quickly, as he conquer'd *Spain*.[2]

So he therefore considered it as suitable for the 'nobly-pensive St. John', the 'dying Wyndham' and Lord Peterborough, the defenders

---

[1] 'Verses on a Grotto by the River Thames at Twickenham', written in the late summer of 1740, just after Sir William Wyndham, the leader of the Hanover Tories died.

[2] 'Imitations of Horace.' First Satire of the Second Book, lines 125–32.

of Liberty. Indeed, the Harmony and Moderation of Bolingbroke's *The Idea of a Patriot King* (1738) are echoed in 'The Essay on Man'.[1] This association between the Grotto and Liberty of progressive Whigs, and of Tories like Wyndham and Bolingbroke who opposed Sir Robert Walpole, is understandable, for it was evidently in this grotto or at the house that some of their most creative hours were spent. Bolingbroke lived quite near at Dawley, where he contrived a *ferme ornée* which was often visited by Voltaire.

> Himself neglects what must all others charm
> And what he built a Palace calls a FARM.[2]

The whole stretch of river, of which Pope's house had a prospect, must have been especially beautiful, and in it lived a remarkable and hospitable community of distinguished people: Lady Suffolk, 'Chloe' of his poems, 'I know a Reasonable Woman, Handsome and witty, yet a Friend',[3] at Marble Hill; Lady Ferrers[4] downstream from Pope; the Earl of Radnor, in whose garden Pope met Warburton in 1740; Kitty Clive, the actress; and after 1747, Horace Walpole at Strawberry. Together with Lord Bathurst and Charles Bridgeman, Pope was consulted by Lady Suffolk in making her landscape at Marble Hill; and visits were exchanged with Frederick, Prince of Wales, at Richmond across the river. Defoe remarks:

> The whole country here shines with a lustre not to be described; take them in a remote view, the fine Seats shine among the Trees as Jewels shine in a rich Coronet; in a near sight they are meer Pictures and Paintings; at a distance they are all Nature, nearhand all Art, but both in extreamest Beauty.[5]

---

[1] 'Epistle 3', lines 283–302.

[2] 'Dawley Farm', of doubtful attribution.

[3] 'On a Certain Lady at Court'. Pope introduced Swift to her in 1726. She later had the honour to receive a letter from Lemuel Gulliver.

[4] Referred to (despite change of sex) in the Epigram,

> My Ld. complains that P— (stark mad with Gardens)
> Has lopp'd three Trees, the Value of three Farthings!

Warton says that this refers to Lord Radnor; but his trees were too far off to spoil any vista of Pope's. It refers to the three walnut trees planted by Lady Ferrers.

[5] *On a Tour thro' the Whole Island of Great Britain* (London, 1724).

How did Pope manage to put into practice, in so small an area as his estate, his Rules—'Contrasts, the management of Surprises and the concealment of Bounds'? It seems that he achieved contrasts through varied planting in irregular patterns and serpentine lines; surprise by the tunnelled entry into the grotto under the Hampton turnpike road (on which a coach can be seen in the engraving on Plate V), and by placing temples and other architectural features to confront one suddenly on turning a corner; and the concealment of bounds by giving the eye an uninterrupted view to infinity by ingenious planting leading through vistas down to the Thames. The lights and shades he managed by 'disposing the thick grove work, the thin, and the openings in a proper manner'.[1] As a painter, he writes, 'you may distance things by darkening them, and by narrowing the plantations more and more towards the end'. In 1713 Pope had taken painting lessons from his friend, Jervas,[2] and thereafter he sees landscape as a painter and judges landscaping by a painter's aesthetic standards. The highest compliment he could pay William Kent was to say that he was 'painter enough to taste the charm of landscape'. How much the poet and painter combine in:

> To build, to plant, whatever you intend,
> To rear the Column, or the Arch to bend,
> To swell the Terras, or to sink the Grot;
> In all, let Nature never be forgot.
> But treat the Goddess like a modest fair,
> Nor over-dress, nor leave her wholly bare;
> Let not each beauty ev'ry where be spy'd,
> Where half the skill is decently to hide.
> He gains all points, who pleasingly confounds,
> Surprizes, varies, and conceals the Bounds.
>   Consult the Genius of the Place[3] in all;
> That tells the Waters or to rise, or fall,

[1] Joseph Spence's *Anecdotes, observations and characters of books and men* (London, 1820).

[2] Charles Jervas (1675–1739), a pupil of Sir Godfrey Kneller, whose portrait of Pope hangs in the National Portrait Gallery. His work was referred to by Horace Walpole as 'wretched daubings' and 'defective in drawing, colouring and composition'. However, Steele in *The Tatler*, 18 April 1709, thought he was the 'last great painter that Italy has sent us'. He was, in fact, Irish.

[3] *Genius loci* of Virgil. *Aeneid*, V.

Or helps th'ambitious Hill the heav'n to scale,
Or scoops in circling theatres the Vale,
Calls in the Country, catches opening glades,
Joins willing woods, and varies shades from shades,
Now breaks or now directs, th'intending Lines;
Paints as you plant, and, as you work, designs.[1]

This was the ideal which he brought to life at Twickenham. At the same time, another poet, Matthew Prior, who also 'loved his estate more than Tully did his Tusculum or Horace his Sabine Field',[2] was laying out a garden at Down Hall, near Harlow in Essex.[3] But this was very different from Pope's, for it was concerned with 'squares, rounds, diagonals and planted Quincunces'. And it is this, on a more ostentatious and vulgar scale, that Pope condemns at 'Timon's Villa' in the same Epistle.[4]

At Timon's Villa let us pass a day,
Where all cry out, 'What sums are thrown away!'
So proud, so grand, of that stupendous air,
Soft and Agreeable come never there.
Greatness, with Timon, dwells in such a draught
As brings all Brobdignag before your thought.
To compass this, his building is a Town,
His pond an Ocean, his parterre a Down:
Who but must laugh, the Master when he sees,
A puny insect, shiv'ring at a breeze!
Lo, what huge heaps of littleness around!
The whole, a labour'd Quarry above ground.
Two Cupids squirt before: a Lake behind
Improves the keenness of the Northern wind.
His Gardens next your admiration call,
On ev'ry side you look, behold the Wall!
No pleasing Intricacies intervene,
No artful wildness to perplex the scene;
Grove nods at grove, each Alley has a brother,
And half the platform just reflects the other.

[1] 'Epistle to Lord Burlington', 'Moral Essays IV', lines 47–64.
[2] Longleat MSS. Prior Papers.
[3] The derelict state of this estate, given him by his patron Lord Harley, is amusingly described in 'The Ballad of Down Hall' (1715).
[4] Lines 99–132.

The suff'ring eye inverted Nature sees,
Trees cut to Statues, Statues thick as trees,
With here a Fountain, never to be play'd,
And there a Summer-house, that knows no shade;
Here Amphitrite sails thro' myrtle bow'rs;
There Gladiators fight, or die, in flow'rs;
Un-water'd see the drooping sea-horse mourn,
And swallows roost in Nilus' dusty Urn.
    My Lord advances with majestic mien,
Smit with the mighty pleasure, to be seen:
But soft—by regular approach—not yet—
First thro' the length of yon hot Terrace sweat,
And when up ten steep slopes you've dragg'd your thighs,
Just at his Study-door he'll bless your eyes.

Some of these details were similar to the landscape at Cannons, Edgware, the great house of James Brydges, 1st Duke of Chandos, and readers naturally thought that this estate and its owner were being directly satirized by Pope. Part of the pleasure grounds of eighty-three acres was indeed enclosed by a wall of over five hundred yards, and had among other objects, a gilded gladiator 'with sword and target', a *jet d'eau*, and a great staircase. Yet Professor George Sherburn, in his scholarly essay,[1] has reached the conclusion that 'it does not seem probable that Pope intended any detail to be so applied' to Cannons, and modern scholarship has accepted this view.[2] Therefore, despite Dr. Johnson,[3] who unfairly wrote that Chandos was sceptical of Pope's denial of any exact reference, there is every reason to believe that it did not specifically refer to Cannons. Indeed, Chandos, for all that Dr. Johnson says, was convinced, and as he was modest, unassuming and generous-minded, he may be believed. 'I have received,' he wrote, 'from the author, two letters on the subject, in which he utterly denies that I was the object he had in view.' Let us leave it at that and side with Switzer, who took 'grove nods at grove' to be equally true of Blenheim. It was a

[1] 'Timon's Villa and Cannons', *Huntington Library Bulletin*, No. 8, October 1935.
[2] The evidence is examined in great detail with the same conclusion by F. W. Bateson in his Twickenham edition of '*Alexander Pope. Epistles to Several Persons*' (London, 1951), Appendix B.
[3] *Lives of the English Poets* (Everyman edition, London, 1946), Vol. 2, pp. 180–1.

composite picture of gigantic Le Nôtre formality and ostentatious vulgarity that Pope censured; and he certainly denied a direct reference, in reply to the letter from the Duke, as well as to Lord Burlington, who was worried by readers' reactions:

nothing is so evident . . . as that the Character of Timon is collected from twenty different absurditys and Improprieties! and was never the Picture of any one Human Creature. The Argument is short. Either the Duke these folks would abuse, *did* all those things, or he *did not*. If he did, he would deserve to be laughd at with a Vengeance; and if he did *not*, then it's plain it cannot be the Duke: and the latter is really the case.[1]

And again, on the next day, to Aaron Hill:

. . . I never imagin'd the least Application of what I said of *Timon* could be made to the D. of Ch——s, than whom there is scarce a more blameless, worthy and generous, beneficient Character, among all our Nobility: . . . I am certain, if you calmly read every Particular of that Description, you'll find almost all of 'em point-blank the Reverse of that Person's *Villa*.

Evidently, in his Epistle to Lord Cobham, a year later, he tried to make amends with 'Thus gracious *Chandos* is belov'd at sight'.[2] And this seems to reflect contemporary opinion of him, if John Gay is to be believed:

> If Chandos with a liberal hand bestow,
> Censure imputes it all to pomp and show;
> When, if the motive right were understood,
> His daily pleasure is in doing good.[3]

But there was no doubt of Pope's dislike of false magnificence, 'the first grand Error of which is to imagine that *Greatness* consists in the *Size* and *Dimension*, instead of the *Proportion* and *Harmony* of the whole'.[4] Once again the artist speaks. Yet Defoe had enjoyed a visit to Cannons, finding 'a vast Variety, the Canals very large and

---

[1] Alexander Pope to the Earl of Burlington, 21 December 1731.
[2] 'Moral Essays', Epistle I, line 113.
[3] Epistle IV. To the Rt. Hon. Paul Methuen, Esq.
[4] 'Moral Essays', Epistle IV, Argument.

noble'. And Hawksmoor, in a tactless endeavour to persuade Sarah, Duchess of Marlborough, to further improvement at Blenheim, had written: 'I cannot but own that the water at Cannons, the Duke of Chandos's is the main beauty of that Situation and it cost him dear, but your Grace may have a Greater Beauty with much less Expence.' Had Pope lived another three years he would have had the satisfaction of seeing Cannons demolished, and his prophecy fulfilled:

> Another age shall see the golden Ear
> Imbrown the Slope, and nod on the Parterre,
> Deep Harvests bury all his pride has plann'd,
> And laughing Ceres re-assume the land.[1]

His own landscape suffered a worse fate. Sir William Stanhope, who bought it after Pope's death in 1744, altered it beyond recognition. Horace Walpole regretted how Stanhope had hacked and hewed the groves,

wriggled a winding walk through them with an edging of shrubs, in what they call the modern taste, and, in short, has desired the three lanes to walk in again—and now is forced to shut them out again by a wall, for there was not a Muse could walk there but that she was spied by every country fellow that went by with a pipe in his mouth.

Fortunately, cuttings of the willow under which Pope sat were sent by Sir William to many places in England and abroad before the tree died in 1801. These scions may be of the lineage of all the Weeping Willows that we know: symbolic of our grief for the loss of such a landscape.[2]

Among the many houses that Pope visited was Lord Digby's Sherborne. This landscape must have had certain formal features, for there were five green terraces and a canal, yet it was much admired by Pope, as the gardens beyond the terraces were irregular. Their beauty, he wrote,

---

[1] 'Moral Essays', Epistle IV, lines 173–6.

[2] Part of the grotto, blackened and ruinous, can still be seen. In 1829 the trees were 'propped with uncommon care and guarded by a holy zeal'. Samuel Felton, *Gleanings on Gardens* (London, 1829).

arises from this Irregularity, for not only the Several parts of the Garden itself make the better Contraste by these sudden Rises, Falls and Turns of ground; but the Views about it are let in, and hang over the Walls, in very different figures and aspects.

The setting, in a great amphitheatre with fine honeysuckles, wilderness of cherry trees, horse-chestnut groves and walks through venerable woods delighted him, and the view of the castle ruins, which were covered in ivy was 'inexpressibly awful and solemn'.

At two of his friends' houses, Pope took an active part in the design of the landscape. The first of these was Prior Park, Bath, of Ralph Allen, 'the noblest man in England', as Pope called him. He stayed there, as at Stowe, sometimes for months at a time, on one occasion completing Part IV of 'The Dunciad'. Allen must have been a delightful host, for among others who visited him were men of such diverse interests as William Pitt, who represented Bath; William Warburton, a 'tall, robust, large-boned' parson, who married Allen's niece and inherited the property; Richard Graves, the local rector; Samuel Richardson; the Rev. John Wesley, and George Lyttelton, who was introduced by Pope to Allen. In the letter of introduction, Pope asks Allen whether he might change the epithet 'low-born' to 'humble' in the couplet which now stands as,

> Let humble *Allen*, with an aukward Shame,
> Do good by stealth, and blush to find it Fame.[1]

In November 1736 Pope shows the selflessness of so many eighteenth-century planters, from which we still benefit, by saying that it pleased him that his trees at Twickenham would afford fruit and shade to others, when he would want them no more; and he goes on to say that he hopes to find Allen in the same employment (planting) at Prior Park, where it would be as pleasing to be able to help as with his own. Again, on 15 May 1740,

> It is my firm resolution . . . to see your Gardens finish'd (ready for Mrs. Allen's Grotto and Cascade the following year) I must

---

[1] 'Epilogue to the Satires', Dialogue I, lines 135–6. Referring originally to his 'low-born' Cornish origins, and the modesty of his charity, which was 'seen farther than his house though it stands on a hill' (Henry Fielding, *Joseph Andrews*, Bk. III, Chap. 6).

inquire, next after hers and your health, after that of the Elms we planted on each Side of the Lawn? and of the little Wood-work to join one wood to the other below, which I hope you planted this Spring.

In the next two years, when he is not paying long visits to the Allens, he is finishing his own grotto at Twickenham for which he received on one occasion as much as six tons of stone from Allen. He is pleased also that Mrs. Allen 'has begun to imitate the Great Works of Nature, rather than those Bawbles most Ladies affect. I hope you have not impoverishd Your Rock to beautify mine.' The details of his own grotto are described in a letter to William Borlas which supplements his account to Edward Blount of fifteen years before.

But Allen's greatest claim to fame, more perhaps than being friend to Pope and host to much talent, is by being the prototype of Squire Allworthy in Henry Fielding's *Tom Jones* (1749), in which the house and grounds of the squire are in part described:[1]

There was an air of grandeur in it that struck you with awe, and rivalled the beauties of the best Grecian architecture; and it was as commodious without as venerable within.

It stood on the south-east side of a hill, but nearer the bottom than the top of it, so as to be sheltered from the north-east by a grove of old oaks, which rose above it, in a gradual ascent of near half a mile, and yet high enough to enjoy a most charming prospect of the valley beneath.

In the midst of the grove was a fine lawn, sloping down towards the house, near the summit of which rose a plentiful spring, gushing out of a rock covered with firs, and forming a constant cascade of about thirty feet, not carried down by a regular flight of steps, but tumbling in a natural fall over the broken and mossy stones, till it came to the bottom of the rock; then running off in a pebbly channel, that with many lesser falls winded along, till it fell into a lake at the foot of the hill, about a quarter of a mile below the house on the south side, and which was seen from every room in the front. Out of this lake, which filled the centre of a beautiful plain, embellished with groups of beeches and elms, and fed with sheep, issued a river, that for several miles was seen to meander through an amazing variety of

[1] Book I, Chapter I.

meadows and woods, till it emptied itself in the sea, with a large arm of which, and an island beyond it, the prospect closed.

On the right of this valley opened another of less extent, adorned with villages, and terminated by one of the towers of an old ruined abbey, grown over with ivy, and part of the front, which remained still entire.

The left-hand scene presented the view of a very fine park, composed of very unequal ground, and agreeably varied with all the diversity of hills, lawns, wood, and water, laid out with admirable taste, but owing less to art than to nature, could give. Beyond this the country rose into a ridge of wild mountains, the tops of which were above the clouds.[1]

This was Prior Park, with the omission of the prospect of Bath, the sea, and the Palladian bridge by the water—which in 1749 had not been built, and cannot therefore be seen in Walker's engraving (Plate VI).[2] The indefatigable Dr. Pococke was enchanted by it all when on a visit in 1754; beautiful gardens 'laid out in a wilderness with a piece of water in the middle from which there is a descent' through lawns and woods, opening up a prospect of Bath. He also mentions a new Gothic building, a statue of Moses with his hand striking the rock, and below it the cascade. The scene obviously had all the characteristics so beloved of Pope, Thomson, and Shenstone —irregularity in the descent of the stream, variety in the meadows and woods, the old ruined abbey, diversity, and, above all, the 'admirable taste, owing less to art than to nature'.

In the next paragraph in *Tom Jones*, Squire Allworthy is pictured as he strolls on his terrace at dawn, 'second only to the sun in glory', a piece of hyperbole for which Fielding apologizes, quickly bringing

---

[1] F. Homes Dudden in *Henry Fielding* (1952) points out that Fielding is most likely describing a composite prospect—from Tor Hill, Glastonbury, and from the house at Prior Park. From Tor Hill the 'old ruin'd abbey' would be Glastonbury; the sea would be the Bristol Channel with Stert Island in Bridgwater Bay; the ridge of 'wild mountains' would be Mendips or Quantocks. As Tom Jones was associated with Glastonbury, this seems the best explanation.

[2] The third and last of the bridges slightly influenced by Palladio's design for a three-arch bridge with portico and colonnades, for Venice. The first and finest is at Wilton, designed by Lord Pembroke and Roger Morris, 1736; and the second at Stowe. The foundation stone of this one at Prior Park was laid by Ralph Allen in 1751. Unlike the others, it is not placed on any main axis, but spans the lake in the romantic landscape.

us to the breakfast-table. Nevertheless, the inference is felt that such scenes fittingly accompany benevolence of mind and a peaceful life; and as the novel progresses Tom never meets another man as humane as Mr. Allworthy, nor does Fielding describe another setting as gracious as his. Indeed, once more he delightedly recalls it:

At Eshur, at Stowe, at Wilton, at Eastbury and at Prior Park days are too short for the ravished imagination; in some of these, art chiefly engages our admiration while we admire the wondrous powers of art in improving nature; in others, nature and art contend for our applause, but, in the last, the former seems to triumph. Here Nature appears in her richest attire, and Art dressed with the modestest simplicity attends her benignant mistress.[1]

But, like others, it did not last long, for although Mrs. Gertrude Warburton, Allen's niece who inherited, died in 1796, after another twenty years the twelve miles of woods planted by Ralph Allen had been decimated by the 'licentious fury of the axe', and the 'house with all its present contiguous beauties was but a mere *skeleton*'.[2] This may partly have been the result of Capability Brown's clearing.

From Allen's town house in Lilliput Alley, Bath, there is a prospect up to Hampton and Claverton Downs,[3] on which, two years before his death, he employed Sanderson Miller to design what has come to be known as Sham Castle. The project was William Pitt's idea as he called on Miller to build for Allen 'a very considerable Gothick object which is to stand in a fine situation on the Hills near Bath'.[4] It stands today, symmetrical and clean, like a toy-soldier's fort, with open Gothic arches flanked by the fronts of two castelled towers, with large quatrefoil arrowslits. Like Tintern Abbey, it now has no overtones of melancholy,[5] for when an 'ivy-mantled tower' is

---

[1] *Tom Jones*, Book XI, Chap. 9.

[2] Pierce Egan, *Walks through Bath* (Bath, 1819), p. 201.

[3] Now blocked by a brewer's yard.

[4] William Pitt to Sanderson Miller, 30 October 1755, from the Pay Office.

[5] As a result of the misguided efforts of certain City Councillors in 1929. Since then the original 'ivy-mantled tower' has been so cleaned up that Gray would not recognize it.

laid bare, and the action of the weather repaired, the structure can never be more than an eye-catcher or focal point in a landscape.

Alfred's Hall,[1] on the estate at Cirencester of Allen, 1st Earl Bathurst, was never clean like this, perhaps because Pope shared in its design. Its irregular castellated walls, Gothic windows, broken doorways, and a shell of a tower, framed in black evergreens pierced by melancholy light, are the forerunners of a setting for the Gothic novel. It is a mistake to apply the epithet 'sham' to such buildings, for the word has bogus connotations. What their builders intended was to establish a scene which, by a medieval replica in decay, would encourage thoughts of the transitoriness of this life, in addition to being a focal point in a vista: the philosophic as partner to the aesthetic. Alfred's Hall is the perfect example. From 1718, for twenty years letters passed and visits were exchanged between Pope and Lord Bathurst, who had this common interest in landscaping, though Cirencester Park was more a Fontainebleau-type forest with broad rides than a landscaped park. In July 1718 Pope tells Lord Bathurst that he is the best company and that his newly made Oakley Wood is the best place in which to enjoy that company. Five years later Bathurst writes to Pope that he is resolved to 'begin the alteration of my wood house, and some little baubling works about it, which you shall direct as you will'. And exactly ten years later Mrs. Pendarves writes to Swift that Bathurst has 'greatly improved the wood House, which you may remember but a cottage, not a bit better than an Irish cabin. It is now a venerable castle, and has been mistaken by an antiquarian for one of King Arthur's . . .' He cannot have noticed 'Alfred's Hall' neatly lettered above the entrance.

Soon Pope is describing Bathurst's 'enchanted Forest' and regarding himself as 'the Magician appropriated to the place, without whom no mortal can penetrate into the Recesses of those sacred Shades'.[2] The genius of the place was undoubtedly sylvan, for Bathurst was a forester who planted beech, oak, elm, horse-chestnut, wild cherry and yew, and by joining 'willing woods' unified the whole.

---

[1] For a full description of this and other buildings in Cirencester Park, see Barbara Jones's excellent account in *Follies and Grottoes* (London, 1953), pp. 20–22.

[2] Alexander Pope to Robert Digby, May 1722.

But the course of true landscape love did not always run smoothly. Bathurst writes to Lady Suffolk in 1734 that Pope was endeavouring to find faults, but could not, 'and instead of admiring (as he ought to do) what is already executed, he is everyday drawing a plan for some building or other and then is violently angry it is not set up the next morning'. And Pope, on his side, could write to Robert Digby some years earlier[1] that he had little or no ideas about 'the hanging Gardens of *Babylon*, or the Paradise of *Cyrus*, and the Sharawaggis of *China*', but that he thought Lord Bathurst might have, for 'they were certainly both very *Great* and very *Wild*'. Evidently Lord Bathurst did not take this as laudatory, for the letter has apparently been textually revised by him.[2] Nevertheless, in August 1736, Bathurst sends Pope his plans for a building (cupola)[3] to 'answer three walks', to be painted blue or gilded as Pope wishes. By this time Oakley Wood and a grand avenue, five miles long, according to Mrs. Pendarves, were well established, though she qualifies the beauty of the avenue by pointing out that Lord Bathurst had not realized that 'too great a length destroys the greatness it was intended to promote . . . because length diminishes height and is destructive of stateliness'. So, as Burke later stated, moderate length is grander. Certainly one hopes, on going the full length of this avenue today, that a building of equal majesty will reward one at the end. But such is not the case: the house is neither magnificent nor terminating the avenue, though, like all the garden buildings, it glows with lichened Cotswold stone. Yet the trees, planted as if along some giant's ride in the woods, have a majesty which symbolizes their planter, a grand old man who at the age of eighty-three introduced himself to Sterne by saying that he had lived all his life with

geniuses of that cast [Pope and Swift]; but have survived them; and, despairing ever to find their equals, it is some years since I closed my accounts, and shut up my books, with thoughts of never opening them again: but you have kindled a desire in me of opening them

---

[1] 12 August (1725?).
[2] George Sherburn, ed., *Correspondence of Alexander Pope* (London, 1956), Vol. II, p. 314 n.
[3] The Hexagon.

once more before I die; which I now do; so go home and dine with me.[1]

A small rusticated stone pavilion with the inscription 'Pope's Seat' commemorates this friendship.

The unique combination of artist and writer in Kent and Pope produced unique landscapes. Though small, Twickenham and Rousham were unlike others, and established a Taste which neither Brownian nor Picturesque schools could wholly supplant. The nice balance in which Art decently clothed Nature was not found in the naked lawns of Brown nor in the overdressed Gothic of the Picturesque. And never again does the art of landscaping receive such powerful support, in drawings and words, as from the pen of Alexander Pope.

[1] Lewis Perry Curtis, ed., *Letters of Lawrence Sterne* (Oxford, 1935): Letter 185, of March 1767, to Mrs. Daniel Draper.

3

Stourhead, Hagley and the Leasowes: Mid-Century

> The most laborious Endeavours of Art had been
> used to make it appear like the beautiful product of
> wild, uncultivated Nature.
>
> MRS. LENNOX, *The Female Quixote* (1752)

THE most beautiful landscaping in England, although the trees are in decline, may still be said to be at Stourhead on the Wiltshire-Dorset border. For ten years from 1741 the owner, Henry Hoare, had both the means and the leisure to create this landscape, until, in 1765, it was described by Horace Walpole as 'one of the most picturesque scenes in the world'.[1] Today this Claudesque picture is worthy of Walpole's hyperbole, for it radiates a unique calm and beauty. What was the background of Henry Hoare, the banker, that may have accounted for his planning and carrying out this work? Little is known of his early life. His father died in 1725 when Henry was twenty, but he did not inherit the estate and live at Stourhead until his mother died in 1741. In the intervening years he spent many thousands of pounds on completing the Palladian house which his father had employed Colen Campbell to design. The pictures he bought are of interest in relation to the creation of his landscape, for there are many mythological subjects and landscapes, although the artists are typical choices of a gentleman of means and taste at that time. In 1727 he refers to 'two views

---

[1] Horace Walpole, *Journals of Visits to Country Seats*, ed. Paget J. Toynbee, Walpole Society, Vol. XVI (1927–8).

of Venice, two views and the Ruins of Rome, and a Cascade at Tivoli'. In the next year he buys a 'large Landskip' by John Wootton, who in middle age went to Rome, afterwards painting landscapes with the glow of Claude and Gaspar Poussin, having previously been famous as an animal painter. His prices, according to Horace Walpole, were high at twenty to forty guineas for a horse.[1] The 'large Landskip' is with four others of Wootton's in the house. Then, for the next forty years, Henry Hoare bought works by Nicholas and Gaspar Poussin, Claude, Annibale Caracci, Pannini, Zuccarelli, Carlo Maratti, Carlo Dolce, and Sebastien Ricci. On his mother's death, he and his wife and family came to live at Stourhead and, immensely rich as he was, he started to plan the landscaping of the plantation. But two years later his wife died, followed in 1751 by his only surviving son. This second bereavement was especially tragic, for he had found that the young man was beginning to show a critical interest in the arts. He wrote to his father from Aix in the year before his death:

The Claude you desire me to describe is remarkable for having a Jupiter and Europa in the foreground; it is a sea-port with Trees on the left-hand, and on the right, a Castle on the top of a Rock projecting into the sea, which you see through some trees. It is a pleasant picture but not a warm one. Neither that nor any of the others are in good preservation enough for you to buy.

During these tragic years Henry Hoare seems to have directed all his energies into the creation of his landscape. The magnitude of his achievement is staggering: firstly, because the terrain which he tackled, though there was water, was largely barren downland, typical of Salisbury Plain, and secondly, because he anticipated the work of professional landscapers, such as Capability Brown, by some years, although the influence of William Kent at Rousham, and Pope at Twickenham must be acknowledged. Fortunately, Henry Hoare found six springs and ponds, and damming these, he formed a chain of lakes, eventually clothing their steep banks in beech, oak and fir.[2] At the entrance to the landscape stands the village church of

---

[1] Horace Walpole, *Anecdotes of Painting*, John Wootton (Strawberry Hill, 1762–71).
[2] As at Pergusa, Sicily, described in Ovid's *Metamorphoses*, Book V, lines 338–9; *'silva coronat aquas, cingens latus omne, suisque frondibus | ut velo Phoebeos submovet ignes'*.

V. Pope's house at Twickenham: engraved by A. Heckell, 1749.

Gimmingham, W. S. delin. fecit

Fecit R. Allen Sculp.

PRIOR PARK the Seat of Ralph Allen Esq. near Bath. — PRIOR PARK la Residence de Ralph Allen Campagnie de Bath

VI. Prior Park, engraved by Anthony Walker, 1750

Stourton, with its squat tower, and near it he added another genuine Gothic feature, a medieval cross, which he purchased in 1768 from the city of Bristol, after it had been dismantled and was lying un-cared-for. As William Hazlitt remarks, 'You descend into Stourton by a sharp winding declivity, almost like going underground between high hedges of laurel trees'.[1] Then suddenly the view opens and Claude's landscape, 'Coast View of Delos with Aeneas' (Plate VII*a*),[2] unfolds before you. Across the water, in the middle distance, is the hexastyle Corinthian temple, the Pantheon; in the right foreground is the Roman Doric Temple of Flora, and on the left is the stone bridge (Plate VII*b*). The placing of the water reflecting the setting sun, and the three architectural features are exactly as in Claude's composition. It wants but Anius, Anchises, Aeneas, and Ascanius to be standing outside the Doric temple as they are in Claude's landscape. Both Ovid and Virgil relate the incident on which the picture is based.[3] Anius, the king and priest of Delos, is receiving Aeneas at the temple and showing him the holy site and the two trees to which Latona clung when giving birth to Diana and Apollo. The National Gallery catalogue attri-butes it to Virgil's *Aeneid*, but Marcel Röthlisberger in his *Claude Lorrain. The Paintings, Vol. 1. Critical Catalogue* (1961), suggests that it is closer to Ovid than Virgil, for Anius is making an appropriate gesture as if to guide Aeneas on a tour of the place. This detail is not mentioned by Virgil. Nevertheless, the gesture might equally be one of welcome, mentioned by Virgil but not Ovid: '*veterem Anchisen agnovit amicum*'.

Evidently Henry Hoare had the *Aeneid* in mind, for over the door of the Temple of Flora is the inscription: '*procul o, procul este, profani*'[4] —the words cried out by the Sibyl before she led Aeneas into the underworld to seek his father, Anchises. So, like Dante in *The Divine Comedy*, let us choose Virgil to guide us, and continue round the lake, through the plantations of great trees which form the

---

[1] *Criticisms on Art and sketches of the Principal Picture Galleries in England* (London, 1844).

[2] The National Gallery, London. Henry Hoare might have seen it when it moved round sale rooms in his time.

[3] Ovid, *Metamorphoses*, XIII, lines 631–5. Virgil, *Aeneid*, Book III, lines 80–84.

[4] Virgil, *Aeneid*, Book VI, line 258.

backcloth for other more dramatic flowering shrubs, rhododendron
and azalea, polychromatic in spring, planted by Henry Hoare's
successors. After about half a mile, on the other side of the lake, the
path descends into a long tunnel, which is startlingly lighted by
shafts in the walls, leading to the grotto, the finest of its kind in
England. This is not a grotto like Pope's, of scallops, conches, fel-
spar, quartz and corals, bright and glittering, but of flint and tura,
a form of Bath limestone from which the softer parts have been
worn away by the action of water. In an alcove lies John Cheere's
whitened lead statue of the sleeping Nymph, one arm wreathing
her head, elegantly propped up, and amply encased in drapery that,
on examination, shows a 'sweet disorder'. Many authorities have
attributed the derivation of this statue to the Roman copy, in the
Vatican Museum, of the Greek original of Ariadne. Yet the position
of Cheere's nymph with her right arm wreathing her head is not the
same as the Roman Ariadne, whose right arm crosses her breast,
with her hand resting on her left shoulder. The Stourhead nymph
most closely resembles another sleeping Ariadne in the garden of
the Villa Medici at Rome. This appears in the background of
Velasquez's painting of the Villa Medici garden of 1630 (reproduced
on p. 177 of *Velasquez. A Catalogue Raisonné of his Oeuvre*, by José
López-Rey, London, 1963), and was referred to by John Evelyn in
his *Diary* on 18 January 1645 as 'that incomparable figure of the
dying Cleopatra', as she was then called.[1] Under the Stourhead
figure flows the clear spring water of the source of the River Stour
which streams into a moon-cold marble bath. Along the border of
this is Pope's translation of the Latin inscription which he quoted
in his letter to Edward Blount when speaking of his own grotto at
Twickenham.[2] Were she awake, the Nymph could look, as we can,
through the mammoth-tusk tufa aperture, at the Temple of Flora
on the opposite shore, with the five-arched stone bridge[3] in the
middle distance—as pleasing a scene as she could wish for. Deeper
still in this melancholy spot, again lighted in baroque fashion from

[1] Also referred to by Horace Walpole, when visiting Stourhead, as 'Cleopatra
without the asp'.

[2] It is a common inscription in Italian gardens.

[3] Henry Hoare 'took it from Palladio's bridge at Vicenza'. Henry Hoare to Lady
Bruce, 23 October 1762 (Tottenham House Archive).

above, sits the great figure of the River God, from whose urn
another spring flows. As soon as we step into the daylight again we
see the Rustic Cottage, a pretty Gothic conceit, whose porch and
bow windows should be smothered in vines and creepers, but which,
for some reason, has been swept and cleaned until it has a prophy-
lactic by-pass neatness. Farther up stands the splendid Corinthian
temple, the Pantheon, which houses the great marble Hercules of
Rysbrack, dated 1756, his 'chef-d'oeuvre, and exquisite summary of
his skill, knowledge and judgement'.[1] Flanking him in the circular
interior are two other marble statues by Rysbrack—Flora and an
antique Livia Augusta dressed as Ceres. 'Few buildings exceed the
magnificence, taste and beauty of the temple', writes Horace
Walpole. But it was too pagan for his contemporary, the Reverend
John Wesley, who may perhaps have noted the Venus Callipicia,
who twists sensually, like an apsara, in a niche at the side of the
portico.[2] However, it is difficult to equate aesthetic criticism with
Wesley's reasons for disliking these statues: he 'could not admire
the images of devils', he said, nor should mankind 'reconcile statues
with nudities either to common sense or common decency'.[3] From
this temple, after crossing one bridge which separates the two
largest lakes, and another Cyclopean bridge, one climbs, as at
Cumae, to the Temple of the Sun. This is a steep and hard ascent,
evidently more difficult when constructed, for Henry Hoare with
the *Aeneid* in mind, wrote to Lord Bruce in December 1765: 'I have
made the passage up from the Sousterrain Serpentine & will make
it easier of access *facilis descensus Averno.*' From this height, on the
circular temple's colonnade, it is possible to look along the full
length of the lake to the obelisk with its sun on top, and down to
the turf bridge at the entrance to the gardens.

However, Stourhead's landscaping is more perhaps than just a
setting based on Claude's 'Coast View of Delos with Aeneas' or his
'Sacrifice to Apollo', and more than a series of compositions from
many different *points de vue.* Just as Book VI of the *Aeneid* is not only

---

[1] Horace Walpole, *Journals of Visits to Country Seats* (The Walpole Society, 1927).

[2] Similar to the Venus 'pulling up her smock, and looking backwards at her
buttocks', seen by Evelyn at the Farnese Palace. *Diary,* 25 January 1645.

[3] John Wesley, *Journal,* ed. N. Curnock (London, 1909), Vol. VI (12 September
1776).

a narrative of a journey but a deep moral and philosophical investigation into the meaning of life and death, so the path from the Temple of Ceres to the Temple of Apollo may be an allegory of the journey through life, with certain definite 'archetypes of the collective unconscious' on the way.

Sir Richard Colt Hoare, the historian and Henry Hoare's grandson, advises us about the right route for walking through the grounds. 'We must keep to the right-hand walk, which will lead us to a small Temple with a Doric portico.'[1] This is, of course, the Temple of Flora, or the Temple of Ceres, as its architect, Henry Flitcroft, called it. Mr. Woodbridge writes:

No wonder that the temple of the Earth-Mother who dominates the infancy of man, stands at the beginning of the garden. Within an arched recess, opposite the entrance, stands a large white urn on a pedestal. Round the urn is a carving in relief of a Bacchanalian procession. On either side are the marble heads of two young men, each on a column. . . . Above the 'altars' on the walls to the right and left of the door, are circular niches containing classical female busts, maternal in character. . . . Thus the temple of the mother also contains the division of the sexes. But it is the female, raised above the altar, who is dominant. The young men on whom she looks down have not her air of assurance. Indeed, they do not appear fully masculine, and one at least, appears tragic: like those youthful gods who died each year that the earth might become fertile.[2]

After the walk around the head of the lake comes the grotto, where lies the sleeping beauty who has to be awakened. 'The princess who must be won', continues Mr. Woodbridge, 'is one aspect of what Jung calls "the anima" . . . which is conservative, and clings in a most exasperating fashion to the ways of earlier mankind. Therefore it likes to appear in historic dress, with a predilection for Greece and Egypt.' Near her is the River God, presumably Pater Stour, another of Jung's archetypes associated with the anima, for instance in Prospero and Miranda. He is 'the superior master and teacher, a pointer of ways, the pre-existent meaning in chaotic life,

---

[1] Sir Richard Colt Hoare, MS. Memoirs (Stourhead).
[2] Kenneth Woodbridge enlarges on this in *Henry Hoare's Paradise*, Art Bulletin (March, 1965).

the father of the soul'.[1] Next, in the adytum of the Pantheon, is Hercules, the hero who frees the princess, the fully developed man 'unlike the young men in the temple of Ceres'. Thereafter, in the Temple of the Sun, all the life span can be viewed. It is the Temple of Light or Consciousness, without which the whole work of creation of the landscape could not have been.

These may not have been conscious associations of Henry Hoare's. Yet he must have known, in his tragic bereavements, that he could find consolation in the creation of 'delightful scenes, whether in nature, painting or poetry', which 'have a kindly influence on the body as well as the mind, and not only serve to clear and brighten the imagination, but are able to disperse grief and melancholy, and to set the animal spirits in pleasing and agreeable motions'.[2] So he 'proceeded *con spirito* upon a widely extended scale'.[3] It seems likely that as William Kent directed the details of the landscaping, in addition to the buildings and ornaments of his landscape, so Henry Flitcroft, who himself succeeded Kent as master mason in 1748, acted similarly at Stourhead. He is known to have designed the three key features of the landscape, and in one of the few letters to Henry Hoare that remains he reveals that he must have been responsible for more than just the buildings.

My next shall bring you sections of the proper Moulding for this Building and after that the Temple of Ceres: with the Rocky Arch in which I propose to place the River God; and a sketch how I conceive the head of the lake should be formed. 'Twill make a most agreeable Scene with the Solemn Shades about it and the variety of other agreeable circumstances.[4]

Dr. Pococke, on his travels in July 1754, describes the 'Temple of Hercules, not yet finished, with a grand portico of the Corinthian or Composite Order'.[5] Before the trees reached their full height the

[1] C. G. Jung, *The Integration of the Personality*, translated by S. M. Dell (London, 1940).

[2] Joseph Addison, *The Spectator*, No. 411, 21 June 1712.

[3] Sir Richard Colt Hoare, MS. Memoirs (Stourhead).

[4] Henry Flitcroft to Henry Hoare, from Whitehall, 25 August 1744 (Stourhead Archive).

[5] Dr. R. Pococke, *Travels thro' England*, ed. J. J. Cartwright, Camden Society (London, 1889).

proximity of the buildings may have been too evident. Indeed, Sir Richard Colt Hoare[1] thought the fashion in his grandfather's time was to overcrowd nature 'by buildings not in harmony with each other'. By 1779 in addition to the buildings already mentioned there were a Gothic Greenhouse, a Turkish Tent of 'painted canvas . . . the inside blue and white in mosaic',[2] a hermitage and a rustic cottage.

The National Trust, which received the estate from the Hoare family in 1946, has admirably restored and planted. But in days when we have a plethora of horticultural colour it would be wise to remember that 'the middle colour of the Seven Primary ones and consequently the most agreeable to the Organ of Sight is also the general Colour of the Vegetable Kingdom'.[3] How, for example, would Flitcroft and Henry Hoare react to the banks of pretty, pale hydrangeas now so prominent in front of the Pantheon? Would they think that these set the mood that they wished for? I suspect that their ghosts wander on an early summer morning, as the mists rise from the lake, and the reflections of trees and temples begin to darken the waters, or when, in 'October twilight the water mirrors the sky', for those are the times to watch the drifting swans: not when the rhododendrons bring in the gay busloads.

At the same time that Henry Hoare was working at Stourhead another landowner of comparable wealth, but of greater influence in the world, was engaged on his estate at Hagley in Worcestershire. George Lyttelton, of the Cobham cousinhood of Pitts, Grenvilles, and Wyndhams, 'amiable, absent-minded, of unimpeachable integrity and benevolent character',[4] styled by Pope as 'true to virtue, as warm as true',[5] was also implicitly recognized as patron of James Thomson in 'The Seasons', although the work was not actually dedicated to him, as was Fielding's *Tom Jones*. Despite the success of the poem, after the publication of the four parts between 1726 and 1730, James Thomson was poor and benefited from the patron-

---

[1] R. Colt Hoare, *History of Modern Wiltshire* (London, 1822).
[2] Mrs. P. Lybbe Powys, *Passages from the Diaries. 1756–1808*, ed. E. J. Climenson (London, 1899).
[3] David Hartley, *Observations on Man* (London, 1749).
[4] *Dictionary of National Biography*.
[5] 'Imitations of Horace', Ep. I, i, line 30.

age of Frederick, Prince of Wales, to whom he had been introduced by Lyttelton. Perhaps with Somerville's query in mind,

> Why should the Muse, born so divinely fair,
> Want the reforming toilet's daily care?

Thomson and Lyttelton, himself a poet, revised 'The Seasons' at Hagley in 1743, and republished it with illustrations by William Kent.

The poem's popularity at the time may now surprise us. Joseph Warton placed it with Milton's and Pope's verse in 'diffusing a general taste for the beauties of nature and landscape'. Cowper spoke of it warmly, and Coleridge found a much-thumbed copy in a pub. In the Augustan Age it was rare for the poetic Muse to go out of doors for over 5,000 lines of blank verse, and she was evidently enjoying herself at Hagley and elsewhere. Caught by the novelty of the situation, Thomson's readers were stirred by his love of all that visually makes a landscape—the changes of colour, texture, and movement of sky, trees or earth. It is difficult to paint in words, but his readers thought that he had been successful.

> Behold yon breathing prospect bids the Muse
> Throw all her beauty forth. But who can paint
> Like Nature? Can imagination boast,
> Amid its gay creation, hues like hers?
> Or can it mix them with that matchless skill,
> And lose them in each other, as appears
> In every bud that blows? If fancy then
> Unequal fails beneath the pleasing task,
> Ah, what shall language do? ah, where find words
> Tinged with so many colours . . .[1]

Having since followed Wordsworth in 'The Prelude', we know that Thomson had neither his narrative interest nor his philosophic insight, when walking over the same ground; but the eighteenth century was happy to follow Thomson's 'thoughts continual climb', not knowing how his heart might have leapt. What appealed most were Thomson's excursive pictures of the natural scene, in storm or

[1] 'Spring', lines 467–79.

calm, at home and abroad, and the constant topographical-reflective passages. Much of 'Summer' and 'Autumn' is really a travelogue with snatches of the geography of South America, Abyssinia, or Lapland, and the history of Ancient Greece and Rome thrown in to spice it. In none of these places does Nature in the raw, as in primeval Africa, appeal to him. The Savage is not yet Noble.

> Love dwells not there,
> The soft regards, the tenderness of life,
> The heart-shed tear, the ineffable delight
> Of sweet humanity: these court the beam
> Of milder climes . . .[1]

which, of course, includes Britain. Thomson's repeated patriotic eulogies and optimistic faith in Britain do not allow one to forget the author of the song, 'Rule Britannia' (1740),[2] which, as Southey said, was 'the political hymn of this country as long as she maintains her political power'.

> Rich is thy soil, and merciful thy clime;
> Thy streams unfailing in the Summer's drought;
> Unmatched thy guardian-oaks; thy valleys float
> With golden waves;[3]

Altogether, in the four parts, there are only three direct references to landscaping. The first, in 'Spring', is to Hagley of his patron, which he visited for the first time in 1743; the 'place I most desire to see', he writes in July to George Lyttelton.

In the meantime I will go on correcting 'The Seasons', and hope to carry down more than one of them with me. The muses, whom you obligingly say I shall bring along with me, I shall find with you—the muses of the great simple country, not the fine-lady muses of Richmond-hill. I have lived so long in the noise, or at least in the distant din of the town, that I begin to forget what retirement is: with you I shall enjoy it in its highest elegance and purest simplicity. The mind will not only be soothed into peace, but enlivened into harmony. My compliments attend all at Hagley, and particularly her who gives it charms to you it never had before.

---

[1] 'Summer', lines 890–4.   [2] From 'Alfred'.   [3] 'Summer', lines 1446–9.

In 'Spring', he describes George Lyttelton, accompanied by his young wife, Lucy, walking through Hagley amid such a scene of beauty that he, like Contentment,

> feels an inward bliss
> Spring o'er his mind, beyond the power of kings
> To purchase. Pure Serenity apace
> Induces thought, and contemplation still.
> By swift degrees the love of nature works,
> And warms the bosom; till the last, sublimed
> To rapture and enthusiastic heat,
> We feel the present Deity and taste
> The joy of God to see a happy World![1]

Despite the reference to Enthusiasm, Thomson is as sure of the truth of feelings induced by Nature, if regulated, as was Shaftesbury. Contentment and Serenity are *summum bonum*. Yet the scene which Thomson describes is not as regulated as one might think.

> There along the dale
> With woods o'erhung, and shagged with mossy rocks,
> Whence on each hand the gushing waters play,
> And down the rough cascade white-dashing fall
> Or gleam in lengthened vista through the trees,[2]

It is a picturesque scene which he enjoys, and certainly one which he prefers, as Il Penseroso, to the 'wide-extended walks, The fair majestic paradise of Stowe', to which he refers in 'Autumn'. This is likewise the season which he prefers: 'The spirits are not then dissipated with the gaiety of Spring and the glaring light of Summer, but composed into a serious and tempered joy.'[3] No 'glaring light' but an autumnal glow dominates many of Claude's landscapes, and there are influences, as Professor Manwaring[4] has pointed out, which are very evident in Thomson's descriptions, for Thomson had been on the Grand Tour and therefore must have seen these or other similar poetic conceptions of ideal landscape. Autumn is the season that brings a philosophic melancholy whose effects he clearly

---

[1] 'Spring', lines 895–903.   [2] 'Spring', lines 909–13.
[3] James Thomson to George Lyttelton, 14 July 1743.
[4] Elizabeth Manwaring, *Italian Landscape in Eighteenth Century England* (New York, 1925).

described. It is not 'loathed Melancholy', or the black melancholia of Elizabethan usage, but more as Evelyn used the word when he described the royal park at Brussels: 'nor is it less pleasant than in the most solitary recesses, so naturally it is furnish'd with whatever may render it agreeable, melancholy and country-like'.[1] For Thomson, it is a 'Sacred Influence' which 'inflames Imagination', exalts 'swelling Thought and induces sympathies of Love and Friendship dear'. Thomson is at his best here:

> Oh! bear me then to vast embowering shades,
> To twilight groves, and visionary vales,
> To weeping grottoes, and prophetic glooms;
> Where angel forms athwart the solemn dusk,
> Tremendous, sweep, or seem to sweep along;
> And voices more than human, through the void
> Deep-sounding, seize the enthusiastic ear.[2]

He does not feel that the Gloom is 'too much'; although he uses the question in order to move on to Stowe, where

> Not Persian Cyrus on Ionia's shore
> E'er saw such sylvan scenes, such various art
> By genius fired, such ardent genius tamed
> By cool judicious art, that in the strife
> All-beauteous Nature fears to be outdone.

This is certainly not Nature helping Art, and Art enriching Nature, but rather Nature conflicting with Art to the detriment of both. Thomson shows more enthusiasm for

> The negligence of Nature, wide, and wild
> Where, undisguised by mimic art, she spreads
> Unbounded beauty to the roving eye.

Not for him, Cobham's[3] 'verdant files of order'd Trees' at Stowe; though he is not always consistent. For at the end of his effusively optimistic poem, 'Liberty', he links Stowe with the more natural landscaping which we know he admired.

---

[1] *Diary*, 8 October 1641.   [2] 'Autumn', lines 1030–6.

[3] The first Lord Cobham was George Lyttelton's maternal uncle, and in 1752, on becoming Earl Temple, was possibly the richest man in England.

> See! Sylvan scenes where art alone pretends
> To dress her mistress, and disclose her charms—
> Such as a Pope in miniature has shown,
> A Bathurst o'er the widening forest spreads,[1]
> And such as form a Richmond, Chiswick, Stowe.[2]

Perhaps it was fortunate that death prevented Thomson from seeing all George Lyttelton's later improvements at Hagley, for some features might have been like 'cool, judicious art'. Unlike Dyer, he was, for example, no great lover of ruins and when in Rome was critical of

> the falling poor remains
> Of what exalted once the Ausonian shore.[3]

There are about thirty more lines in 'Autumn' in which is described the landscaping at Vanbrugh's Eastbury[4] of Bubb Dodington, 'Where simple Nature reigns and every View Diffusive, spreads the pure Dorsetian Downs'. Possibly 'simple Nature' reigned in the distant prospect; but the gardens were all Art, being designed by Bridgeman with strictly formal parterres, oblong basin, symmetrical walks and groves.[5] Thomson could not forget that Bubb Dodington had been Maecenas to him. At the end of this section are the best lines in the poem: magnificent lines, reminiscent of, but better than, some of Virgil's Second Georgic:

> Oh Nature! all-sufficient! over all
> Enrich me with the knowledge of thy works;
> Snatch me to heaven;. . . .
>
> .   .   .   .   .
>
> But, if to that unequal, if the blood
> In sluggish streams about my heart forbid
> That best ambition, under closing shades
> Inglorious lay me by the lowly brook,
> And whisper to my dreams.

---

[1] Oakley woods of Allen, 1st Lord Bathurst, at Cirencester.
[2] 'Liberty', Part V, lines 696–700.   [3] 'Liberty', Part I, lines 41–42.
[4] Eastbury: five miles from Blandford, completed 1738, demolished 1782.
[5] Gough drawings in the Bodleian Library.

Like Henry Hoare, George Lyttelton suffered three bereavements in a short time: his beloved Lucy, *'uxori dilectissimae'* of
Roubiliac's monument, died in childbirth in 1747,[1] James Thomson
in the next year, and his father in 1751. Thereafter, at about the
same age as Henry Hoare, he set himself to improving his estate,
although he had started in his father's lifetime. The change between
1751 and 1756 is described at length by that inveterate traveller,
Dr. Richard Pococke,[2] afterwards Bishop of Meath. During the
course of years there is hardly a new piece of landscaping in England
that Pococke does not visit and write about in much detail, noting
minute improvements as much as omitting human details. He
visited Hagley in June 1751, a few months before Sir Thomas
Lyttelton's death. There he saw a new plantation of trees on the
hill to the east, a shady walk and a hermitage in the middle of the
wood to the south, and 'large lawns' as well as a 'ruined castle'.
This is mentioned by Horace Walpole after a visit in 1753:

. . . enchanting scenes . . . a hill of three miles, but broke into all
manner of beauty; such lawns, such wood, rills, cascades and a thick-
ness of verdure quite to the summit of this hill, and commanding such
a vale of towns and meadows, and woods extending quite to the Black
Mountain in Wales, that I quite forgot my favourite Thames! Indeed
I prefer nothing to Hagley but Mount Edgecumbe. There is extreme
taste in the park. The seats are not of the best, but there is not one
absurdity. There is a ruined castle, built by Miller, that would get
him his freedom, even of Strawberry: it has the true rust of the
barons' wars. Then there is such a scene of a small lake, with cascades
falling down such a Parnassus! with a circular temple on a distant
eminence; and there is such a fairy dale, with more cascades gushing
out of the rocks! And there is a hermitage so exactly like those of
Sadeler's prints, on the brow of a shady mountain, stealing peeps into
the glorious world below! And there is such a pretty well in a wood,

---

[1] James Granger in his 'Ode to Solitude' was sympathetic:

> And late in Hagley you were seen,
> With bloodshed eyes and sombre mien,
> Hymen his yellow vestments tore,
> And Dirge a wreath of cypress wore.

[2] Richard Pococke, *Travels thro' England*, Camden Society (London, 1888).

like the Samaritan woman's in a picture of Niccolo Poussin! And there is such a wood without the park, enjoying such a prospect![1]

Plate VIII is most likely the picture to which Horace Walpole refers. It is doubtful if he ever saw the original painting, for it certainly never came to England, but he would have known the composition from the engraving. The round tower on the brow of the hill resembles Miller's ruined castle, which Shenstone described to Lady Luxborough as 'one entire Tow'r, and three Stumps of Towers, with a ruin'd Wall betwixt them . . .' (6 June 1748). As the stones of the ruined castle were taken from near-by Halesowen Abbey, which was being dismantled, it can never have looked new, as Miller's Sham Castle at Bath does today. To encourage the appearance of antiquity

the large mossy stones which have seemingly tumbled from the tottering and ruinous walls, are suffered to lie about the different parts of the building in the utmost confusion. This greatly preserves its intention and confirms the common opinion of every stranger of its early date; while, to carry a stronger face of antiquity, ivy is encouraged to climb about the walls and turrets, and it now so closely embraces those parts with its glossy arms, that it is impossible to look upon it without a suggestion of its being ancient as it really appears.[2]

This is pure Picturesque, as was the description of the hermitage in the woods, 'on the brow of a shady mountain, stealing peeps into the glorious world below'.[3] It was made with the roots of trees with a seat round it covered with matting, and in this quiet, retired spot were engraved Milton's concluding lines from 'Il Penseroso':

> And may at last my weary age
> Find out the peaceful hermitage,
> The Hairy Gown and Mossy Cell,
> Where I may sit and rightly spell
> Of every Star that Heav'n doth shew,
> And every Herb that sips the dew;

[1] Horace Walpole to Richard Bentley, September 1753.
[2] Contemporary Guide to Worcestershire.   [3] Richard Pococke, op. cit.

Till old experience do attain
To something like Prophetic strain.
These pleasures, *Melancholy* give,
And I with thee will choose to live.

When Dr. Pococke paid his second visit, in September 1756, there were great changes evident. A 'fine house with four fronts of freestone' had been built to Sanderson Miller's austere Palladian design. Perhaps it was mistaken judgement on Lyttelton's part not to take the advice of Horace Walpole to employ John Chute of The Vyne, one of the architects of Strawberry. The grounds were extended to include the area where the old house and garden were. Additional features were 'a beautiful cascade falling down the rocks;[1] a grotto where the water runs; a statue of Venus of Medici as coming out of a fountain' and a stream running from it, to the right of which was a mossy seat with the inscription

Ego laudo ruris amoeni
Rivos et musco circumlita saxa nemusque.[2]

Another seat was under an oak, 'adorned with turning honey-suckle'; an urn sacred to the memory of Pope; a statue of Apollo; a rotunda on a height with a dome supported by eight Ionic pillars; a half-octagon building on an eminence with the inscription:

Ingenio Immortali
Jacobi Thomson
Poetae Sublimis
Viri Boni
Aediculam hanc, in secessu, quam vivus dilexit
Post mortem ejus constructam
Dicat dedicatque
Georgius Lyttelton

Even the hermitage had further additions, including a seat 'adorned

---

[1] G. B. Hill, ed., *Boswell's Life of Johnson* (Oxford, 1950), Vol. 5, p. 456: Samuel Johnson (17 September 1774) thought the park wanted water, and had only one temporary cascade.
[2] Horace, Epistles, I : x, 7.

    I joy to sit where streams meand'ring rove,
    O'er plains and moss-grown rocks, and through the grove.

with bones made in thin snail shells split in two', and appropriately
inscribed

Sedes Contemplationis
Omnia Vanitas

Pococke also mentions a 'rough Dorick portico' which must have
been the Temple of Theseus, designed by James 'Athenian' Stuart,
an interesting building architecturally, as it was the first Greek
Doric building in this country. Around this was a beautiful shrubbery, full of curious plants such as 'orange trees and other exoticks';
and lastly a column to the memory of Frederick, Prince of Wales,
to whom Thomson was grateful for patronage, and Lyttelton
indebted for office. It must indeed have been 'the finest ground in
which nature is helped by art, with the greatest taste, in the most
elegant manner . . .'[1] with its great beech woods tumbling down
the steep hill to the house, its cascades, hermitage, sham castle,
Temple of Theseus, rotunda, and seats with limitless prospects to
the Welsh border.

Perhaps the obelisk, which still stands, is ironically suitable in
grounds owned by the Lytteltons, for was not Frederick, Prince of
Wales, a cricketer? And did not the nineteenth-century Lytteltons
puncture the family portraits while at winter cricket practice in the
Long Gallery? Today the only well-kept section of Hagley is the
cricket field adjoining the house. Elsewhere, chicken coops sprawl
near the ha-ha, ruined oaks and broken seats lie untended, barbed
wire fences bisect vistas, derelict drains indicate one-time cascades,
the urn to Pope's memory is overturned, lorries roar near by, and
the octopus of building estates clutches the perimeter. It is impossible to imagine it as 'an object of pilgrimage', as its guide-book
expresses it, and hard to find the soul of a great landscape into which
the iron of Birmingham has entered. Though 'the Cambrian
Mountains like far Clouds' still 'skirt the blue Horizon', George
Lyttelton would not recognize it. Thomson's paragon, Sir Industry,
has won.

Within four miles of Hagley, to the north-east of Halesowen, a
friend of George Lyttelton's, William Shenstone, the poet (1714–63),

---

[1] Richard Pococke, op. cit.

designed and executed a landscape which brought him more fame than his verses. For a few years before 1745 (when he took over his father's estate, the Leasowes)[1] until his death, he stayed there, quietly reflective like Horace on his Sabine Farm, writing lyric poetry, entertaining his friends and improving his grounds. Samuel Johnson, in his *Lives of the English Poets*, was critical of his activities:

from this time he began to point his prospects, to diversify his surface, to entangle his walks, and to wind his waters; which he did with such judgment and such fancy, as made his little domain the envy of the great and the admiration of the skilful; a place to be visited by travellers, and copied by designers.

But Johnson continues pontifically with the dictum that landscaping should be considered as an 'innocent amusement' to be treated as a sport rather than as 'the business of human reason'; to which Richard Graves, Shenstone's friend from his Pembroke College, Oxford, days retaliated with the epigram:

> Bred up in Birmingham, in Litchfield born,
> No wonder rural beauties he should scorn.

Shenstone never had an income of more than £300 a year, which was insufficient for landscaping on the grand scale, as at Hagley or Stourhead, though in eighteenth-century terms it was not negligible. Oliver Goldsmith's parson was 'passing rich with forty pounds a year' in his modest mansion with its overgrown garden, though Sweet Auburn was in Ireland, where living was cheaper. Yet at the Leasowes Shenstone had an excellent natural site, with fine prospects over Worcestershire and Shropshire, a house pleasantly sited on a hill and no shortage of springs or water. William Pitt[2] (later Earl of Chatham), on looking at some of the old oaks and beeches, remarked that Nature had done everything for him, to which Shenstone, remembering that his cascades had been 'absolutely no more than a mere ditch',[3] replied 'that he hoped that

---

[1] Old English *lǽs* meaning pastureland.
[2] William Pitt 'improved' his own villa at Enfield Chase (sixty-five acres) in 1747.
[3] Richard Graves, *Recollection of some particulars in the life of the late William Shenstone* (London, 1788).

VII. (*a*) 'Coast View of Delos with Aeneas' by Claude Lorrain.

VII. (*b*) Entrance to the gardens, Stourhead, Wiltshire.

VIII "The Samaritan Woman at the Well", engraved by Nicholas Poussin

he had done something for Nature too'.[1] Compared with Hagley it was a small area, as Pembroke College is to Christ Church; but, as Lancelot Brown would later have said, it had 'capabilities'. The house, a medium-sized farmhouse, backed by trees to the north, stood in the centre of what was an inverted triangle of ground with its apex high on a hill, with streams running down dingles along the two sides to a pool along the base. Throughout this area he planned a *ferme ornée*, with walks, taking in a series of views to the Clee Hills, the Wrekin and, on a clear day, the Welsh mountains. Along these walks he placed features such as memorial urns to his friends, alive or dead (Thomson, Lyttelton, and Somerville), as well as statues, and seats with inscriptions. It was essentially a terrain in which one walked, in which 'the effeminate indulgence of a carriage was not possible'.[2] At the start one passed a ruined ivy-clad Gothic priory, then went on into a grotto,

> *Intus aquae dulces, vivoque sedilia saxo,*
> *nympharum domo*[3]

('The haunt of Nereids, fram'd by nature's hands'), followed by a root-house, and after going round the top of the hill, perhaps resting at a seat from which one could see three counties, one dropped down through a wood in which there was a delightful cascade, for 150 yards, which was dedicated to Virgil. This is the bare outline of a landscape that enchanted all except Horace Walpole, who was disdainful of its 'insipidity'. Shenstone's friend, the poet and publisher Robert Dodsley, has described it in verse, after his first visit in 1754:

> The bursting torrent tumbles down the steep
> In foaming fury; fierce, irregular,
> Wild interrupted, cross'd with rocks and roots
> And interwoven trees, till, soon absorbed,
> An opening cavern all its rage entombs.
> So vanish human glories.

---

[1] Quoted by Richard Graves in *Columella*, Chap. XX (London, 1779).

[2] Joseph Heely, *Letters on the Beauties of Hagley, Envil and the Leasowes* (London, 1777).

[3] Virgil, *Aeneid*, Book I, line 167. This quotation was also used at Stourhead. It associates the grotto with the African shore on which Aeneas landed.

No Naiad's leading step conducts the rill;
Nor sylvan god presiding skirts the lawn
In beauteous wildness with fair-spreading trees,
Nor magic wand has circumscribed the scene,
'Tis thine own taste, thy genius that presides.

Some years later he also wrote an uncritical encomium in prose of the scene—even a distant glass factory appears like a pyramid—but he summed up what must have been its chief characteristic: 'the hand of art is in no way visible either in the shape of the ground, the disposition of the trees, or (which are numerous and striking) the romantic fall of the cascades'.[1]

In his essay, *Unconnected Thoughts on Gardening*, Shenstone outlines what, in fact, he achieved at the Leasowes. The essential was a Variety in a series of pictures—variety in tone, texture and position of objects, so placed that one reacted on another. Groups of trees and sweeps of lawn, urns, seats, and other architectural features would contrast with scars of rock or other natural objects to form compositions from different viewpoints. He was also interested in the relationship in scale of objects to the whole composition. 'Taste in gardens etc. has little more to do than to collect the Beauties of Nature into a compass proper for its own observation.' No particular painters are mentioned from which one might determine the type of composition to which he referred. Although he was a water-colourist himself, might his lack of knowledge of landscape painters be because he disliked the Grand Tour, on which he never went?

Deluded Youth! that quits these verdant plains
To catch the follies of an alien soil!

('Elegy XIV')

Ruins, Shenstone says, have variety in the texture of their surface and also inspire scope for the imagination in their decayed magnificence. Straight lines, for the past fondness for which he could not account, have no variety, as Hogarth remarked. So avenues, if used, should show the art of distancing, by a gradual tonal diminution of distinctness through the conjunction of different trees: starting,

---

[1] Robert Dodsley, *A Description of the Leasowes* (London, 1773).

for example, with yew, and grading through fir to almond-willow or silver osier. On the 'tour' of the grounds no spot should be seen twice from the same viewpoint. Novelty (Pope's 'Surprise') was essential, and this could be achieved by woods suddenly opening to reveal a prospect, or a corner being suddenly turned to show an urn or obelisk, in scale and form rightly contrasting with its surroundings. Like Burke, a copy of whose *Inquiry into the Origin of our Ideas on the Sublime and the Beautiful* he possessed, he links Beauty with Smoothness, and Grandeur with Simplicity. Shenstone's method in the Essay is indeed unconnected, repetitive and rarely particularized, except, for example, in his abhorrence of small circular clumps of firs (*pace* Kent and Brown), which when placed in the middle of a lawn reminded him of 'a coronet placed on an elephant or camel's back'. Most of these tenets of Naturalism are taken up by the Picturesque followers at the end of the century, and, in the main, the Leasowes appealed to them.

Shenstone's achievement in his verse was to fuse this environment to a virtuous life: guided by Shaftesbury, and Pope in his 'Essay on Man', he thought that 'the most important end of all poetry was to encourage virtue, and cyclically, that virtue grew from the landscape that was the inspiration for the verse. It was doubtful, says Whately, 'whether the spot inspired his verse; or whether in the scenes which he formed, he only realized the pastoral images which abound in his songs'.[1] Unfortunately, little of Shenstone's verse is more than second-class. Although in his 'Elegies', for which he is best known, ideas are expressed which other poets later make memorable, there is really nothing more than moralizing, and no real philosophy of Nature.

> En'n now sagacious foresight points to show
> A little bench of heedless bishops here,
> And there a little chancellour in embryo
> Or bard sublime, if bard may e'er be so
> As Milton, Shakspear, names that ne'er shall dye!

predates by a few years Gray's 'mute inglorious Milton' and 'village Hampden'. And also, in the same poem,

[1] Sir Thomas Whately, *Observations on Modern Gardening* (London, 1771).

> Enjoy, poor imps, enjoy your sportive trade
> For never may ye taste more careless hours,

was written before

> Alas, regardless of their doom
> The little victims play!
> No sense have they of ills to come,
> Nor care beyond today.

Yet the whole of the 'The Schoolmistress' (1737, revised 1742), which Pope thought his best poem, though written 'in imitation of Spenser in its language and tenderness of sentiment', is infinitely less memorable than either Gray's Ode or his Elegy. Nearly a third of Shenstone's poem is taken up with a detailed description of an incident in which the schoolmistress uses her birch on some unfortunate child who has failed in his history lesson; how she 'looses his brogues' till his 'dainty skin shows', then 'levels her aim', and how the 'bum y-galled boy' is then isolated.[1] Admittedly Shenstone censures her with 'Beware, ye Dames . . .'; but the incident and her actions do not seem to agree with her 'passing much time in truly virtuous deed' in her thatched cottage with

> trim rosemarine, that whilom crown'd
> The daintiest garden of the proudest peer.

Sir Walter Scott said that from childhood he had read Dodsley's account of the Leasowes with the greatest joy. He envied Shenstone more for the pleasure of accomplishing the objects detailed than for the 'possession of pipe, crook, flock, and Phyllis to boot'. Pastoral ballads did not appeal to Samuel Johnson, who was sickened at the mention of pastoral paraphernalia, and fortunately, as Shenstone matured, he wrote ballads of another type, although they were not at the time popular. In one of these ('Elegy XXVI') the pathetic fallacy seems to have been stretched to a more mawkish extreme

---

[1] In more recent times another poet, Wilfred Blunt, presented some birch trees to the headmaster of Christ's Hospital near by. They have not been used for the purpose he suggested, but, on growing to maturity, help to break a corner of a red-brick quadrangle.

than parts of Tennyson. After Jessy, the heroine, has been undone by her lover, the flowers reproach her with

> Hope not to find delight in us, they say,
> For we are spotless, Jessy, we are pure.

Despite Ruskin finding 'perfection of truth and tenderness of imagination' in this passage, the ballad was little read, even in Victorian times. Likewise,

> Lo! not an hedge-row hawthorn blows
> Or humble harebell paints the plain
> Or valley winds, or fountain flows,
> Or purple heath is ting'd in vain

with its foretaste of Wordsworth, has not earned Shenstone a place in *The Oxford Book of English Verse*, or altered posterity's agreement with Walpole and Gray in their estimates of the 'water-gruel bard',[1] about whom Gray wrote that he 'trusts to nature and simple sentiment, why does he no better? He goes hopping along his own gravel-walks, and never deviates from the beaten paths for fear of being lost.' But Walpole's and Gray's dismissal of his landscape was unfair. The influence of the Leasowes on all whose incomes did not enable them to 'improve' on the grand scale was universal. During Shenstone's lifetime his estate was often visited by the Lytteltons, their friends, including James Thomson, and their relations, the Pitts and Grenvilles.

> And distant sounds foretold th'approach
> Of frequent chaise and crowded coach,
> For sons of taste and daughters fair,
> Hasted the sweet surprise to share,
> While Hagley wonder'd at their stay
> And hardly brook'd the long delay.[2]

---

[1] Matthew Green in 'The Spleen' (1737) has a curious apostrophe to this food made by boiling pearl barley in water:

> Hail! water-gruel, healing power
> Of easy access to the poor;
> Thy help love's confessors implore,
> And doctors secretly adore.

[2] Richard Jago, 'Labour and Genius'.

Parties of such diverse people as Adam Smith, William Pitt, Oliver
Goldsmith, Edmund Burke, and John Wesley; and his literary
friends of the Warwickshire coterie, among whom was Sanderson
Miller, might have been conducted round by the poet, clad in his
plain blue coat and scarlet waistcoat that he invariably wore, and
accompanied by Lucy, his whippet, who sits at his feet in Edward
Alcock's portrait in the National Portrait Gallery. He was even
pleased to show his work to the local inhabitants, until 'the liberty
his good nature granted was soon turned into licentiousness; the
people destroying the shrubs, picking the flowers, breaking down
the hedges and doing other damage'.[1]

Shenstone was a 'simple, elegant and amiable'[2] bachelor who had
many lifelong friends, among whom was the Reverend Richard
Jago, the poet, who had known him from his schooldays at Solihull
School, where the two main interests of Shenstone's life seem to
have already shown, for he helped Jago both with his verses, and also
to 'scoop rude grottoes in the shelving bank'. Later in life Jago held a
living near Sanderson Miller in Warwickshire, and there he wrote
his poetic appreciation of Miller's landscaping, which included the
building of Radway Tower, to commemorate the place on the
summit of Edgehill, where Charles I raised his standard before
the battle that opened the Civil War. The long poem, 'Edgehill; or,
the Rural Prospect delineated and moralized' (1767), is more topographical than 'Grongar's Hill' or 'Cooper's Hill', and has none of
their quality. In the course of it he manages to mention some of the
history and geography of most of the country seats in Warwickshire, and even the characteristics of the chief towns, including
Bremicham, alias Birmingham, in correct but uninspired penta-
meters. Of Radway he writes:

> Thanks, Miller! to thy Paths
> That ease our winding steps! Thanks to the fount,
> The trees, the flowrs, imparting to the sense
> Fragrance, or dulcet sound of murmuring rill,
> And stilling ev'ry tumult in the breast!
> And oft the stately wood, and oft the broken arch,

---

[1] James Woodhouse, the neighbouring cobbler and poet, whom Shenstone be-
friended.
[2] Thomas Whately, *Observations on the Art of Gardening* (London 1771).

Or mould'ring wall, well taught to counterfeit
The waste of time, to solemn thought excite,
And crown with graceful pomp a shaggy hill.
So virtue paints the steep ascent to fame
So her aerial resistance displays.

This last image is from Shaftesbury, for Jago, like Shenstone, was influenced by his thought.

Seek not with fruitless cost, the level plain
To raise aloft, nor sink the rising hill.
Each has its charms, though diff'rent; each in kind
Improve, not alter. Art with art conceal.
Let no strait-terrac'd lines your slopes deform;[1]

But Charles Lyttelton thought Jago's poem was 'diluted' and 'obscure', though it had 'pretty lines'; and indeed it was strange that in referring to Radway and its inhabitants Jago said nothing more than to comment on Miller's having made the ascent of Edgehill easy. Miller's tower and thatched cottage were the admiration of his friends, among whom were William Pitt, George Lyttelton, Lord North, and Lord Dacre. This lofty octagonal tower, built in splendid stone from a near-by quarry, is still a prominent feature of the southern Warwickshire landscape. Unfortunately the attitude expressed some fifty years ago by the authors of *An Eighteenth Century Correspondence to Sanderson Miller of Radway* is still common. 'To our modern ideas', they write, 'it seems an absurd extravagance to have spent so much on a building that served no other purpose than an "object" in and from which to survey a fine prospect, and as a summer-house in which to picnic.' Dr. Pococke echoed contemporary enthusiasm by saying that Miller had 'made a fine lawn up the hill, with shady walks round it, up to the ruined castle on Edgehill' and had 'erected a very noble Round tower which is entire, to which there is an ascent as by a ruine, and there is a very fine octagon Gothic room in it, with four windows and four niches, and some old painted glass in the windows'.

Another friend of Shenstone's for many years was the Reverend Richard Graves, whose novel *The Spiritual Quixote* or *The Summer*

---

[1] Richard Jago, op. cit.

Ramble of Mr. Geoffrey Wildgoose (1722) is the precursor of *Humphry Clinker* in its irony and letter form. Mr. Wildgoose, the hero, is a burlesque portrait of Whitefield, the Methodist, whom the author had known at Pembroke College, Oxford. The enthusiasm of the early Methodists in their encounters with what they considered evil-doing is ridiculed throughout. When Mr. Wildgoose and his companion Jerry Tugwell stop in Hagley village at an inn the local inhabitants think that Wildgoose, who wears a black coat and will not have a drink, is a parson. He is, however, forced to listen to the gossip of the innkeeper, who tells them of the housekeeper of the Lytteltons, who is 'the d-ndest b-tch in all England'. They move on quickly to Halesowen, where they are at once informed that Shenstone's Folly is the name the 'common people give to any work of taste, the utility of which exceeds their comprehension'. (The novel is full of such irony.) On entering the grounds they see the poet 'in his own hair' giving directions to some labourers who are working overtime in order to finish a 'receptacle for a cataract of water'. They are then shown round by the owner. Mr. Wildgoose's reactions are not dissimilar from Wesley's in real life at Stourhead: a garden should be considered only as an amusement and not be allowed to engross our attention. The next morning, having entertained them overnight, Shenstone is surprised to find their rooms empty; but there is a note on the table from Mr. Wildgoose.

I am called hence by the Spirit: in the visions of the night it was revealed to me. I must own that, like good Publius, you have received and lodged us courteously and my bowels yearn for your salvation! But, my dear friend, I am afraid you have set up idols in your heart. You seem to pay a greater regard to Pan and Sylvanus than to Paul or Silas. You have forsaken the fountains of the living Lord, and hewn you out cisterns, broken cisterns, that will hold no water: but my conscience beareth testimony against this idolatry. Bel boweth down, Nebo stoopeth. I have delivered my own soul and will pray for your conversion.

> Your brother in the Lord,
> Geoffrey Wildgoose.

Shenstone expresses further surprise at this letter, but on going into his estate finds the sluices opened, the reservoirs empty, and the leaden statue of the Piping Faun thrown down. However, he consoles himself with the thought that Lord Dartmouth and his guests, whom he is expecting that day, will find the incident amusing. In the meantime, Jerry Tugwell, like the second clown-gravedigger at Elsinore, starts to ask questions of Mr. Wildgoose, for he expected a warrant out for their arrest. Mr. Shenstone, he reasons, seemed 'a sensible gentleman' who would not be so foolish as to 'worship images as the Papishes do'. He adds as a final piece of reasoning: 'Why, there is our squire has got a naked thing-emybob stands up in the middle of the grove (it is either Virgin Mary or Fair Rosamond or Dinah that was ravished by the Jacobites)', yet he had never heard that the squire worshipped it. But Mr. Wildgoose gives him no satisfactory answers and they continue on their way to Birmingham.

Richard Graves satirized Shenstone in *Columella*, another novel (Plate IX). Two friends of Columella (Shenstone), having just arrived on a visit, are surprised to find their 'philosophical friend, with a faggot-stick in one hand, and a book in the other, his hair about his ears, and one stocking about his heels'. The cause of his anxiety is some pigs which have routed up his primroses and peri-winkles. On the brow of the hill is the Sibyl's temple, 'ruinated like that at Tivoli', while in the valley the Gothic tower of the parish church appears above the trees. Coplestone Warre Bampfylde (1719–91) was himself a landscape gardener on his estate at Hester-combe near Taunton, where there are still the remains of a steep cascade and a Doric temple; and on an urn, recently overturned, is an inscription, dated 1786, to Henry Hoare of Stourhead, comparing him to Virgil.

As well as tending to his own landscape, Shenstone was able to help his friends with theirs; these included Lady Luxborough, his chief correspondent, at Barrels, Henley-in-Arden, and Lord Stam-ford at Enville near by. This must have been a picturesque setting, with a humble thatched cottage, 'with its little circular lawn in front, and the graceful clustering trees that verge the area, and form a perfect canopy over the building.'[1] These, writes Joseph Heely,

---

[1] Joseph Heely, *Letters on the Beauties of Hagley, Envil and the Leasowes* (London, 1777).

have 'greater powers to charm the eye of taste than the most magnificent temple, loaded with all the finery art can give'. There was also a chapel dedicated to Shenstone, a Gothic Shepherd's Lodge, a rotunda, an Octagon Boat House, and even a Gothic billiard-room in which, incongruously, there was a small organ and busts of Homer and Cicero, presumably to improve the standard of play. But all of these are either in ruins or non-existent today, and the trees have been felled.

Shenstone's influence spread farther—to the marquis de Girardin, at Ermenonville, his château thirty miles north-east of Paris. To lay out gardens in England may mean, as we shall see, destroying older landscapes; but in France it certainly meant a disastrous sweeping away of formal gardens near the house if the whole was to be 'improved' and made into a *jardin à l'anglaise*. The marquis at Ermenonville required a romantic landscape, so asked Shenstone's advice. The result was magnificent of its sort, and later became famous for its association with Rousseau, who not only spent the last few months of his life there (in 1778) but had earlier chosen it as the ideal landscape in which to place Julie, the heroine, and her lover, Saint-Preux, of his novel *La Nouvelle Héloise*, written in the late 1750s. It was a time of change in Rousseau's life: '*jusqu'alors l'indignation de la vertu m'avait tenu lieu d'Apollon; la tendresse et la douceur d'âme m'entinrent lieu cette fois*'.[1] In this setting one would expect to find, in the course of the novel, more of Rousseau's love of freedom in Nature and a converse hatred of all formality in landscaping. He expresses this freely elsewhere in his works; and except for Rousseau's not allowing any buildings in his landscape, this passage might have come from Shenstone.

L'erreur des prétendus gens de goût est de vouloir de l'art partout, et de n'être jamais content que l'art ne paroisse. . . . Que signifient ces allées si droites, si sablées, qu'on trouve sans cesse, et ces étoiles, par lesquelles, bien loin d'étendre aux yeux la grandeur d'un parc, comme on l'imagine, on ne fait qu'en montrer mal-adroitement les bornes?

In Letter XXIII, to Julie in *La Nouvelle Héloise*, Rousseau cites Pet-

---

[1] J. J. Rousseau, *Confessions*, 487 (Penguin Books edition, London, 1953).

rarch, who had earlier stated exactly what Rousseau wished for in
the natural scene:

> *Qui non palazzi, non teatro o loggia*
> *Ma'n lor vece un'abete, un faggio, un pino,*
> *Tra l'erba verde e'l bel monte vicino,*
> *Levan di terra al ciel nostr' intelletto.*

Yet despite Julie's Elysium at Clarens (Ermenonville), and the novel
being much referred to by later English writers on landscaping,
there is, in fact, little expression of Rousseau's ideas of freedom in
Nature, except, possibly, for Saint-Preux's references to the grandeur of mountains, which may have helped to relieve the eighteenth
century of some of its horror of them. There is much more, at length,
of Saint-Preux's erotic emotions, in relation to the natural scene,
rather than an expression of aesthetic sensibility. It was a strange
novel for *le citoyen de Genève* to have written.

The marquis erected a mausoleum temple of Pastoral Muses,
with inscriptions to Shenstone, Thomson, and other poets. Surrounding this was landscaping which must have been formed by
the marquis with Shenstone's *Unconnected Thoughts* in his hand.
Four years after Shenstone's death, the marquis published his
essay, '*De la Composition des Paysages*'. In this he stressed the necessity
for Variety in the assemblage of colours and in a negligence of grace
and nature. And, like Shenstone, he advocated an elegance of
outline through the management of happy contrasts of light and
shadow that gave projection and relief to chosen objects. Both
Shenstone and he wrote as poets and painters rather than as architects and gardeners.

> *Nous nous trouvâmes au pied d'une colline, plantée irrégulièrement d'arbres*
> *mégaux et de bois épais. Au fond de cette sombre et agréable vallée coule un*
> *ruisseau, qui fait de petites cascades, et qui murmure hautement sur les*
> *cailloux: c'est là que l'art, sans se montrer nulle part a parfaitement secondé*
> *la nature. Des roches, des racines, des arbres isolés, rencontrés au milieu du*
> *sentier, et qu'il faut tourner vous arrêtant, avec un sentiment de surprise et de*
> *plaisir.*

But his whole landscape is, in fact, dominated by the spirit of
Rousseau, whose sarcophagus rests on L'Ile des Peupliers in the

middle of the lake: '*Ici Repose l'Homme de Nature. J. J. Rousseau*'. It is ironic that the benevolent Shenstone should have influenced the last setting of that tortured anglophobe.

In 1763, after a visit to Enville, Shenstone caught a severe chill and in a short time was dead. For some years the Leasowes continued to be a place of pilgrimage. Mrs. Thrale, her husband, and Dr. Johnson called on a cold and rainy day in September 1774. After walking round, Johnson thought it 'the next place to Ilam',[1] and Mrs. Thrale wrote that of all places in the world it would be her choice to live in, so lovely were the woods, walks and cascades, and so 'unartificial' was it. She even preferred it to Hagley, which 'should be reserved for the gardener to show on a Sunday to travelling fools and starers'. Sir George's gardeners seem to have been efficient guides, for John Talbot, writing from Lacock in September 1754 to Sanderson Miller, says he had visited Hagley, where the gardener, in the owner's absence, showed them around very well and 'as he either approv'd of our faces, or expected a suitable Fee, was a good Cicerone'. In the same letter he remarks on the 'Horrid Massacre', by a 'Shrewsbury man', of Miller's Gothic summer-house at Enville. After Shenstone's death, the Leasowes had eight owners in thirty-seven years. Oliver Goldsmith remarks on the devastation wrought by a button manufacturer who bought it, thinking that as it was 'a beauty in a button to be of a regular pattern, so the same regularity ought to obtain in a landscape', so he clipped hedges, cut down trees and made 'vistas upon the stables and hog-sties'.[2] As can be seen in Plate X, the stones in the foreground are on the banks of the lake into which the streams flowed. This drawing was engraved for *The Modern British Traveller* about sixteen years after Shenstone's death, in which time the 'button manufacturer' mentioned by Oliver Goldsmith had cut down many of the trees, as is evident in the engraving. The next owner was a ship's captain who erected Chinese temples. This was especially ironic, for Shenstone had inscribed the base of his statue of Venus with the words:

---

[1] This was high praise. See pp. 169–70 for Ilam and Dr. Johnson.

[2] Oliver Goldsmith, 'Unacknowledged Essays', Essay XXVI, 'The History of a Poet's garden', first published in the *Westminster Magazine* (1773).

> And far be driven the sumptuous glare
> Of gold from British groves;
> And far the meretricious air
> Of China's vain alcoves.

One owner pulled down the house to enlarge it, and, during the absence of another,

> young men tried their strength by setting their shoulders to obelisks, and old women demonstrated their wisdom by carrying home pieces of the seats to their fires; a robust young fellow sent Mr. Somervile's urn a-spinning down the hill; a vigorous iconoclast beheaded the piping fawn at a blow.[1]

Recently, for some years, wide-legged men and women have hit golf-balls along bunkered fairways around the house, boys have raced their bicycles along tarred roads in the dells, and stumps of trees and corrugated iron have littered the copses. The spire of Halesowen church, in which Shenstone is buried, still links earth to heaven. In the distance the Wrekin stands inviolate.

> O Earth! to his remains indulgent be,
> Who so much care and cost bestow'd on thee![2]

[1] Hugh Miller, *First Impressions of England and her People* (London, 1847).

[2] From 'Verses left on a Seat, the Hand Unknown', after Shenstone's death. Quoted in *A Collection of Poems*, ed. R. Dodsley (London, 1773).

4

Longinus and the Philosophic Background

It has been the fate of arts to be enveloped in
mysterious and incomprehensible language . . .

SIR JOSHUA REYNOLDS, *Discourse VII*

THE aesthetic tradition of Shaftesbury was taken a step
further by the common-sense philosophical discussions of
Francis Hutcheson,[1] a Scottish disciple of his. In his
Inquiry into the Original of our Ideas of Beauty and Virtue (1725)
Hutcheson thought that he had found a universal and absolute
Beauty. This he defined as having the qualities of Uniformity
amidst Variety, based largely on examples from nature, such as
birds, beasts and flowers. To the man of taste, this beauty was
immediately recognizable, for he would have developed a further
passive sense, beyond his usual five, which would enable him to
find pleasure therein: and this was achieved not through education
but by superior powers of perception. This view was mercilessly
satirized in James Bramston's poem, 'The Man of Taste', which was
written in reply to Pope's 'Epistle to Lord Burlington' (1731).

> No youth did I in education waste
> Happy in an Hereditary Taste.
> Writing ne'er cramped the sinews of my thumb,
> Nor barb'rous birch e'er brushed my brawny bum,

---

[1] Hutcheson was born in County Down, whither his grandfather had emigrated
from Ayrshire, but he himself studied in Scotland, and from 1729 was Professor of
Moral Philosophy at Glasgow University.

> My guts ne'er suffered from a college-cook
> My name ne'er entered in a buttery-book,
>
>   .   .   .   .   .   .
>
> Nature's my guide, all Sciences I scorn.

Yet Hutcheson was willing to grant to Art a Comparative Beauty of its own, derived from the imitation of Nature. So, for example,

> strict regularity in laying out gardens in Parterres, Vistas, parallel Walks is often neglected to obtain an imitation of Nature even in some of its Wildernesses. And we are more pleased with this Imitation especially if the scene is large and spacious than the more confin'd exactness of regular works.

As in Addison's *Spectator*, No. 412, Hutcheson exempts Grandeur and Novelty from this definition of Beauty, and in this he is followed by Hogarth and Burke, who both enlarge on his central theme of Uniformity and Variety.

But before Hogarth's and Burke's contributions in the 1750s another exhaustive study in verse was published. Mark Akenside in 'The Pleasures of Imagination', a didactic poem of two thousand lines of blank verse, paraphrases much of Longinus, the first-century Greek philosopher in his reference to the origins of Sublimity and Beauty. The poem was written when Akenside was 23 and was well received after publication by Dodsley. Gray thought it 'infected with the Hutchinson-Jargon';[1] Pope thought him 'no everyday writer'; Shenstone told Jago that the poem was worth reading despite its expensive production; but Samuel Johnson could not get through it. Its main theme is a discussion concerned with those intellectual qualities which form the imagination, and in his first Book in the first version of the poem (1744), he chooses three stimulants of that imagination.

> Know then, whate'er of nature's pregnant stores,
> Whate'er of mimic art's reflected forms
> With love and admiration thus inflame
> The powers of fancy, her delighted sons

---

[1] Thomas Gray to Thomas Wharton, 26 April 1744. He means Francis Hutcheson.

To three illustrious orders have referr'd;
Three sister-graces, whom the painter's hand,
The poet's tongue confesses; the sublime,
The wonderful, the fair.

When he came to revise the poem (1757) he reduced the three
'illustrious orders' to two—the sublime and the beautiful, as in
Burke, whose *Inquiry* he may have read, for it had been written a
year or two before its publication in 1756. Akenside, after so long
an interval, not surprisingly is unable to preserve the freshness of
the original, and it tends to become more correct and moral. This is
evident in the revision of the passage quoted previously:

Know then, whate'er of the world's ancient store,
Whate'er of mimic art's reflected scenes,
With love and admiration thus inspire
Attentive fancy, her delighted sons
In two illustrious orders comprehend,
Self-taught. From him whose rustic toil the lark
Cheers warbling, to the bard whose daring thoughts
Range the full orb of being, still the form,
Which fancy worships, or sublime or fair
Her votaries proclaim.

It would have been more understandable for him to have had
only two divisions in his first version, for in his delineations and
examples of beauty he is largely concerned with the dualism of
the sublime and the beautiful. Sublimity, as in Longinus, is exemplified by majestic forms, wide horizons and large rivers; Beauty is
found in smooth, colourful, and cheerful objects, as in Addison's
Spectator, No. 412:

beauty, which immediately diffuses a secret satisfaction and com-
placency through the imagination, and gives a finishing to everything that is great or uncommon. The very first discovery of it strikes
the mind with an inward joy, and spreads a cheerfulness and delight
through all its faculties.

This series on Imagination, which lasted in the *Spectator* for eleven
daily numbers, undoubtedly influenced Akenside as much as did the
moral discussions of Shaftesbury.

IX. *Columella* by Richard Graves. Frontispiece to Vol. 1.

View of LEASOWES near Hales-Owen in SHROPSHIRE, including the Priory & Seat of the late Will.ᵐ Shenstone Esq.ʳ

Designed by R. Jardine

> . . . for Truth and Good are one,
> And Beauty dwells in them, and they in her,
> With like participation.

This passage, which reflects much from Shaftesbury's *Characteristicks*, remains unchanged in Akenside's revision in 1757.

Like many others in the century, he endeavours to find an attribution for supreme taste, whereby the pleasures of the imagination may be enjoyed to the full. Is taste not

> . . . a discerning sense
> Of decent and sublime, with quick disgust
> From things deform'd or disarrang'd, or gross
> In species? This, nor gems, nor stores of gold,
> Nor purple state, nor culture, can bestow;
> But God alone, when first his active hand
> Imprints the secret bias of the soul.

At first sight it appears that Akenside attributes all to the divine Parent; but in his exemplification he cites the peasant who 'with rude expression and untutor'd airs' may be stirred by the beauty of a sunset, yet in vain 'without fair culture's kind parental aid'. So it seems that taste is a divine faculty bred by education. As usual, this begs the question. Batty Langley recommended ruins, 'either painted upon canvas, or actually built in that Manner with bricks and covered with plastering' to terminate walks.[1] Yet neither his generation nor any other has accepted this as a divinely inspired recommendation, combined with an empiric taste. In fact, it is no nearer the mark than James Cawthorn's wild shot: "Tis sense, 'tis nature, and 'tis something more.'

Also preceding Hogarth's and Burke's analyses of Beauty was David Hartley's *Observations of Man* (1749). He again cites uniformity and variety as the principal sources of beauty in nature and art. But his is largely an ethical work in which the pleasures of the imagination are secondary in importance to the acts of the benevolent and pious man. In a section dealing with these pleasures, he shows the influence of the Platonist, Longinus, for Hartley, like all his successors, distinguishes between the emotions inspired by

---

[1] *New Principles of Gardening* (London, 1728).

Grandeur and those of Beauty. A precipice, or cataract or mountain of snow, for example, is grand or sublime, and at first may bring reactions of fear and horror, but these will eventually pass to pleasure.

Another Scot in the Shaftesbury tradition was David Hume (1711–76), who, although acknowledging that a unanimity of taste was non-existent, was willing to ascribe to the man of taste an additional sense.[1] And this sense, by which one could cultivate a delicacy of taste for the fine arts, could improve the whole temper of the mind. For these emotions induced by the study of beauty, 'draw off the mind from the hurry of business and interest; cherish reflection; dispose to tranquillity; and produce an agreeable melancholy, which of all dispositions of the mind, is the best suited to love and friendship'. Here is that same agreeable melancholy of John Evelyn, enjoying its finest hour as a prescription for the good life. In thinking that the cultivation of this sense of delicacy of taste could be acquired without education, Hutcheson differs from Hume, who states that it is cultivated by aesthetic practice—from experience in comparisons in art and by checks through 'good sense' on prejudice, both of which faculties are the key-stone of education. For Hume thought that excesses occur only in uneducated minds, 'disordered by frenzies of enthusiasm'. He cites as example the French monk whose cell windows opened on to a noble prospect: so he vowed never to look at it again, lest it might corrupt him.

After much preparation, Hogarth's *Analysis of Beauty* was published in 1753. It was written with the intention of fixing the fluctuating ideas of the man of taste. As Hogarth was an artist, with greater powers of observation, possibly, than any of his contemporaries, his empirical ideas, though briefly stated, which are the result of a lifelong study of the principles of beauty, have more validity than those of the moral philosophers. His original sub-title was 'Forms linearly considered', and his starting-point was the principle that beauty consisted of a synthesis of uniform, curving or waving lines. These would form 'swelling figures' that would be pleasing to the eye not just on account of their surface, but because the inward contents of the areas formed by the lines are of equal

---

[1] *Essays, Moral, Political and Literary* (London, 1759).

importance. It is as if a shell had been scooped out and so viewed from all angles, 'as we walk round it', for the eye enjoys both movement and rhythm. It follows that this movement of line, viewed from every angle, is of especial importance in landscaping.

His essential principles were six in number: Fitness, Variety, Uniformity, Simplicity, Intricacy, and Quantity, and they mutually interacted. Fitness, in bulk and proportion, implied a structural soundness; Variety was a 'composed variety' without too many contrasts, for 'variety uncomposed, and without design, is confusion and deformity'. This could be exemplified by perspective views with their gradual lessening, as in pyramidic form. Serving to give Fitness were Uniformity and Regularity or symmetry. The problem was similarly discussed by Montesquieu later: '*Une longue uniformité rend tout insupportable . . . s'il est vrai que l'on ait fait cette fameuse allée de Moscou à Petersbourg, le voyageur doit perir d'ennui, renfermé entre les deux rangs de cette allée . . .*'[1]

The spirit longs for symmetry even though it might appear a contradiction; and paradoxically, says Hogarth, the eye, despite being delighted by 'exactness of counterparts', eventually longs for Variety.[2] Hogarth exemplified this common avoidance of regularity by showing how a painter might place a tree or the shadow of a cloud to break the equalities and parallelisms of a Palladian building. This principle was often practised by contemporary landscapers, and was further exploited by the Picturesque school. Simplicity 'without Variety' said Hogarth, 'is wholly insipid'. A pyramid, for example, is more interesting than a cone, though built of straight lines, for the eye travels both upward and around it. For the same reason, Hogarth preferred an oval to a circle, a triangle to a square, and a pyramid to a cube. An egg shows even more variety; but the quintessence of infinite variety in waving lines is a pineapple, as used by Wren on the exterior of St. Paul's Cathedral. As the eye enjoys pursuing a 'wanton kind of chase', Intricacy is essential. Hogarth's concept of Quantity is similar to that used later by Burke; huge shapeless rocks are horrific, awful and sublime, where-

[1] Charles Louis de Montesquieu, *Sur le Gout. Oeuvres posthumes* (London, 1783).

[2] Shakespeare, who was thought by Hogarth to have the deepest penetration into nature in all literature, had summed up all the 'charms of beauty in the words infinite variety'.

as objects with form and fitness in large quantities bring pleasure. As large objects, he lists, incongruously, a grove of high trees, Windsor Castle, the façade of the Louvre, elephants, whales and robes of state. He constantly protests against an excess, which produces an impropriety or lack of fitness, such as a large wig on an old man, or even in a 'rough shock dog' which is an incongruous mixture of 'a muff and a sensible friendly animal'![1] All these principles are fully illustrated, so that there can be no doubt of his exact meaning.

He is most quoted for his linear precepts. Straight lines are dull, for they vary only in length; a waving line, on the contrary—the line of beauty—has two curves contrasted with lively movement, and is therefore more ornamental. But most interesting to the eye is the three-dimensional serpentine line which waves and winds at the same time in different directions, and thus encloses in itself infinitely varied contents. This is what he calls the line of grace, like a 'fine wire properly twisted round the elegant and varied figure of a cone' (Plate XI). He shows that natural, as well as human, forms are often composed of this line, which, to avoid excess, should not bulge too much in its curvature, but be only '*il poco piu*'. So although rococo is in the main asymmetrical, being filled with 'C' scrolls and curves of much variety and intricacy, yet Hogarth's serpentine line, having a more gradual wave which takes into account the proportion of the whole, is more than mere surface decoration and therefore preferable. And this line he observed universally in Nature, which was, he said, 'simple, plain and true in all her works: and those who strictly adhere to her laws, and closely attend to her appearances in their infinite varieties, are guarded against and prejudiced bias from truth'. He quotes 'Paradise Lost' (which he illustrated, for Milton was one of his favourite authors) to show Milton's love of this serpentine line in his description of the informal first garden.

> So vary'd he, and of his tortuous train
> Curl'd many a wanton wreath, in sight of Eve,
> To lure her eye.

[1] The shock dog was fashionable in the 1750s. It was about the size of a miniature poodle, was white with black or red roan markings, and had a soft, curly coat with a top-knot.

The term 'serpentine' had been used for some years. In the early 1730s Queen Caroline had had Kensington Gardens landscaped to include a mount and a serpentine stream. Nevertheless, Samuel Richardson in his *Familiar Letters* (1741), writing an imaginary letter from a young lady in town to her aunt in the country, remarks that it is 'a noble piece of water called the Serpentine River, but for what reason I know not (it being a strait, and not winding piece)'. In *The Gentleman's Magazine*, April 1733, Queen Caroline was ludicrously compared with Eve, who was indeed less satisfied with her garden. There is also the inevitable expression of the fashionable francophobe attitude towards regular and formal gardening.

> A River waves thorough the Happy Land,
> And ebbs and flows at Caroline's command.
> No costly fountains, with proud Vigour rise,
> Nor with their foaming waters lash the Skies.
> To such false pride, be none but Louis prone,
> All she lays out in Pleasure is her own.
> Here nothing is profuse, nor nothing vain;
> But all is noble, and yet all is plain:
> So happily do Art and Nature joyn,
> Each Strives which most shall add to the Design.
> In such a State were our first Parents plac'd
> And Eve, like CAROLINE the garden grac'd;
> Had she such Constancy of Mind possest
> She had not fell, but we had still been blest.

In the year that the *Analysis of Beauty* was published Queen Caroline and Bridgeman constructed a canal in St. James's Park, but it was not until Nash in 1830 that it was made serpentine. In the meantime the Rev. William Mason's symbol of a serpentine path as liberty seems absurdly far-fetched and bathetic.

> Smooth, simple Path! whose undulating line
> With sidelong tufts of flow'ry fragrance crown'd,
> 'Plain in its neatness',[1] spans my garden ground;
>
> .   .   .   .

---

[1] Milton's translation (Fifth Ode of Horace, Lib. I) of '*simplex munditii*'.

Liberal though limited, restrained though free,
Fearless of dew or dirt, or dust, I rove,
And own those comforts, all deriv'd from thee!
Take then, smooth Path, this tribute of my love,
Thou emblem pure of legal liberty![1]

In his final chapters Hogarth discusses light and shade with reference to perspective, and his conclusions here, as with those on linear forms, were directly relatable to landscaping.

Edmund Burke's *Enquiry into the Origin of our Ideas of the Sublime and Beautiful*, written before he was 21, was published three years after Hogarth's work. In his definition of Sublimity, Burke takes much from Longinus, who had dealt largely with Rhetoric, yet Burke manages with some success to transpose Longinus's terms to fit his own aesthetic theories. Awe-inspiring grandeur rather than elegance, the chief quality of Longinus's Sublimity, may be applied to oratory or landscape, and in either way elevate our thought. According to Longinus, it might be achieved, in speaking or writing, by a command of full-blooded ideas, inspired by vehement emotion, but controlled by proper construction in its three main features: amplification, variation, and climax. (This also may be applied to landscaping, for any scene should lead through varied rhythms to a climactic point or focus.) Throughout *On the Sublime* Longinus confines himself to literary matters, which he rarely exemplifies by visual references, except for one instance when he mentions the Nile, Danube, and Rhine as exciting admiration by their grandeur and sublimity—a quality never possessed by a small stream. Burke takes up Admiration as one of the qualities inspired by Sublimity, and adds Dread and Mystery as being equally strong. He outlines five chief characteristics of Sublimity: the first is a Vastness of Dimension in Depth or Height or Length, and of these three Depth is the most effective in inspiring awe, especially when it includes the perpendicular, with a rugged or broken surface. Length is the least effective.[2] The second quality of Burke's, which

[1] Sonnet XII, 'To a Gravel Walk' (1797).
[2] 'I have ever observed that colonnades and avenues of trees of moderate length, were without comparison far grander than when they were suffered to run to immense distances.' This is referred to by Mrs. Pendarves (later Mrs. Delany) when she writes of Bathurst's avenue at Cirencester: *vide* p. 47.

is similar to Longinus's Amplification,[1] is Infinity, which produces 'a delightful horror' as the imagination is infinitely extended. His example in this instance is of a Rotund form which has no boundary fixed and which has a uniformity that does not check the imagination. Burke's next quality he calls Difficulty, by which he does not mean a baroque contrivance after the pattern of Hogarth, but a 'rudeness of the work' such as in Stonehenge or any structure which has required much effort to erect it and which is without art. And lastly, comes Magnificence and Darkness or associations with dark and gloomy colours. But mere Grandeur or Magnificence, as Longinus pointed out, runs a risk if left to itself or is 'abandoned to the impetus of uninstructed enterprise', for it needs the 'stay and balance of scientific method'. Presumably this means that art should control the 'splendid confusion' which would otherwise ensue. The close connexion between the Gothic novels and the landscapers of the Picturesque is very evident in these qualities. The 'delightful horror', and awe produced by scenes of Vastness, and Difficulty in dark colours are, in fact, their main tenets; and the terrain in Wales or some of its border counties, where its chief apostles lived, is excellently suited, in climate and topography, to realizing their ideals.

In dealing with the qualities of Beauty, Burke does not rely on Longinus, except in so far as many are antithetical to the Sublime. Here the main inspiration is not awe but love, and this 'demands no assistance from our reasoning, so proportion and measurement play no part'. Thus, in the footsteps of Shaftesbury, it is easy to walk into the happy, informal garden championed by the feelings, leaving behind that cold reason which by its rules of proportion has turned trees into pillars or pyramids, hedges into walls or screens, and all planning into a symmetrical order.

The beautiful is to be found in smallness and smoothness, as in the skins of animals and coats of birds, or in smooth leaves, slopes and streams. In the next quality, Gradual Variation, Burke and Hogarth agree, except that Burke will not accept angular figures, for they are too much the product of our reasoning. His last two essentials, which are both antitheses of the Sublime, are Delicacy

[1] Not very clear in Longinus, as there is a lacuna in Chap. 2.

and its expression in clear, bright, and diversified colours. For example, the myrtle, vine, and jasmine are as delicate and beautiful as the oak, ash, and elm are majestic and sublime. In summing up, he again states that beauty does not affect us through the 'languid and precarious operation of our reason', but is governed by love and passion.

During the great Scottish renaissance that produced David Hume, Francis Hutcheson, Adam Smith, Allan Ramsay, Kames, Boswell, and the Adam brothers, the ideas of Burke were remodelled to suit the Scottish intellectual scene by Dr. Hugh Blair (1718–1800), who was appointed Regius Professor of Rhetoric and Belles-Lettres at Edinburgh in 1762. In his lectures on Longinus he first applies his principles to landscape rather than literature, and much of what he says is identical to Burke: Vastness produces Sublimity, and darkness and loneliness increase it. He is the typical Scottish Ossian Romantic—'the hoary mountain, and the solitary lake; the aged forest, and the torrent falling over the rock', all produce an emotion that is delightful but 'altogether of a serious kind': 'a degree of awfulness and solemnity even approaching to severity . . . very distinguishable from the more gay and brisk emotion raised by beautiful objects'. A Gothic cathedral is sublime because of its size, height, 'awful obscurity', strength, antiquity, and durability. Again, in his fifth lecture on Beauty, he repeats Burke in claiming delicate colour and graceful variety as its two main attributes. Here he quotes Hogarth at some length, summarizing, presumably for the benefit of his students, the distinctions between the line of beauty and the line of grace, and with the inevitable illustration of a straight canal being an insipid figure compared with the meanders of rivers.

Some of his lectures are occupied with lengthy and pedantic criticisms of Addison's style in the *Spectator*, Nos. 411, 412, and 413, which deal with the pleasures of the imagination in the natural scene. The felicity of some of Addison's thought may sometimes be obscured by tortuous writing, but it should not have been necessary for Blair to comment, for example, on the careless interjection of the adverb 'only' in the passage: 'By greatness, I do not only mean the bulk of any single object, but the largeness of a whole view, considered as one entire piece.' And in dealing with landscaping,

Hugh Blair often uses the same dark palette as his cousin, Robert Blair, the author of that mortuary poem 'The Grave'. These 767 lines of blank verse were the precursors of Young's 'Night Thoughts', and in their ghostly solitude of the lonely churchyard were the inspiration of much of the picturesque school of the Gothic novel.

Another influence on Hugh Blair was Henry Home, Lord Kames, author of *The Elements of Criticism* (1762), of whom Boswell, ever anxious to champion Scotland, once boasted to Samuel Johnson: 'But, Sir, we have Lord Kames', to receive the snub, 'You *have* Lord Kames. Keep him; ha, ha, ha! We don't envy you him.'[1]

Yet Johnson thought that *The Elements of Criticism* was 'a pretty essay . . . though much of it is chimerical'.[2] But today it seems humourless and tired writing, which shows none of the vigour of the author, a Scottish judge who lived to the age of eighty-six, and was noted for his coarse humour, being the prototype of the 'acute, metaphysical judge' in *Redgauntlet*. He endeavoured to divide Beauty into two classes: Intrinsic, involving only the single act of vision, apart from any other factors, and Relative, which depended upon a consideration of the use of the object. In this latter half he thought that Simplicity should be the rule, and that such fripperies as triumphal arches, Chinese houses, obelisks, cascades and fountains were out of place in a garden.

In his view, Taste was the result of study rather than of native sensibility, and all his approach to the subject is more rational than Shaftesbury's, for feeling seems absent from his examination. It is perhaps nearer to Reynolds's 'Reason must ultimately determine everything; at this minute it is required to inform us when that very reason is to give way to feeling.'[3]

In another essay, on 'Gardening and Architecture', Kames invents the astounding simile that 'a garden, in France and Italy, is disposed like the human body, alleys like legs and arms answering each other; the great walk in the middle representing the trunk of the body'. He was an admirer of William Kent's work, but was evidently unable to see how much Kent owed to French gardening.

---

[1] James Boswell, *Life of Johnson* (Oxford, 1934), Vol. II, p. 53.
[2] ibid., Vol. I, p. 394.   [3] *Discourse XIII*.

Versailles, said Kames, showed no unity in design, was unnatural, 'and its groves of jets d'eau, statues of animals conversing in the manner of Aesop, water issuing out of the mouths of wild beasts gave an impression of fairy-land and witchcraft'. Voltaire quickly dashed to the defence of the great French garden and there seems little that Kames could have replied to his criticisms:

> *M. Home donne toujours son opinion pour une loi, et il étend son despotisme sur tous les objets . . . ses arrêts . . . sur les jardins ne nous permettent pas de douter qu'il ne soit de tous les magistrats d'Écosse le mieux logé, et qu'il n'ait le plus beau parc. Il trouve les bosquets de Versailles ridicules; mais s'il fait jamais un voyage en France, on lui fera les honneurs de Versailles, on fera jouer les eaux pour lui, on le promènera dans les bosquets, et peut-être alors ne sera-t-il pas si dégouté. Après cela, s'il se mocque des bosquets de Versailles, et des tragédies de Racine, nous le souffrirons volontiers: nous serons que chacun à son gout. . . .*[1]

Kames's taste in literature was unusual, for he regarded Congreve's *The Mourning Bride* (1697) as the most perfect drama. Fortunately Congreve is remembered for his comedies of manners and not for dramas in which captive princesses ask their lovers to 'Kill me, kill me, dash me with thy chains, Tread on me' or 'Drag me, and harrow the earth with my bare bosom'. *The Mourning Bride* is a seventeenth-century equivalent of the horrors of *Tamburlaine* or *Titus Andronicus*: a mute Moor swallows a message; a queen takes poison; a king in disguise is murdered; a head is severed from a dead body; but all is well in the end, for the bride's husband reappears.

Nevertheless, in dealing with landscape matters, Kames is less eccentric. Although he disliked the Gothic style, he preferred Gothic ruins to Grecian, for the Gothic suggests the triumph of time over strength, whereas the Grecian shows the triumph of barbarity over taste.[2] He anticipated Repton in recommending the regularity of a parterre near the house, because the garden, being an accessory, ought to partake of the characteristics of the principal object.

In stating that a beautiful environment brings with it a gaiety

---

[1] '*Lettre à un Journaliste*'. Article in the *Gazette littéraire de l'Europe* (1764).

[2] Hume's Gothic Tower on Calton Hill, Edinburgh, should therefore arouse different feelings from its Grecian companions.

and harmony of mind in the spectator as well as a rectitude of manners, he joins the followers of Shaftesbury. Fortunately, in recent times, educational establishments have found homes in some of the best English landscaped parks, as at Bretton Hall, Newton Park, Prior Park, Radley, Stowe, Bryanston, and Milton; and one hopes that these surroundings will prove the truth of Kames's observation:

> It is a sad truth that the young student, familiarized to the dirtiness and disorder of many colleges pent within narrow bounds in populous cities, is rendered in a measure insensible to the elegant beauties of art and nature . . . good professors are not more essential to a college than a spacious garden sweetly ornamented but without anything staring or fantastic, so as upon the whole to inspire our youth with a taste no less for simplicity than for elegance.

Kames then gives Oxford as a model. Unfortunately, two hundred years later, the dirt and disorder that Kames condemned has brought about the situation that he wished to avoid: the College gardens alone being oases of quiet. Besides, has not Kant denied that love of beauty leads to a moral disposition, and averred that 'connoisseurs in taste not only often but generally are given up to idle capricious and mischievous passions'?

Although he hated bogus connoisseurs in taste, Sir Joshua Reynolds, in his Discourses delivered as President of the Royal Academy between 1769 and 1790, did not go as far as Kant in his condemnation. These connoisseurs might remember a few names of painters, and a few unnecessary rules of the Academy, and they were in no way fitted to proclaim a standard of taste. Reynolds relates how with one such mock connoisseur he visited the Cartoons at Hampton Court, and was subjected to the typical cant of the time when the so-called connoisseur stopped in front of Raphael's 'St. Paul preaching', and remarked how much better it might have been had the art of Contrast and the flowing line of Grace and Beauty been known in Raphael's time! But Reynolds constantly asserted his belief in the reality of a genuine standard of taste: not an intuitive taste with which one might be born, but an acquired taste after wide reading in literature and moral philosophy, and a continual comparative criticism of the works of the greatest artists. And if this was governed by a reasonableness of outlook it should result in a standard by which beauty might be unmistakably perceived. He also stressed how the intrinsic quality of this beauty was its ability to please at first sight. This is not the narrow reason of the connoisseur, guided by the Rules of the Academy; but a wider exercise of the faculty which must work 'even in the midst of the highest flights of fancy and imagination'.

In his unexpected eulogy of Vanbrugh as an architect, he again strikes at 'the petulant sarcasms of factious men of letters' who have criticized Vanbrugh. One of Vanbrugh's fortes was to understand perfectly 'the conduct of a background', so that none of his buildings start out of the landscape abruptly or crudely, without 'expectation or preparation'. This is indeed a characteristic of his major works. But Reynolds only grudgingly acknowledges gardening as having the possible status of an art; for if all art were banished from the garden, as it was by the followers of the Picturesque, then, says Reynolds, it ceases to be a garden! Nor would he acknowledge 'Nature dressed with Art' as a fit subject for a landscape painter. With reference to sculpture, in Discourse X, he indirectly criticizes the Picturesque, by using the term as a synonym for 'all that partakes of fancy or caprice . . . and which is incompatible with that sobriety and gravity' that should be the chief characteristic of sculpture. One feels that his emphasis upon reason, which will produce a measured Variety and Novelty, a regulated and unaffected Simplicity in all things, is too carefully contrived. Just as in his portraits, the faces of his sitters are often dead white because the carmine has faded out, so these Discourses reflect an academic light which has dimmed with the years. No longer do we believe that 'Reason, without doubt must ultimately determine everything; at this moment it is required to inform us when that very reason is to give way to feeling'. And to show the importance of this belief, Reynolds isolated the sentence as a complete paragraph.

Brown and his followers must have relished Reynolds's repetition, in Discourse III, of Aristotle, that nature was not perfect and that the power of discovering what is not perfect can only be acquired by one experienced in seeing her defects. Brown considered that he could create, in landscaping, as perfect an abstract idea of natural forms as any artist; and he took pains neither to copy Nature too closely nor to leave her blemishes. Like Claude, Brown managed to retain qualities of quietness and repose in the scenes which he created, and like Reynolds he thought that taking nature as he found it seldom produced beauty.

Despite his admiration for Burke's *Enquiry*, Reynolds is off the main track of eighteenth-century writers on aesthetics, for, above all, reason leads him to an intellectual admiration for the great masters. But in describing taste as acquired rather than inherited, and in claiming the man of taste to be cultivated, sensitive and reasonable, he does not deviate far from the course already set, which continued to the end of the century.

Another Scot completed the succession of eighteenth-century philosopher-aestheticians. Archibald Alison (1757–1839), an indolent parson, in his *Spectator*-type 'Essays on the Nature and Principles of Taste' (1790), reiterated much that had been said, and, in his references to the Sublime, was much quoted by Payne Knight, Uvedale Price, and their contemporary Picturesque followers. Alison limits the Emotion of Taste, by which we perceive whatever is beautiful or sublime, by ascribing it as only possible to those in the higher stations of life, as in the liberal professions. It is a strange slant in the psychological approach to the imagination, that ideas and associations can be appreciated only by those who have been academically educated. For the full functioning of this emotion the imagination is excited, according to Alison, after a pleasing perception. Landscaping as scenery is therefore beautiful to the man of taste only in so far as it arouses emotions of cheerfulness, serenity or melancholy. But it is easier to understand his assertion that in order to make or enjoy landscaping the principles of composition should be known, for to produce a unified and harmonious scene nature must be improved by subtraction here and addition there. As Whistler subsequently remarked, 'Seldom does Nature succeed in making a picture.'[1]

Alison deviates little from the way cut by his predecessors, except in so far that he acknowledges Hogarth's serpentine forms as

[1] *The Gentle Art of Making Enemies* (London, 1890).

beautiful only if the lines are small and elegant, for the associations they arouse are delicate and tender. And in this conclusion he shows how far he and his fellow philosophers are removed from modern aesthetic theories which are firm in the belief that art does not derive its beauty from any associational representation. Because Hogarth, as an artist, stated this inherently, his *Analysis* has ultimately more value than all the works of philosophers, judges, parsons, and dons. Yet the much-stated distinctions of Longinus between the Sublime and the Beautiful and the dissertations of Shaftesbury on the emotions of Taste and Morals were themes with variations which were constantly played by all landscapers of every school in the second half of the century.

5

Literary Reactions to Lancelot Brown

> The gardens and lawn seem from the windows of
> this spacious house to be as boundless as the mind of
> the owner, and as free and open as his countenance.
>
> SAMUEL RICHARDSON,
> *Sir Charles Grandison,* Vol. 6, Letter 5

THE greatest of the professional landscapers was Lancelot
Brown (1715–83), a Northumbrian, who gravitated to
Stowe as a kitchen gardener during the improvements of
William Kent. At the height of his fame he was the most sought-
after improver in the country, and in 1764 became royal gardener
at Hampton Court. With his admirers and clients, amateur and
professional, he planned hundreds of estates, some of which still
survive, despite urban encroachments, as one of the basic features of
the English scene. He was not a painter like William Kent, but
thought of landscape in literary and intellectual terms. Meeting by
chance his friend Hannah More[1] in Hampton Court gardens in the
year before his sudden death, he spent two hours explaining to her
his theories on which he had based his life's work in landscaping,
and he employed literary and grammatical allusions to illustrate his
meaning.

Now THERE, (pointing a finger), I make a comma, and pointing
to another spot where a more decided turn is proper, I make a colon;
at another point (where an interruption is desirable to break the

---

[1] She was staying at the time with the widowed Mrs. Garrick at Hampton
House.

view) a parenthesis—now a full-stop, and then I begin another subject[1]

Perhaps he was showing her the few alterations he had carried out in the palace gardens some years earlier; but however he demonstrated, it was as intellectual a concept as any from Burke, whose tenets of the Beautiful he so closely followed.

Yet his imagination was never bounded by this syntactical ideology. In the Garricks' small estate, for example, he had been set a problem some years earlier, and had solved it brilliantly. Hampton House was separated by the turnpike road from the lawns of the riverside frontage, as was Pope's house at Twickenham. How could Garrick join this house[2] with the waterside lawns, on which he had built a graceful octagon temple, with Greek Ionic portico, to house Roubiliac's statue of Shakespeare? He thought of a bridge; but Brown designed a tunnel which was really a long grotto, containing a bath-house and its spring. To emerge, in summer, from the cold, murky gloom of the arch on to the bright lawns beside the shining river must have been an enchanting experience. Fortunately, Mr. Garrick reported that Samuel Johnson, *arbiter formae*, sealed the matter by expressing his approval of the project with 'David, David, what can't be overdone, may be underdone.' The tunnel was used, and, in the temple, Garrick kept various relics of Shakespeare. These included a chair made from the wood of a large mulberry tree which, in a strong local tradition, had been planted by Shakespeare in the garden of his house, New Place, at Stratford. In 1756 a 'sacreligious priest' living there had the tree cut down.[3]

Again, working on a small scale many years later for another friend of Hannah More's, at Sandleford Priory in Berkshire, Brown

[1] Hannah More to her sister, 31 December 1782.

[2] Hampton House, now divided into flats, is known as Garrick's Villa. The Temple is owned by Hampton U.D.C., and the Shakespeare statue is in the British Museum.

[3] 'There stood here till lately the house in which Shakespeare lived, and a mulberry tree of his planting . . . the tree so large that it would shade the grass plot in your garden, which I think is more than twenty yards square . . . a certain man . . . has cut down the tree, and piled it as a stack of firewood, to the great vexation, loss and disappointment of the inhabitants; however, an honest silversmith bought the whole stack of wood, and makes many odd things of this wood for the curious, some of which I hope to bring with me to town.' Letter of a visitor to Stratford (1760).

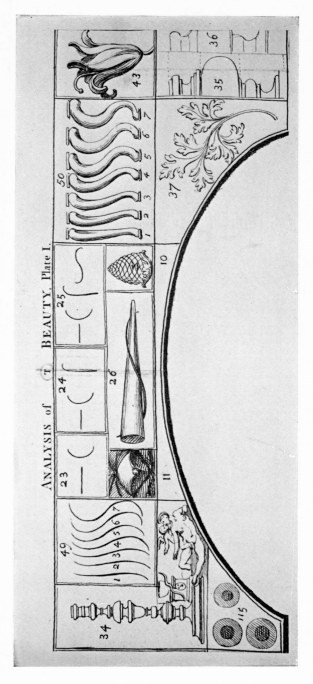

XI. The Line of Beauty or Grace from *The Analysis of Beauty* by William Hogarth, 1753.

sensibly suited his designs to his employer's taste. She was Mrs.
Elizabeth Montagu,[1] who wrote to Hannah More in 1782 that
there were 'no temples to heathen gods' or 'proud bridges . . . used
by the wantonness of wealth', but work which helped to provide
employment for poor weavers who were out of work in Newbury.[2]

Brown's larger landscapes today are such that a painter would
delight in: sweeping turf, accented by groups of majestic trees,
gentle slopes to a river or lake which reflects the tones and forms of
the trees, and, in the far distance, rising ground joining skyline and
infinity. Standing in the shadow of one of his dark cedars near the
house, one can trace these distances and recessions in every direction. And this is the plan which he often followed, his ideal being to
bring to life an improvement on rough Nature, whom he regarded
as a raw goddess who was always striving for perfection, but who
never achieved it without the Aristotelian dressing of man's divinely
rational faculties. So he aimed at the perfect form by selecting the
best from Nature, thereby eliminating any 'false accidents' in her
form that she might have made. His typical work had a belt of trees
around the perimeter, enclosing the whole area, as if to create an
Arcadia separated from the harsh world. The inner edge of this belt
was irregular and serpentine, receding or projecting according to
the contours of the ground, and softened by clumps of trees, planted
in pairs or trios. In general, there were elms, oaks, and beeches,
according to the locality, with firs as wind-breaks later to be
removed, and, sometimes, Lombardy poplars to make vertical
accents similar to cypresses in Italy. Where possible, the middle
distance was enlivened by water in the form of a lake or stream
dammed to a level below that of the base of the trees in order to
reflect fully their outlines and shadows. The edges of this water
were concealed, either by planting, by a slope, or by some architectural feature such as a small bridge. The view from the house was
uninterrupted, as a ha-ha was concealed; and the clumps entered

[1] 'Queen of the Blues' and founder of the Blue Stocking Clubs of literary ladies
who met, as Boswell said, 'to participate in conversation with literary and ingenious
men, animated by a desire to please'. However, it was apparently Mr. Stillingfleet,
a popular member, whose sombre stockings gained the name for the clubs.
[2] One of the virtues of English landscape gardening and the admiration of
foreigners: *vide* Owen Cambridge's article in *The World*, 3 April 1755.

the scene as wing screens forming receding perspective. Mr. Russell Page,[1] in recently replanning Longleat with Lord Bath, analyses the exact siting of Brown's trees in that park. Many, he says, had been planted 'using lines or right angles or wedge shapes exactly as though they (the planters) were designing wings for theatrical scenery', because they realized that rotund mature forms of trees had initially to be rectilinear. Brown also considered the view in reverse and from all angles, so that from the farthest bound to the house and everywhere one walked was carefully planned. It is still possible to realize this in many of his parks, for though few of his trees remain, his successors have often replanted identically: and his detailed plans often remain in the libraries of the houses.

He was ruthless in clearing, though he sometimes had the good sense to leave mature avenues of trees, as at Corsham and Chillington, even though they might not fit into his master plan. His critics were many, referring to him as Brown the 'kitchen gardener' who swept away parterres to produce acres of barren lawn, as at Blenheim and Claremont, and who inconveniently concealed such mundane areas as vegetable gardens. William Cowper pictures him at work:

> Lo, he comes!
> Th'omnipotent magician, Brown, appears!
> Down falls the venerable pile, th'abode
> Of our forefathers—a grave whisker'd race,
> But tasteless. Springs a palace in its stead,
> But in a distant spot; where, more expos'd,
> It may enjoy th'advantage of the north,
> And aguish east, till time shall have transform'd
> Those naked acres to a shelt'ring grove.
> He speaks. The lake in front becomes a lawn;
> Woods vanish, hills subside, and vallies rise:
> And streams, as if created for his use,
> Pursue the track of his directing wand,
> Now murm'ring soft, now roaring in cascades—
> Ev'n as he bids! Th'enraptur'd owner smiles.
> 'Tis finish'd, and yet, finish'd as it seems,

[1] *The Education of a Gardener* (London, 1962), p. 26.

Still wants a grace, the loveliest it could show,
A mine to satisfy th'enormous cost.[1]

And the theatre audience in 1740 at David Garrick's first play,
a frolic called *Lethe or Esop in the Shades*, laughed at the satirical reference to Brown and his works when uttered by old Lord Chalkstone,
a part later to be a favourite of Garrick's. The gouty peer is one of
a succession of mortals who is about to be ferried by Charon; and on
the shores of the Styx, addressing the philosopher, Esop, he looks
through his 'glass' at the Elysian Fields,

Which by the way Mr. Esop, are laid out most detestably—no
taste! No fancy in the whole world! Your river there, what d'ye call
it? Aye, Styx—why, 'tis as straight as Fleet-ditch. You should have
given it a serpentine sweep, and sloped the banks of it. The place
indeed has fine *Capabilities*; but you should clear the wood to the left,
and the clump of trees to the right; in short, the whole wants variety,
extent, contrast, inequality. (Going towards the orchestra, stops
suddenly, and looks into the Pit.) Upon my word, here's a fine
Hah-hah! And a most curious collection of evergreens and flowering
shrubs.

Brown's methods were again satirized in Colman and Garrick's
The Clandestine Marriage (1766). This play received a Royal Com-
mand Performance four years later, and afterwards an order from
George III that Zoffany should commemorate, in a conversation
piece, a scene in which Mrs. Baddeley, who had so charmed the
King, plays the part of the young Fanny Sterling. With her is Lord
Ogleby, an amiable old peer very similar to Lord Chalkstone, who
is 'ridiculously aping the graces of youth' in thinking that Fanny
Sterling is in love with him, whereas she is secretly married to
another. This scene is set in the garden of Mr. Sterling, a rich
merchant, who has recently carried out 'improvements'. The
'smack-smooth' lawn, the path 'twisting and turning' like a worm,
the 'spire' terminating the prospect, and Canton, the humorous
Swiss valet, who is about to interrupt, may all be seen in Zoffany's
painting (Plate XII). In an earlier scene in the play these improvements of Mr. Sterling are exactly itemized as he proudly shows

[1] 'The Task', Book III, lines 765–83.

them to Lord Ogleby, Mrs. Heidelberg his sister, and Fanny, his niece.

Lord Ogleby. Great Improvements indeed, Mr. Sterling! wonderful improvements! The four seasons in lead, the flying Mercury, and the basin with Neptune in the middle, are all in the very extreme of fine taste. You have as many rich figures as the man at Hyde-Park Corner.[1]

Mr. Sterling. The chief pleasure of a country-house is to make improvements, you know, my Lord. I spare no expence, not I.—This is quite another-guess sort of a place than it was when I first took it, my Lord. We were surrounded with trees. I cut down above fifty to make the lawn before the house, and let in the wind and sun—smack-smooth—as you see.—Then I made a green-house out of the old laundry, and turned the brew-house into a pinery.—The high octagon summer-house, you see yonder, is raised on the mast of a ship, given me by an East-India captain, who has turned many a thousand of my money. It commands the whole road. All the coaches and chariots, and chaises, pass and repass under your eye. I'll mount you up there in the afternoon, my Lord. 'Tis the pleasantest place in the world to take a pipe and a bottle,—and so you shall say, my Lord.

Lord Ogleby. Ay—or a bowl of punch, or a can of flip, Mr. Sterling! for it looks like a cabin in the air.—If flying chairs were in use, the captain might make a voyage to the Indies in it, if he had but a fair wind.

Canton. Ha, ha, ha, ha!

Mrs. Heidelberg. My brother's a little comacal in his ideas, my Lord!— But you'll excuse him.—I have a little gothick dairy, fitted up entirely in my own taste.—In the evening I shall hope for the honour of your Lordship's company to take a dish to tea there, or a sullabub warm from the cow.

Lord Ogleby. I have every moment a fresh opportunity of admiring the elegance of Mrs. Heidelberg—the very flower of delicacy, and cream of politeness.

Mrs. Heidelberg. O, my Lord! (Leering at Lord Ogleby)

Lord Ogleby. O, madam! (Leering at Mrs. Heidelberg)

Mr. Sterling. How d'ye like these close walks, my Lord?

---

[1] Henry and John Cheere, who at their 'shop' at Hyde Park Corner made 'the Gods of Athens and of Rome' in lead and stone. Henry was knighted for his public service in the year of the production of *The Clandestine Marriage*.

Lord Ogleby. A most excellent serpentine! It forms a perfect maze, and winds like a true lover's knot.

Mr. Sterling. Ay, there's none of your straight lines here—but all taste—zig-zag—crinkum-crankum—in and out—right and left— to and again—twisting and turning like a worm, my Lord!

Lord Ogleby. Admirably laid out indeed, Mr. Sterling! one can hardly see an inch beyond one's nose anywhere in these walks.—You are a most excellent oeconomist of your land, and make a little go a great way.—It lies together in as small parcels as if it was placed in pots out at your window in Grace-church street.

Canton. Ha, ha, ha, ha!

Lord Ogleby. What d'ye laugh at, Canton?

Canton. Ah! que cette similitude est drole! So clever what you say, mi Lor!

Lord Ogleby (*To Fanny*). You seem mightily engaged, Madam, What are those pretty hands so busily employed about?

Fanny. Only making up a nose-gay, my Lord!—Will your Lordship do me the honour of accepting it? (presenting it.)

Lord Ogleby. I'll wear it next my heart, Madam!—(aside) I see the young creature dotes on me!

.   .   .   .

Mr. Sterling. I'll only show his Lordship my ruins, and the cascade, and the Chinese bridge, and then we'll go in to breakfast.

Lord Ogleby. Ruins, did you say, Mr. Sterling?

Mr. Sterling. Ay, ruins, my Lord! and they are reckoned very fine ones too. You would think them ready to tumble on your head. It has just cost me a hundred and fifty pounds, to put my ruins in thorough repair. This way, if your Lordship pleases.

Lord Ogleby. (Going, stops) What steeple's that we see yonder? the parish church, I suppose?

Mr. Sterling. Ha, ha, ha! that's admirable. It is no church at all, my Lord! it is a spire that I have built against a tree, a field or two off, to terminate the prospect. One must always have a church, or an obelisk, or something to terminate the prospect, you know. That's a rule of taste, my Lord!

Lord Ogleby. Very ingenious, indeed. For my part, I desire no finer prospect than this I see before me. (Leering at the women) Simple, yet varied; bounded, yet extensive. Get away, Canton! (Pushing Canton away) I want no assistance.—I'll walk with the ladies.

Mr. Sterling. This way, my Lord!

But what Brown's generation could laugh at, our own should cherish. At Bowood he planted over 100,000 trees which may have looked insignificant at the time when the young Lord Lansdowne was reproved for jumping over one of them; but today they are the embodiment of his 'sweet pastorals and elegant elegiacs'. Most of his patrons gave him a free hand, some perhaps being frightened by his bluff, direct manner with its accompanying flippancy. 'The first peer that experiences it, laughs to conceal his being angry at the freedom; the next flatters him for fear of being treated familiarly; and ten more bear it because it is *so like Browne*.'[1] Even royalty succumbed, and he was commissioned to redesign Bridgeman's layout at Richmond, thereby receiving the unqualified approval of William Mason in his 'Heroic Epistle' to Sir William Chambers. It is acidly satiric of Chambers and all his Chinese works, and also of any form of formal gardening. In this passage he is delighted with Brown's actions at Richmond:

> Come then, prolific Art, and with thee bring
> The charms that rise from thy exhaustless spring;
> To Richmond come, for see, untutor'd Brown
> Destroys these wonders which were thy own.
> Lo, from his melon-ground the peasant slave[2]
> Has rudely rush'd and levell'd Merlin's Cave;
> Knock'd down the waxen Wizzard, seiz'd his wand,
> Transform'd to lawn what late was Fairy land;
> And marr'd with impious hand, each sweet design
> Of Stephen Duck and good Queen Caroline.[3]

The 'sweet design' was a thatched Gothick house-cum-grotto of William Kent's, erected in 1735. Stephen Duck was a Wiltshire labourer, turned poet, ordained priest, commissioned Yeoman of the Guard to Queen Caroline, and responsible for the safety of her grotto. He finally drowned himself in the Thames.

> Thus shall Tradition keep my Fame alive;
> The *Bard* shall die, the *Thresher* still survive.

[1] Horace Walpole to the Countess of Ossory, 1 October 1773.

[2] This refers to Sir William Chambers's remark about Brown: 'Peasants emerging from the melon-ground to take the periwig and turn professor.'

[3] Charlotte Caroline of Brandenburg-Anspach (1683–1737), consort of George II.

Yet this one-time farm-hand became a better poet than many who had less dramatic lives. His 'Description of a Journey to Marlborough, Bath, Portsmouth etc.' written in 1736 is by no means the 'dull narration of a tedious Muse', and is of interest in showing how far Allen's landscaping had progressed before he had started to build Prior Park.

> A vary'd Scene! For Nature here displays
> A thousand lovely Charms, a thousand Ways:
> Allen attends, to dress her beauteous Face,
> With Handmaid Art improving ev'ry Grace,
> Now forms the verdant Walk or sunny Glade,
> Or pours the Waters o'er the steep Cascade;
> Or now contracts 'em with judicious Skill,
> And leeds 'em gently murm'ring down the Hill.

Queen Caroline was anything but 'good', and Pope never forgave her for her heartless treatment of Frederick, Prince of Wales. She 'made great pretensions to Learning and Taste with not much of the former and none of the latter'.[1] Her grotto, in which there were books, inspired many bad verses including Matthew Green's of that title. It was called Merlin's Cave (Plate XIII), though it was certainly not a cave. In it were six Tussaud-like figures in wax incongruously arranged: Merlin, with his secretary seated at a table; Elizabeth of York,[2] with Queen Elizabeth and two more out of Ariosto, as he had praised certain ancestors of the house of Brunswick.

> Lord! how we strut thro' *Merlin's* Cave, to see
> No Poets there, but *Stephen*, you, and me.[3]

The Gentleman's Magazine printed a few squibs which adequately express contemporary opinion of this 'unintelligible puppet-show'.[4]

> This indigested Pile appears
> The Relict of a thousand years;

[1] Horace Walpole, Notes to William Mason's 'Heroic Epistle to Sir William Chambers' (1757).
[2] Henry VII's queen.
[3] Alexander Pope, 'Imitations of Horace', 2 Epistle, ii, 139. He refers to Colley Cibber, Duck and himself as being the only live 'poets' in the grotto at that moment.
[4] Horace Walpole, op. cit.

> As if the Rock, in savage Dance,
> Amphion hither brought by Chance.
>
> .   .   .   .   .   .
>
> Now Stephen, touch the sounding String,
> To praise this Fabrick be thy Part,
> In Strains as innocent as Art:
> Pure native Wit will copy best
> A rural beauty when undrest.

And another, full of numerical detail:

> Three holes there are, thro' which you see
> Three seats to set your A—e on;
> And Idols four—of Wizzards three,
> And one unchristian Parson.

So it was not considered a disaster, after Queen Caroline's death, for Brown, like a 'peasant slave', to raze such a monstrous conceit to the ground. But Sir William Chambers's jealousy of Brown was harder to erase, and his *Dissertation on Oriental Gardening* (1772) was largely aimed at Brown, who had also displaced him as the architect of Lord Clive's new Claremont. Fifteen years earlier Chambers had produced his *Designs for Chinese Buildings* and this had started what Hogarth called 'paltry imitations of Chinese buildings', a vogue which was popular chiefly on account of its novelty. The seeds had been sown by William Temple in *The Garden of Epicurus* and had been blown across the Channel by winds which had passed over the Chinese landscapes of Louis XIV, inspired by Jesuit travellers' tales. At sixteen Chambers had been to China as a merchant seaman cadet and had returned with details of the Chinese methods of landscaping. In his *Dissertation on Oriental Gardening* he says that they distinguished three different species of scenes which they called pleasing, horrid, and enchanted. Evidently the enchanted scenes were similar to romantic picturesque; Horror, a Chinese variant of Sublimity was introduced by 'impending rocks, dark caverns and impetuous cataracts' as well as ruined buildings and 'gloomy woods, gibbets, crosses, wheels and the whole apparatus of torture' which could be seen from the roadside.

This was an easy target for William Mason's satirical arrows:

> Now to our lawns of dalliance and delight
> Join we the groves of horror and affright;
> This to achieve no foreign aids we try,
> Thy gibbets, Bagshot! shall our wants supply.

Mason's poem, of only 146 lines, was immediately popular, and went through fifteen editions in two years. Such details as those concerned with the more fantastic social customs of China—the pickpockets, sharpers, eunuchs, etc., who were used in festivals for the diversion of his Imperial Majesty and his ladies—were easily transferable as topical references to the English scene, thereby exposing their absurd inappropriateness as much as certain details of the landscaping. Chambers's paper-thin structure was quickly pierced, and Lancelot Brown prevailed, but still not without satirical references. Thomas Percy of *Reliques* fame is gravely ironic of an estate before and after improvement.

> Ye pleasing thickets, artless bow'rs
> Fair remains of ancient taste!
> Whose winding paths, the vernal hours
> Once with every flowret grac'd!
> Tho' sad forsaken now ye lie,
> Ye once could feast the smell, and charm the eye.

Then the new owner succeeds:

> See the future Plan they draw!
> Taste and elegance attend.
> Each charm to heighten, each veil to flaw,
> Neatness, beauty, grace to lend.
> ART brings the level and the Line
> While nature prompts and guides the whole Design.

> Walls expand and tortur'd yews expire;
> Bloomy shrubs unfold their dyes;
> Dull avenues no longer tire;
> Lawns expand, and clumps arise;
> New vistas catch the distant seat
> And every scene is beauteous, new or great.[1]

[1] 'Ode on the Death of Augustus, Earl of Sussex, And the Improvements design'd at Easton Mauduit. August 20th 1758.'

Robert Lloyd in 'The Cit's Country Box', 1757, reveals the influence of both Brown and Chambers on the typical city councillor and his wife who improved the grounds of the house which they had just bought some 'three or four miles from town'. She speaks:

> 'Twould come but to a trifling price
> To make it quite a paradise;
> I cannot bear those nasty rails,
> Those ugly broken mouldy pales:
> Suppose, my dear, instead of these
> We build a railing, all Chinese,
> Although one hates to be exposed;
> 'Tis dismal to be thus enclosed;
> One hardly any object sees—
> I wish you'd fell those odious trees.
>
> .   .   .   .   .
>
> Our house, beholders would adore,
> Was then a level lawn before,
> Nothing its view to incommode,
> But quite laid open to the road;
> While ev'ry trav'ller in amaze,
> Should on our little mansion gaze,
> And pointing to the choice retreat,
> Cry, that's Sir Thrifty's country seat.
> No doubt her arguments prevail,
> For madam's TASTE can never fail.

The estate was further embellished by Gothic and Chinese temples, zigzag bridges of William Halfpenny's designs, and 'the Gods of Athens and of Rome' made by the Cheeres. The city tradesman and his wife were thrifty, like John Gilpin, so their improvements did not involve them in vast rebuilding of the terrain. Brown's richer patrons were satirized in James Bramston's 'Man of Taste' (1733); though written some years earlier it applies:

> Does it not merit the beholder's praise,
> What's high to sink? and what is low to raise?
> Slopes shall ascend where once a green-house stood,
> And in my horse-pond I will plant a wood.
> Let misers dread the hoarded gold to waste,
> Expence and alteration shew a TASTE.

At Claremont or Blenheim, his levelling naturally encountered criticism. Sometimes the terrain lent itself to improvement (had 'capabilities' as he would say), and at others there was much grubbing of hedges, burying of land drains and carving away high ground. At Moor Park any remaining terraces of the 'perfect garden'[1] were swept away, and high ground was constructed in the middle distance like 'so many artificial molehills'.[2] Samuel Johnson evidently realized none of this, for after passing a few hours at Moor Park with the owner, Admiral Lord Anson,[3] he composed an epigram commemorating the Ionic Temple of the Winds which the Admiral had so appropriately erected:

> *Gratum animum laudo; qui debuit omnia ventis*
> *Quam bene ventorum surgere templa jubet!*[4]

Much of Brown's work has qualities directly attributable to Burke's definition of Beauty: smoothness and gentleness in lawns, slopes and plantations; Gradual Variation in serpentine linear patterns, and a brightness, openness, and clarity throughout. If there is sometimes a vastness of dimension that one might associate with the Sublime, it does not inspire awe or dread, for the imagination is never infinitely extended. And always in his perspective views there is a Variety giving a Fitness which Hogarth would have extolled. It is impossible to mention all the estates on which he worked, but the best make an impressive list, in which are many of the great houses of the Whig noblemen: Addington, Alnwick, Althorp, Ampthill, Ashburnham, Ashridge, Belvoir, Berrington, Blenheim, Bowood, Broadlands, Burghley, Cardiff Castle, Castle Ashby, Charlecote, Chatsworth, Claremont, Combe Abbey, Compton Verney, Corsham, Croome, Eaton, Edgbaston, Hampton Court, Harewood, Heveningham, Himley, Holkham, Ickworth, Ingestre, Longleat, Lowther, Luton Hoo, Milton Abbey, Moor Park, Nuneham Park, Prior Park, Radley, Ragley, Sandleford,

---

[1] Sir William Temple's estimate.   [2] Horace Walpole.
[3] Author of *A Voyage Round the World* (London, 1748), died 1762.
[4] A grateful mind I praise! All to the winds he owed
And so upon the winds a Temple he bestowed.
The Temple was destroyed recently during building operations.

Sherborne, Stowe, Syon, Tottenham Park, Trentham, Wardour, Warwick, Wilton, Wimpole, and Wynnstay.

One of these might have been the setting for Samuel Richardson's Grandison Hall, the seat of the aristocrat and egotistical young paragon, Sir Charles Grandison; for, as described by Miss Lucy Selby, it had all the best features of a Brownian landscape. A serpentine stream, a cascade, noble prospects, mature clumps, sunk fences, temples, seats, and a gardener's rustic villa are all eulogized, as well as the tenets of infinity, variety and openness. As Richardson paints his hero in idyllic colours, unmixed with the muddy tones of vice and folly, so it is clear that he intended this description to epitomize the perfect setting, even though it is seen through the rose-coloured glasses of a sentimental woman. Yet it is hard to understand how Samuel Johnson could have thought that there was 'more knowledge of the heart in one letter of Richardson's, than in all *Tom Jones*'.[1] To raise doubts one has but to compare this letter with Fielding's description of Squire Allworthy's park.[2]

This large and convenient house is situated in a spacious park; which has several fine avenues leading to it.

On the north side of the park flows a winding stream, that may well be called a river, abounding with trout and other fish, the current quickened by a noble cascade, which tumbles down its foaming waters from a rock, which is continued to some extent in a ledge of rockwork rudely disposed.

The park is remarkable for its prospects, lawns and rich appearing clumps of trees of large growth, which must therefore have been planted by the ancestors of the excellent owner; who, contenting himself to open and enlarge many fine prospects, delights to preserve, as much as possible, the plantations of his ancestors, and particularly thinks it a kind of impiety to fell a tree that was planted by his father.

On the south side of the river, on a natural and easy ascent, is a but plain villa, in the rustic taste, erected by Sir Thomas; the flat roof of which presents a noble prospect. This villa contains convenient lodging-rooms, and one large room in which he used sometimes to entertain his friends.

The gardener's house is a pretty little building. The man is a sober, diligent man; he is in years, has a housewifely good creature of a wife.

[1] James Boswell, *Life of Johnson* (6 April 1772).   [2] See pp. 43–44.

Content appears in the countenances of both. How happy must they be!

The gardens, vineyards, etc., are beautifully laid out. The orangery is flourishing—everything indeed is that belongs to Sir Charles Grandison. Alcoves, little temples, seats are erected at different points of view; the orchard, lawns, and grass-walks have sheep for gardeners; and the whole being bounded only by sunk fences, the eye is carried to views that have no bounds.

The orchard, which takes up near three acres of ground, is planted in a peculiar taste. A neat stone bridge in the centre of it is thrown over the river. It is planted in a natural slope, the higher fruit-trees, as pears, in a semi-circular row first; apples at further distances next; cherries, plums, standard apricots, etc., all which in the season of blossoming, one row gradually lower than another, must make a charming variety of blooming sweets to the eye from the top of the rustic villa, which commands the whole.

The outside of this orchard next the north is planted with three rows of trees, at proper distances from each other: one of pines, one of cedars, one of Scotch firs, in the like semi-circular order, which, at the same time that they afford a perpetual verdure to the eye and shady walks in the summer, defend the orchard from the cold and blighting winds.

This plantation was made by direction of Sir Thomas in his days of fancy. We have heard that he had a poetical, and, consequently a fanciful taste.[1]

In real life, Brown's plantations at first must have looked 'bare and bald', but a viewer with the imagination of Gray could enjoy a landscape such as Brown made at Chatsworth even in its early days. This letter to Dr. Wharton was written late in 1762:

. . . the house has the air of a Palace, the hills rising on three sides shut out the view of the dreary neighbourhood, and are covered with wood to their tops: the front opens to the Derwent winding thro' the valley, which by the art of Mr. Brown is now always visible and full to its brim, for heretofore it could not well be seen (but in rainy seasons) from the windows. A handsome bridge is lately thrown over it and the stables taken away which stood full in view between the

[1] *The History of Sir Charles Grandison: in a Series of Letters published from the Originals by the Editor of Pamela and Clarissa* (Oxford, 1936), Vol. 6, Letter 5, p. 25.

house and the river . . . the scene is yet in its infancy . . . but it promises well in time.

Also in the 1760s the trees at Stowe, Richard Temple, Viscount Cobham's show garden of Europe, were reaching maturity when Brown returned there. As early as 1724 Lord Perceval could describe its twenty acres as 'the finest seat in England',[1] although it then had had only eleven years of life. There was no doubt of its fame after Kent had embellished it, laying the foundations for Brown's final work by cutting out the broad central sweep from house to lake, which is the backbone of the plan. This was conceived on a Versailles scale, and though Brown widened and indented the vista, it remained the one constant in the landscape which was justly famous. The twenty acres gradually became nearly five hundred, and by 1744 Mrs. Elizabeth Montagu thought it a paradise beyond description, though she qualified this by remarking on the disagreeable crowding of the many buildings, which nevertheless became dignified on account of their dedication to 'Patriots, Heroes, Lawgivers and Poets'. In that judgement, in which she neglects aesthetic perception for the literary and moral concepts behind the buildings, she is equally as much in accord with the spirit of her age as is John Wesley, who also judged them on his moral grounds. He thought the temples 'miserable', the statues 'coarse', and the paintings in the Temple of Venus 'lewd'.[2]

George Lyttelton remembered this temple more happily in his lyric to his future wife, Lucy Fortescue:

> Fair Venus! whose delightful Shrine surveys
> Its front reflected in the silver lake
> These humble off'rings, which thy servant pays
> Fresh flowers and myrtle wreaths, propitious take.

It is a typical Palladian building of Kent, with quadrants and one room (with the 'indelicate murals' no longer visible) at the back of an Ionic portico; and has been saved from ruin by restoration in the last decade.

[1] Letter to his uncle, Dering, 14 August 1724.
[2] *Journal*, 13 October 1779. He refers to frescoes by the Venetian, Francesco Sleter, illustrating 'The Faerie Queen', of which no trace remains. See his similar reaction to the Pantheon, Stourhead, p. 53.

Unlike Mrs. Montagu, Horace Walpole did not think the 'Albano glut of buildings'[1] was crowded; and he enjoyed the 'sweet scenes'[2] and 'enchanting walks'[3] as early as 1751. When nineteen years later he was staying there he was further moved by the history that the fanes and temples by then enshrined. 'Pope, Congreve, Kent, Gibbs, Lord Cobham, Lord Chesterfield, the mob of nephews, the Lytteltons, Grevilles, Wests' were among others who had 'inhabited, decorated, planned or visited' Stowe.[4]

> Here Congreve, welcome Guest, oft chear'd the Days,
> With friendly converse, or poetick Lays.
> Here Lyttelton oft spreads his growing Wing,
> Delighted in these Shades to rove and sing.[5]

By the middle sixties, when Mrs. Lybbe Powys saw it, the trees had grown and the landscape matured, adding 'infinitely to many picturesque views of porticoes, temples etc. which when originally expos'd at once, with perhaps three or four more seen from the same point, must have had a different and crowded effect'. There were then over four hundred acres and a walk round of over five miles, more than Kew Gardens; and as the buildings were amply spaced apart, the original crowding must not have been so evident. Nor was it just a matter of a display of wealth, for there was evidently that indefinable quality, in the tradition of Pope—taste.

> . . . beneath whose magic wand
> Truth and correctness guide the artist's hand,
> Woods, lakes and palaces are idle things
> The shame of nations and the blush of kings.
> Expense in Vanbrugh, vanity and show
> May build a Blenheim, but not make a Stowe.[6]

[1] Horace Walpole to George Montagu, 22 July 1751.
[2] Paul Whitehead, 'Manners' (1738).
[3] George Lyttelton, 'The Progress of Love', IV.
[4] Horace Walpole to George Montagu, July 1770.
[5] Gilbert West, *Stowe, the Gardens of the Rt. Hon. Richard Lord Viscount Cobham* (London, 1732). cf. Ruskin in *The Seven Lamps of Architecture* (London, 1849), 'the greatest glory of a building is not in its stones . . . it is not until a building has been hallowed by the deeds of men . . . that its existence . . . can be gifted with . . . language and of life'.
[6] James Cawthorn, 'Of Taste' (1755).

Unknown to Cawthorn, Vanbrugh designed many buildings for Stowe, as well as Blenheim. Unfortunately, the best of them, his sturdy Temple of Bacchus, was destroyed to free the site for a school chapel. There is no better guide to the grounds than Laurence Whistler,[1] and to follow him is to see how carefully planned is every building as a key-point to vistas, running back and forth in long axes, with constant surprises en route, and all enlivened by water and enriched with planting. He takes us from Buckingham along the Grand Avenue to its climax at the Corinthian Arch, through which we can see the splendid view to the south front of the house: then over the Oxford Water, recently cleared of reeds, past the twin Boycott pavilions of Gibbs up to the house. From the great south front we look down the wide vista to the lake, on the eastern side of which is a glade called the Elysian Fields. In Kent's time it was bisected by a river and there was a series of carefully planned compositions as in landscape painting. Overshadowed by trees is the circular colonnade of Kent's Temple of Ancient Virtue (*c.* 1734).[2] This used to face a ruin near by called the Temple of Modern Virtue, and this, as Laurence Whistler points out, is the reason for the nomenclature, for the satire illustrates the Whig opposition of Cobham and Pitt to Sir Robert Walpole's political policies. Across a dam is another structure designed by Kent, the Temple of British Worthies. Sixteen busts of worthies, including Bacon, Shakespeare, Locke, Newton, Milton, and Pope, deliberately face the ruins of Modern Virtue.

In a parallel vista, to the east, stands the big, ironstone Gothic Temple of Gibbs, triangular in form with pentagonal towers, so much admired by Horace Walpole; and interesting in being as early as any other Gothic Revival garden pavilion; but it lacks the grace and fancy of later examples. Farther on down the hill is the Palladian bridge across part of the Octagon Lake. It was built soon after and modelled on the one at Wilton, but it is not approached by steps, so seems to stand lower. Unfortunately the school's hard tennis courts block the vista between this and Gibbs's Temple of Friendship, a

[1] *Stowe. A Guide to the Gardens* (London, 1956).
[2] cf. Hawksmoor's Mausoleum at Castle Howard, which was built at the same time.

The Section of MERLIN's CAVE in The Royal Gardens at Richmond.

as Designd by Mr Kent. I. Vardy delin et sculp.

XIII. Merlin's Cave from *Some Designs of Mr. Inigo Jones and Mr. William Kent* by John Vardy, 1744.

XIV. Stowe, The Doric Arch: engraved by Thomas Medland, 1796,
from *A Description of the House and Gardens* by J. Seeley, 1797.

visual key-point, though it has been in ruins for some years. This was dedicated to the 'Boy Patriots', the Opposition Whigs led by Pitt and Lyttelton. Today it is slowly falling apart, and despite being unsafe and out-of-bounds is scored by the initials of other, lesser-known, boys. If we go on westwards we reach the Lake Pavilions and look up the wide vista to the south front of the house. Near by, on an island, is the Congreve Monument (1736) by Kent. After recent clearance, the monkey which surmounts it is no longer strangled by undergrowth as he inspects himself in his mirror. Does he hold it to view himself, possibly through Congreve's satirical eyes, or does he reflect in it the state of the grounds?

> And gazing there beheld his alter'd Look;
> Wond'ring, he saw his Features and his Hue
> So much were chang'd, that scarce himself he knew.[1]

The Eleven Acre Lake is often brightened by the movement of the white sails of the boats of the school sailing club, a scene which would have pleased Humphry Repton. As we pass over the dam with its cascade dividing the lake we can see over the main vista to Vanbrugh's open Rotundo, perfectly placed as an eye-catcher and a viewpoint, for from it one can look across the main vista to the Doric arch (Plate XIV) dedicated to Princess Amelia, who became so ecstatic at the time of Horace Walpole's visit in 1768. It was placed in a straight line with Stowe Castle, which could be seen in the distance, and the Palladian bridge, which was thus delightfully framed. Subsequent planting has obliterated this view, which, according to Horace Walpole, had 'more beauties of light, shade and buildings, than any picture of Albano'. To the north, the view from the Rotundo is not so happy, for at this point the modern school buildings have disastrously started to encroach into the vista, the worst example being the headmaster's seven-bay house, with its neo-Georgian brick façade like many others in fashionable Chelsea.

The last part of the grounds to be completed was the Grecian Valley to the north-east, and here the work of Brown in the serpen-tining of the borders of the trees, the carefully placed clumps and the winding paths is still just recognizable. Facing up this is the majestic

[1] John Dryden, 'Palamon and Arcite', I, lines 562-4.

Temple of Concord and Victory designed by Kent, but not finished until 1763, when it was dedicated to celebrate the triumphs of the Seven Years War, during which Britain had been saved by Pitt. It must have been superb, in its Roman Ionic classicism, its pediments crowned with six statues, until that day in 1926 when sixteen of its columns were cut out to furnish the interior of the new school chapel. It stands today shabbily bricked up like a discarded army hutment. Near by, and fortunately of use to the school as a music school, is the Queen's Building,[1] with its handsome portico of four Corinthian columns at the head of a broad staircase. A few years ago this temple used to make a superb setting for a series of outdoor productions of Shakespeare. In these the rhythms of the verse were spoken by the young Stoic actors with relish, understanding, and freshness. To hear Theseus congratulating the mechanicals on their 'fine tragedy . . . notably discharged'[2] would have pleased Cobham and his Whig literary friends, whose hatred of tyranny and whose admiration for Athenian freedom were reflected in the gracious, orderly, and natural disposition of the grounds, brought to fulfilment by Brown's Grecian Valley.

> . . . Time shall make it grow
> A Work to wonder at—perhaps a STOW.

Yet, symbolically perhaps, the headless trunk of Lord Cobham dominates the scene from the top of James Gibbs's tall column, and few bother to read the inscription which commemorates his creation.

> . . . *Et elegantiori Hortorum cultu His primum in*
> *agris illustrato Patriam ornavit. MDCCXLVII*

The longest verse panegyric of the natural school, modelled on 'The Georgics', is William Mason's 'The English Garden', published in the year of Brown's death. It is in blank verse, then unfashionable, rather than rhyming couplets; for Mason thought that more variety

[1] Originally the Lady's Temple.
[2] Unlike Garrick's version of *Midsummer Night's Dream*, which, in Cibber's words, was 'minc'd and fricasseed into a thing called *The Fairies*' (the artisans were taken out of the play altogether).

was possible in quantity and cadence in blank verse, than in the confinement of the studied arrangement of final syllables and consonants in rhyme. And he thought that this variety was exactly analogous to the freedom from control in natural landscaping and was therefore a more suitable medium. Variety is the key, for she

> Assists the Balance; 'gainst the barren crag.
> She lifts the pastur'd slope; to distant hills
> Opposes neighb'ring shades; and, central oft,
> Relieves the flatness of the lawn, or lake,
> With studded tuft, or island. So to poize
> Her objects, mimic Art may oft attain:
> She rules the foreground. She can swell or sink
> Its surface; here her leafey screen oppose,
> And there withdraw, here part the varying greens,
> And there in one promiscuous gloom combine
> As best befits the Genius of the scene.

He suggests that the young travellers returning from Italy should memorize the scenes 'that taught a Claude to grave his canvas with Hesperian hues', and, after giving them local form, if nature is kind with materials, reproduce them in England.

Much of the poem repeats the traditional themes: the genius of the place to be consulted in order that she might hear the call of art, and the usual condemnation of the French formal garden, brought to England by that 'abject tool of France' Charles II. The poem is long, and some of it suffers from the restricted attitude of the country gentleman to his social inferiors. Mason has no more sympathy than Gray for the 'mute inglorious' Miltons. The children of the labourer living in the cot at the corner of the park should be clothed, provided with leathern scrip and strictly kept to their position in life—looking after the sheep efficiently and decoratively. In Book IV, a tale of Alcander and his Gothic castle by the sea, he indulges in a description which must have pleased the Picturesque school, of a thatched and gloomy cell of a hermit, with no nonsense.

> . . . void of hour-glass, scull and maple dish,
> Its mimic garniture. Alcander's taste
> Disdains to trick with emblematic toys.

Romanticizing the setting, Mason paints even the stoves in the Grecian conservatory in picturesque enamel:

> The glassy penthouse of ignoble form
> High on Ionic shafts he bad it tower
> A proud Rotunda; to its sides conjoin'd
> Two broad Piazzas in theatric curve,
> Ending in equal Porticos sublime.
> Glass rooft the whole, and sidelong to the South
> 'Twixt ev'ry fluted Column lightly rear'd
> Its wall pellucid. All within was day,
> Was genial Summer's day, for secret stoves
> Thro' the pile solstitial warmth convey'd.

Yet, despite these extravagances, the major part of the poem conveys Mason's delight in the natural scene as landscaped by Brown, and he predicts that

> . . . Bards yet unborn
> Shall pay to Brown that tribute fittest paid
> In strains the beauty of his scenes inspire.

No other poets have subsequently come forward, and 'The English Garden' remains to 'preserve the Science' as Horace Walpole remarked in his Notes to it.

Considering other admirable critical writing by Horace Walpole in addition to this, it is surprising that he should have earned a reputation for waspish gossip and superficial social comment. He was unique both as a chronicler of events in his three thousand letters and as an experimenter in Gothic at Strawberry Hill, Twickenham. In his reactions to landscaping he shows a consistent standard of criticism throughout his life. From his visit to Versailles when on the Grand Tour with Gray in 1739, he never changes his ideological standpoint. He believed, as he stated in the Notes for William Mason's 'Heroic Epistle to Sir William Chambers', that 'the imitation of Nature in Gardens, or rather in laying-out of ground, still called Gardening for want of a specific term to distinguish an Art totally new, is Original and indisputably English'. Versailles was therefore 'littered with statues and fountains . . . there are avenues of water-pots who disport themselves much in squirting up cascadelins. In short 'tis a garden for a great child'[1] (a very just estimate of Louis XIV's character). And thirty-five years later he still thought that M. Boutin's garden in Paris was the

completest absurdity . . . a river that wriggles at right-angles through a stone-gutter, with two tansy puddings that were dug out of it, and three or four beds in a row, by a corner of the wall with samples of grass, corn and of *en friche*, like a taylor's paper of patterns.[2]

His work at Strawberry Hill appeared casual, yet nature concealed art in the fourteen acres of the grounds, and in the apparently accidental additions to the house, each of which was carefully studied to make a final picturesque elevation. In June 1753 he wrote to Horace Mann,

This view of the castle is what I have just finished and is the only side that will be at all regular. Directly before it is an open grove, through which you see a field, which is bounded by a serpentine wood of all kinds of trees, and flowering shrubs, and flowers. The lawn before the house is situated on the top of a small hill, from whence to the left you see the town and church of Twickenham encircling a turn of the river that looks exactly like a sea-port in miniature. The opposite shore is a most delicious meadow bounded by Richmond Hill, which loses itself in the noble woods of the Park to the end of the Prospect on the right, where is another turn of the river, and the suburbs of Kingston as luckily placed as Twickenham on the left: and a natural terrace on the brow of the hill, with meadows of my own down to the river, commands both extremities. Is not this a tolerable prospect? You must figure that all this is perpetually enlivened by a navigation of boats and barges and by a road below my terrace with coaches, post-chaises, waggons, and horsemen constantly in motion, and the fields speckled with horses and sheep.

All this (much of which can be seen in Plate XV) shows a most moderate and unextravagant taste, with none of the formality which would have ordained a central axis, or the bareness of Brown which might have swept away more natural planting, or the dense-

---

[1] Horace Walpole to Richard West, July 1739.
[2] Horace Walpole to General Conway, 12 November 1774.

ness of the later Picturesque; and becoming increasingly interested in horticulture, by 1765 he remarks on the scent in June from acacias, honeysuckles, and syringas which he had planted. The architectural, paved terrace was clothed by planting immediately around the house. The paths through the woods revealed variety in their views, and his pleasure in animation of movement showed a warmth of feeling which high walls would have shut out. Considering the estate's 'extreme littleness',[1] it was a triumph of ingenuity, and in the best traditions of English landscape gardening —practical poetry from one who, like Pope and Kent, believed that the 'three new graces, Poetry, Painting and Gardening should unite to dress and adorn Nature'.

At approximately the same time Walpole's cousin, General Conway, was laying out nine hundred acres at Park Place, Henley-on-Thames. It was a romantic spot with steep beech woods dropping to the river and was evidently like an enlarged Strawberry Hill. Such embellishments as forty-five prehistoric stones taken from Jersey, where General Conway was Governor, and placed at Park Place exactly as they had been, may offend modern archaeological sensitivity, yet it was perhaps no worse than the transference of the Elgin Marbles. In her excellent *Horace Walpole. Gardenist* (Princeton, U.S.A., 1943), Professor Chase points out the similarities between some of the features at Park Place and those in Walpole's Hieroglyphic Tale, *Hi-Li* (1785). In both there was a rustic bridge over no water, a lonely tomb where nobody was buried, a subterraneous passage through which the eyes of dogs might be seen shining, and a path along the river. *Hi-Li* naturally has a Chinese setting; but this interest was not long-standing with Horace Walpole, who for the greater part of his life was shocked by the lack of propriety and symmetry in Chambers's variety of Chinese used in landscaping.

Writing of three different classifications of landscaping in his *History of the Modern Taste in Gardening*, he gives us an excellent idea

---

[1] Thomas Gray to Thomas Wharton, 13 August 1754. Walpole eventually acquired more land across the Teddington road to the east of the house, on which he had a Gothic cottage and his pool, Payong, with its goldfish, he so often writes of. The present incumbents of Strawberry Hill, a Roman Catholic Training College, have a habit of showing one a circular stone basin, on the lawn near the house, as Payong.

of contemporary work apart from that of Brown. His first group was tantamount to the park-cum-garden landscape of Strawberry Hill or Park Place; the second was the *ferme ornée*, a combination of utility and beauty as at Philip Southcote's Wooburn Farm, near Weybridge. On these one hundred and fifty acres Southcote raised cattle and farmed; but kept thirty-five adorned with flowers and shrubs— a more successful experiment in farming and landscape gardening than Shenstone's at the Leasowes, which both Horace Walpole and Repton thought was a disparate mixture of cows and cascades, of profit and beauty. /The third type was the 'savage' landscape of Salvator Rosa which was typified by Charles Hamilton's magnificent Painshill, near Cobham. These hundred acres have been described in great detail by Whately and in contemporary guides such as *The Ambulator*, and it was more visited at the time than Stourhead. Vast pine woods, lake, and river, elegant lawns, temples, and hermitage, each view melting into another without abrupt edges or borders, the whole modelled on Rosa and Gaspar Poussin, and which must have justified the praises of contemporaries.

Walpole also describes in his Letters most of the larger estates which he visited, and throughout his life he travelled much. Euston with a fine park but too many clumps; the 'glorious woods' of the Duke of Bedford at Woburn; the 'Albano glut of buildings' at Stowe; Blenheim, like 'a quarry of stone', and Warwick Castle 'well laid out by one Brown', are but a few. His standards of criticism were neither esoteric nor bigoted; and like all great landscapers he deplored the loss of great trees, as at Mount Edgecumbe, where 'the hundred ancient oaks growing exactly where they ought' had been felled 'to make room for a battery';[1] and he always consulted the genius of the place before making a judgement on the landscaping.

In 1783 Brown, 'the second monarch of landscape',[2] died. Although his work does not always show the painter's eye of Horace Walpole or Kent, how often have 'the setting sun and the long autumnal shades enriched the landscape to a Claude Lorrain'[3] in the

---

[1] Horace Walpole to the Countess of Ossory, 16 August 1780.
[2] Horace Walpole to the Countess of Ossory, 8 February 1783.
[3] Horace Walpole to Miss Mary and Miss Agnes Berry, 16 September 1791, referring to the view from Strawberry Hill.

scenes which he created; and how often have these same groves been felled or 'their lawns restored to the ploughshare or defolated by Tyranny or Tax-gatherers'?[1]

[1] Horace Walpole, *Notes to the English Garden* by William Mason.

6

The Repton–Payne Knight Controversy

> To improve the scenery of a country, and to display
> its native beauties with advantage is an art which
> originated in England.
>
> HUMPHRY REPTON, *Sketches and Hints* (1794)

IVE years after Brown's death Humphry Repton, a gentleman
farmer *manqué*, in his middle thirties, who read widely and
painted in water-colours adequately, decided that landscape
gardening should be his life work.[1] Knowing well the works of
Mason, Gilpin, Whately, and Girardin, he was fitted to inherit the
natural tradition. So his friend, Anna Seward, wrote to him a few
months after his decision: 'if you do not transcend your predecessors
in the art you have adopted, it will be strange; you, whom poetry,
painting have so much more beauteously endowed.' In twenty
years his success showed her to be right: he had made over 3,000
sketches for improvements and had produced over 200 Red Books
showing his plans, written and drawn, for estates in all parts of the
country.

Brown was 'truly great' and Repton was quick to defend his
memory from the attacks of Payne Knight and the Picturesque
adherents. Yet his own work differed from Brown's in certain
features; and, as he was a prolific writer, these practices and the
reasons for them are fully set out in his works.[2] He insisted, for

---

[1] Letter to his friend, the Rev. Norton Nicholls, 26 August 1788.

[2] *Sketches and Hints on Landscape Gardening* (London, 1794). *Observation on the theory
and practice of Landscape Gardening* (London, 1803). *An Enquiry into the changes of taste
in Landscape Gardening* (London, 1806). *Fragments on the Theory and Practice of Landscape
Gardening* (London, 1816).

example, that a house needed a formal basis to link it to natural scenes beyond, so where possible he created terraces and parterres rather than allowing lawn to straggle up to the front door, as often happened in Brown's work. Woburn, with its unified connecting wings, parterres, and terraces is the perfect example of Repton's work on the grand scale. Another feature of Brown's work that he disliked was the planting of small clumps of trees on hilltops like 'bonnets'; his own planting was invariably fuller, the trees cascading into the valley below with the natural contours of the ground. He criticized Brown for unnecessary serpentining, pointing out that a straight line if it crosses contours will inevitably curve. But here he seems to have missed the point of Hogarth's line of grace which waves and winds in two ways three-dimensionally, at the same time, and that is precisely what Brown's lines did. Repton never lost sight of usefulness and convenience, so there was never any hiding of kitchen gardens in awkward places; on the contrary, he often placed them near the stables from which manure was easily transportable. In all his designs common sense ruled: no destruction of Gothic buildings because they happened to be unfashionable, no building of Roman porticoes in an unsuitable climate, no sham ruins or grottoes, though he allowed picturesque cottages for estate workers. Although Brown had made himself into an architect who was able to draw elevations, plans, and maps, his patrons may not have understood exactly what he intended as easily as by examining Repton's hinged plates in his Red Books. By the brilliant expedient of a superimposed flap showing exactly what he would alter in the view from the house, through planting, remodelling of ground and building, he was able to convince those for whom he worked that it would indeed be an improvement. These splendid books bound in red morocco came at a time when the whole art of book production, in title-pages and generosity of layout was at its finest: and although the preliminary exordia may have been obsequious, yet he managed to 'sell' his ideas, and a little flattery brought in commissions. Above all, he managed to convince his patrons that he had a practical knowledge of surveying, mechanics, hydraulics, agriculture, and botany, as well as the general rules of architecture and the study of painting.

He realized that Brown's disciples had often distorted or exaggerated their master's characteristics. 'Brown copied Nature, his illiterate followers copied him.' And in many cases they thought that 'greatness of dimension would produce greatness of character', so they produced immeasurable lawn, naked expanses of water, single trees and overbroad roads. Repton thought that lawns by themselves were of little interest, and in many of his Red Book slides cattle or boats are placed in the scene.[1] In the *Enquiry* he distinguished between the 'cheerful lawn' with cattle and the 'melancholy lawn' which had been cut and rolled. Today he would have enjoyed the enlivened scene which occurs when great houses are opened to the public, for he comments with pleasure on the gaiety of the public at Longleat in his time. Although he liked an unbounded prospect in a park landscape, his work is gentler and less ruthless than Brown's, and above all he was willing to acknowledge that the spirit of the place might be romantic and picturesque. Referring to Abbot's Leigh, near Bristol, he is reputed to have written that the 'walks in the woods on both sides the deep ravine will provide the most romantic scenery and these should neither be too highly dressed nor the natural effects injured by too much interference of Art'.[2] In fact, he acknowledged the Picturesque as causing pleasure by the effects of light and shade, tones and hues in colouring, and form in composition.

He was therefore disturbed by the violence of Payne Knight's attack on Brown in his poem 'The Landscape' (1794), for he appreciated much of the work of the Picturesque school and was a personal friend of Payne Knight's. His replies, which will be dealt with in the next chapter, were restrained, yet concealed a depth of feeling which he revealed to his friends. He thought of Payne Knight's words as a 'malicious attack' and unexpected, for he had lived with him

---

[1] cf. Horace Walpole to the Countess of Ossory, 26 December 1793: 'I have an aversion to a park, and especially a walled park in which the capital event is the coming of cows to water.'

[2] MS. in Bristol University Library entitled 'Notes on some general Maxims of Taste in Gardens from Mr. Repton's Report concerning Abbot's Leigh near Bristol' (1814). This may refer to his son, John Adey Repton, who worked in the neighbourhood at that time, but it equally reflects Humphry Repton's outlook.

in some habits of intimacy and had no reason to suspect the contume-
lious treatment of my profession—especially as I am actually endeavouring to raise it in the scale of Polite Arts. But however I may feel
hurt or express those feelings in confidence to my friends, I hope the
publick will see that I coolly defend myself and my predecessor and
you and every lover of Landscape Gardening as distinguished from
Painting, with arguments, with facts and an appeal to experience.[1]

In his Appendix to *Sketches* he replied restrainedly to Uvedale
Price, defending Brown's clumps and belts, which, he said, were
planted for posterity, when their beauty would reach maturity.
And to Payne Knight he pointed out the difference between landscape painting and landscape gardening, and that to deduce that a
landscape and picture could be treated in similar aesthetic terms
was to start from a false premise. Gardening is in motion: the scene,
with its light, changes with different times of day and season, as
well as in its human interest. Also, in any scene in real life the width
of vision required to see it is much greater than in viewing a picture,
which is confined to about 20 degrees to 90 degrees without moving
the head. There were other fundamental differences: the top of a
hill is pleasant for seeing a prospect in real life, but rarely in a
picture; the foreground is not sketchy as often in landscape painting, for a 'gravel walk or close-mown lawn' is more suitable than
Payne Knight's 'large fragments of stone irregularly thrown
amongst briers and weeds' imitating a picture. And lastly, a
dwelling-house should be convenient and comfortable rather than
just a foreground to a rural picture, for which a 'quarry long-
neglected, mouldering abbey, ruined castle or antiquated cot with
a chimney choked with ivy' may indeed be appropriate.

Both schools of landscaping are satirized by Thomas Love Peacock in *Headlong Hall* (1816). Evidently he had read all the details
of the Repton-Payne Knight controversy, either in their original
writings prior to 1815, or in *The Edinburgh Review* which dealt
thoroughly with Payne Knight's 'Inquiry'.[2] Mr. Marmaduke
Milestone and Sir Patrick O'Prism are Peacock's guides, with whom
he views the panorama of the whole bitter landscape discussion,

---

[1] Richard Payne Knight to the Rev. Norton Nicholls, 6 November 1794.
[2] Vol. VII, January 1806.

and his attitude to both of them is droll and ironic. Perhaps because Mr. Milestone is first described as a 'picturesque landscape gardener of the first celebrity', one editor[1] has remarked that Peacock is satirizing in him the ideas of Payne Knight. This is only half the truth. Mr. Milestone, so named on account of Repton's suggestion in the Tatton Red Book that Arms might be put on a stone or obelisk, represents superficially all that Repton stood for. He arrives for a house-party at Squire Headlong's at Llanberis, and before long is giving his advice on improvements to that estate and to Lord Littlebrain's near by. In this extract the interpolations of Miss Tenorina Chromatic represent the foibles of the Picturesque school. Peacock obviously delights in the whole satire of what is Taste. Like Hume and Payne Knight himself, he is sceptical of any positive and absolute standard. Elegant lawns, regular curves, and majestic clumps mean no more to him than gloomy woods, miniature cascades, and moss-covered Gothic. But he has a superficial, amused understanding, and all the jargon of the rivals.

Mr. Milestone. This, you perceive, is the natural state of one part of the grounds. Here is a wood, never yet touched by the finger of taste; thick, intricate and gloomy. Here is a little stream, dashing from stone to stone, and overshadowed with these untrimmed boughs.

Miss Tenorina. The sweet romantic spot! How beautiful the birds must sing there on a summer's evening!

Miss Graziosa. Dear sister! how can you endure the horrid thicket?

Mr. Milestone. You are right, Miss Graziosa: your taste is correct—perfectly *en règle*. Now, here is the same place corrected—trimmed—polished—decorated—adorned. Here sweeps a plantation in that beautiful regular curve: there winds a gravel walk: here are parts of the old wood, left in these majestic clumps, disposed at equal distances with wonderful symmetry: there are some single shrubs scattered in elegant profusion: here a Portugal laurel, there a juniper; here a laurustinus, there a spruce fir; here a larch, there a lilac; here a rhododendron, there an arbutus. The stream, you see, is become a canal: the banks are perfectly smooth and green, sloping to the water's edge: and there is Lord Littlebrain, rowing in an elegant boat.

[1] Richard Garnett, Everyman edition of *Headlong Hall* (London, 1908).

Squire Headlong. Magical, faith!

Mr. Milestone. Here is another part of the grounds in its natural state. Here is a large rock, with the mountain-ash rooted in its fissures, overgrown, as you see, with ivy and moss; and from this part of it bursts a little fountain, that runs bubbling down its rugged sides.

Miss Tenorina. O how beautiful! How I should love the memory of that miniature cascade!

Mr. Milestone. Beautiful, Miss Tenorina! Hideous. Base, common and popular.[1] Such a thing as you see anywhere, in wild and mountainous districts. Now, observe the metamorphosis. Here is the same rock, cut into the shape of a giant. In one hand he holds a horn, through which that little fountain is thrown to a prodigious elevation. In the other is a ponderous stone, so exactly balanced as to be apparently ready to fall on the head of any person who may happen to be beneath: and there is Lord Littlebrain under it.

Squire Headlong. Miraculous, by Mahomet!

Mr. Milestone. This is the summit of a hill, covered, as you perceive, with wood, and with those mossy stones scattered at random under the trees.

Miss Tenorina. What a delightful spot to read in, on a summer's day! The air must be so pure, and the wind must sound so divinely in the tops of those old pines!

Mr. Milestone. Bad taste, Miss Tenorina. Bad taste, I assure you. Here is the spot improved. The trees are cut down: the stones are cleared away: this is an octagonal pavilion, exactly on the centre of the summit: and there you see Lord Littlebrain, on the top of the pavilion, enjoying the prospect with a telescope.

Squire Headlong. Glorious, egad!

Mr. Milestone. Here is a rugged mountainous road, leading through impervious shades: the ass and the four goats characterise a wild uncultured scene. Here, as you perceive, it is totally changed into a beautiful gravel-road, gracefully curving through a belt of limes; and there is Lord Littlebrain driving four-in-hand.

Squire Headlong. Egregious, by Jupiter.

Mr. Milestone. Here is Littlebrain Castle, a Gothic, moss-grown structure, half bosomed in trees. Near the casement of that turret is an owl peeping from the ivy.

Squire Headlong. And devilish wise he looks.

---

[1] William Shakespeare, *Henry V*, 4.1.38.

Mr. Milestone. Here is the new house, without a tree near it, standing
in the midst of an undulating lawn: a white, polished, angular
building, reflected to a nicety in this waveless lake: and there you
see Lord Littlebrain looking out of the window.

Squire Headlong. And devilish wise he looks too. You shall cut me a
giant before you go.

Mr. Milestone. Good. I'll order down my little corps of pioneers.

But before the novel ends Miss Tenorina becomes engaged to the
Squire, so presumably the Headlong estate is saved from the depre-
dations of Milestone. This is balanced by her sister entrancing Sir
Patrick O'Prism, the dilettante painter, whom we shall see in
another chapter as the spokesman of the Picturesque; so the
Reptonian school will not ultimately be driven from the field if
Miss Graziosa gets her way with her husband.

Considering the reasonableness of Repton's practices—his
middle course between the 'bare and bald' and a Salvator Rosa
wildness—it is surprising that another contemporary who must
have seen his Red Books on her visits to country houses should have
been so anti-Repton.

Jane Austen is known to have been interested in the writings of
William Gilpin, and her novels show a knowledge of the Picturesque: so Elizabeth Bennet appraises Pemberley; Henry Tilney
holds forth from Beechen Cliff, and Marianne Dashwood is always a
ready partisan. But in *Mansfield Park* (1814) there are references to
improvements by Repton, who is mentioned by name. All these
references are proposed or carried out by the least pleasant characters in the novel, leading one to believe in an involvement by Jane
Austen with Picturesque, rather than Reptonian landscaping.
James Rushworth, a neighbouring landowner of the Bertrams of
Mansfield Park, a 'heavy young man, with not more than common
sense', who 'if he had not £12,000 a year would be a stupid fellow',
wishes to improve Sotherton, his estate. He has no ideas himself,
yet is fascinated to the point of boring others by his friend Smith's
park, which has been improved in the Repton manner. 'The
approach *now* is one of the finest things in the country. You see the
house in the most surprising manner', he tells his listeners at Mansfield Park. Then he goes on to declare what a 'dismal old prison' is

his own house in comparison. The assembled company, which appears interested in his schemes, consists of Lady Bertram, the mistress of Mansfield, with Edmund, her ordinand son, and Maria and Julia, her daughters; Fanny Price, her niece; Mrs. Norris, her sister; Dr. Grant, the rector; his wife and her half-sister, Mary Crawford. After Mrs. Norris has protested at his referring to Sotherton as a prison, Rushworth continues:

'It wants improvement, ma'am, beyond any thing. I never saw a place that wanted so much improvement in my life, and it is so forlorn, that I do not know what can be done with it.'

'No wonder that Mr. Rushworth should think so at present,' said Mrs. Grant to Mrs. Norris, with a smile; 'but depend upon it, Sotherton will have *every* improvement in time which his heart can desire.'

'I must try to do something with it,' said Mr. Rushworth, 'but I do not know what. I hope I shall have some good friends to help me.'

'Your best friend upon such an occasion,' said Miss Bertram calmly, 'would be Mr. Repton, I imagine.'

'That is what I was thinking of. As he has done so well by Smith, I think I had better have him at once. His terms are five guineas a day.'

'Well, and if they were *ten*,' cried Mrs. Norris, 'I am sure *you* need not regard it. The expense need not be any impediment. If I were you, I should not think of the expense. I would have everything done in the best style, and made as nice as possible.'

Mrs. Norris, who is one of the most detestable characters in any of the novels, is here anxious to suggest money being spent, provided that it is not her own. In the continuation of the discussion she is shaped with a sharp irony which is rare in this gravely moral novel. There is no doubt of Jane Austen's attitude towards attempts at improvements on such a scale and by such a woman. She continues:

'It would be too ridiculous for me to attempt any thing where I am now, with my little half acre. It would be quite a burlesque. But if I had more room, I should take a prodigious delight in improving and planting. We did a vast deal in that way at the parsonage; we made it

Published according to Act of Parliament by G. Kearsly at N.º 46 in Fleet Street, Aug.t 1775.

P. Sandby R.A pinx.t   M. A. Rooker sculp.t

South View of STRAWBERRY-HILL, the Seat of the Hon.ble M.r Walpole.

XV. South Front of Strawberry Hill by Paul Sandby: engraved by M. A. Rooker, 1775.

XVI. (*a*) South Front of Harlestone Park before Improvement by
Humphry Repton.

XVI. (*b*) South Front of Harlestone Park after Improvement by
Humphry Repton.

a quite different place from what it was when we first had it. You young ones do not remember much about it, perhaps. But if dear Sir Thomas were here, he could tell you what improvements we made; and a great deal more would have been done, but for poor Mr. Norris's sad state of health. He could hardly ever get out, poor man, to enjoy anything, and *that* disheartened me from doing several things that Sir Thomas and I used to talk of. If it had not been for *that*, we should have carried on the garden wall, and made the plantation to shut out the churchyard, just as Dr. Grant has done. We were always doing something, as it was. It was only spring twelvemonth before Mr. Norris's death, that we put in the apricot against the stable wall, which is now grown such a noble tree, and getting to such perfection, sir,' addressing herself then to Dr. Grant.

'The tree thrives well beyond a doubt, madam,' replied Dr. Grant. 'The soil is good; and I never pass it without regretting that the fruit should be so little worth the trouble of gathering.'

'Sir, it is a moor park, we bought it as a moor park,[1] and it cost us—that is, it was a present from Sir Thomas, but I saw the bill, and I know it cost seven shillings, and was charged as a moor park.'

'You were imposed on, ma'am', replied Dr. Grant; 'these potatoes have as much the flavour of a moor park apricot, as the fruit from that tree. It is an insipid fruit at the best; but a good apricot is eatable, which none from my garden are.'

'The truth is, ma'am,' said Mrs. Grant, pretending to whisper across the table to Mrs. Norris, 'that Dr. Grant hardly knows what the natural taste of our apricot is; he is scarcely ever indulged with one, for it is so valuable a fruit, with a little assistance, and ours is such a remarkably large, fair sort, that what with early tarts and preserves, my cook contrives to get them all.'

Mrs. Norris, who had begun to redden, was appeased, and, for a little while, other subjects took place of the improvements of Sotherton. Dr. Grant and Mrs. Norris were seldom good friends; their acquaintance had begun in dilapidations, and their habits were totally dissimilar.

After a short interruption, Mr. Rushworth began again.

'Smith's place is the admiration of all the country; and it was a mere nothing before Repton took it in hand. I think I shall have Repton.'

---

[1] The 'Moor Park' apricot was also called 'Anson's' and 'Temple's' after owners of that estate where Sir William Temple first grew it.

At this point, Lady Bertram, a woman devoid of many positive ideas, makes her one contribution:

'. . . if I were you, I would have a very pretty shrubbery. One likes to get out into a shrubbery in fine weather.'

Perhaps Fanny Price, who was often forced to entertain Lady Bertram, has been reading to her from Cowper, for he was Fanny Price's favourite author, whose love of picturesque natural scenes, whether shady avenues or semi-wild shrubberies, was frequently declared.

> Our fathers knew the value of a screen
> From sultry suns; and, in their shaded walks
> And long protract'd bow'rs, enjoy'd at noon
> The gloom and coolness of declining day.
> We bear our shades about us; self-depriv'd
> Of other screen, the thin umbrella spread,
> And range an Indian waste without a tree.
> Thanks to Benevolus[1]—he spares me yet
> These chestnuts rang'd in corresponding lines;
> And, though himself so polish'd still reprieves
> The obsolete prolixity of shade.[2]

After thanking Lady Bertram for her suggestion, which had, in fact, been his intention to carry out, Rushworth continues with repetitive details of his friend Smith's estate. At the end of this account he draws in Fanny Price, who is the good, unsophisticated poor relation of the Bertrams, to protest at the felling of an avenue; this time she directly refers to Cowper. She and Edmund, her future husband, are the only entirely good and blameless characters among those present, so she may to some extent be identified with the authoress, to whose sympathies it is an additional pointer. Rushworth, who is 'not usually a great talker', continues the subject:

'Smith has not much above a hundred acres altogether in his grounds, which is little enough, and makes it more surprising that the place can have been so improved. Now, at Sotherton, we have a good seven hundred, without reckoning the water meadows; so that I

---

[1] John Throckmorton of Weston Underwood.   [2] 'The Task', Book I, lines 255–65.

think, if so much could be done at Compton, we need not despair. There have been two or three fine old trees cut down that grew too near the house, and it opens the prospect amazingly, which makes me think that Repton, or anybody of that sort would certainly have the avenue at Sotherton down; the avenue that leads from the west front to the top of the hill you know . . .'

Fanny . . . who had been attentively listening, now said in a low voice,

'Cut down an avenue! What a pity! Does not it make you think of Cowper? "Ye fallen avenues, once more I mourn your fate un-merited." '[1]

He smiled as he answered, 'I am afraid the avenue stands a bad chance, Fanny.'

'I should like to see Sotherton before it is cut down, to see the place as it is now, in its old state; but I do not suppose I shall.'

Edmund Bertram then suggests that Rushworth himself should conduct the improvements: but he, not surprisingly, avers that he has no 'eye or ingenuity for such matters', and that Repton is the man for the job, for he could finish it and then the work could be looked at for the first time. Fanny says that she would like to see the progress of any such work, and here Mary Crawford enters the discussion by describing the horrors of being involved in such improvements at her uncle's 'cottage' at Twickenham. In fact, it was from this very house that she had recently been forced to depart when her uncle had introduced his mistress into the house, after the death of her aunt. The association of improvements with lack of strength of character and even vice, continues to build up in the novel. The cottage 'being excessively pretty, it was found necessary to be improved; and for three months we were all dirt and confusion, without a gravel walk to step on, or a bench fit for use'.

Then the subject of the arrival of Mary Crawford's harp is dis-cussed, during the course of which the seventy miles to London is mentioned, thereby giving us a clue to the location of Mansfield. After which, Mrs. Grant suggests that her brother, Henry Craw-ford, is the man to advise on improvements at Sotherton.

---

[1] William Gilpin in his *Observations on the Western parts of England, relative chiefly to picturesque beauty* (London, 1798), also quotes these lines from 'The Task', Book 1.

'My dear Henry, have *you* nothing to say? You have been an improver yourself, and from what I hear of Everingham, it may vie with any place in England. Its natural beauties, I am sure, are great. Everingham as it *used* to be was perfect in my estimation; such a happy fall of ground, and such timber! What would I not give to see it again!'

The remark is illogical, for if Everingham was 'perfect' before he improved it, what would be the point of altering it? However, Henry Crawford replies with a compliment, declaring that he is not fitted for a job of this scale. This does not ring true, for he has an income of £4,000 a year, and Everingham must have been a considerable estate. The irony of his concern for Rushworth's future happiness, if taken in general rather than in specific landscaping terms, is revealed later in the novel when he is cited as co-respondent after persuading Maria Bertram, by then Mrs. Rushworth, to leave her husband.

Crawford speaks of Everingham, in reply to Mrs. Grant:

'In extent it is a mere nothing—you would be surprised at its insignificance; and as for improvement, there is little for me to do; too little—I should like to have been busy much longer.'

'You are fond of this sort of thing?' said Julia.

'Excessively: but what with the natural advantages of the ground, which pointed out even to a very young eye what little remained to be done, and my consequent resolutions, I had not been of age three months before Everingham was all that it is now. My plan was laid at Westminster—little altered perhaps at Cambridge, and at one and twenty executed. I am inclined to envy Mr. Rushworth for having so much happiness yet before him.'

The group is unanimous in thinking that Crawford should advise on Sotherton, and Rushworth arranges for them all to visit him, to hear Crawford's suggestions on the spot. So, on a hot summer's day, about a fortnight later, they bowl down the hill in a barouche towards the house. Fanny's first thought is for the situation of the avenue which may be cut down. She is curtly told that it is of oak and is on the other side of the house. During the course of their walk round Henry Crawford's observations are neither lengthy nor profound. He sees 'walls of great promise', which on one side of the house bounded the lawn, then there was a

planted area, a bowling-green, and beyond the bowling-green a long terrace walk, backed by iron palisades, and commanding a view over them to the tops of the trees of the wilderness immediately adjoining. It was a good spot for fault-finding.

But we do not hear of the faults which Crawford is presumed to have found. Instead the party moves off to the shade of the wilderness to get out of the heat. After going up a 'considerable flight of steps' they reach the wilderness, which is 'a planted wood of about two acres, and though chiefly of larch and laurel, and beech cut down, and though laid out with too much regularity, was darkness and shade, and natural beauty, compared with the bowling-green and the terrace'.

Fanny, being delicate, tires first of her serpentine wanderings, and is escorted to a shady bench 'looking over the ha-ha into the park'. The others move off, and she is left alone. Perhaps she remembers her beloved Cowper:

> We tread the wilderness, whose well-roll'd walks,
> With curvature of slow and easy sweep—
> Deception innocent—give ample space
> To narrow bounds.[1]

She has ample time to muse, for after about twenty minutes Rushworth, Henry Crawford, and Maria Bertram return. They have apparently not decided on any exact improvements, though Crawford is 'full of ideas and projects', which are accepted in their entirety by Rushworth, who has no ideas of his own. Then Maria sees the iron gate which leads into the park, and less than half a mile away is a knoll from which they might with advantage look back at the house. Unfortunately the gate is locked, and Rushworth has forgotten to bring the key. He returns to the house to get it, but takes so long that Maria becomes impatient.

'Yes, certainly, the sun shines and the park looks cheerful. But unluckily that iron gate, that ha-ha, give me a feeling of restraint and

[1] 'The Task', Book I, lines 351–4.

hardship. I cannot get out, as the starling said.' As she spoke, and it was with expression, she walked to the gate; he followed her.

'Mr. Rushworth is so long fetching this key!'

'And for the world you would not get out without the key and without Mr. Rushworth's authority and protection, or I think you might with little difficulty pass round the edge of the gate, here, with my assistance; I think it might be done, if you really wished to be more at large, and could allow yourself to think it not prohibited.'

'Prohibited! nonsense! I certainly can get out that way, and I will. Mr. Rushworth will be here in a moment you know—we shall not be out of sight.'

'Or if we are, Miss Price will be so good as to tell him, that he will find us near the knoll, the grove of oak on the knoll.'

Fanny, feeling this to be wrong, could not help making an effort to prevent it. 'You will hurt yourself, Miss Bertram,' she cried, 'you will certainly hurt yourself against those spikes—you will tear your gown—you will be in danger of slipping into the ha-ha. You had better not go.'

But she crosses, and soon they are out of sight on their circuitous way to the knoll. Their action in breaking out over iron spikes and around the locked gate is wholly symbolic of their future life. By running away with Crawford after her unsuccessful marriage to Rushworth, Maria again crosses the spikes of convention and the locked gate of propriety, to find herself ostracized by society, beyond the ha-ha. And it is significant that Henry Crawford, the improver in the Repton manner, is the partner to this conduct. The 'elegance, propriety, regularity and harmony' of Mansfield has been and will be ultimately unaltered by any improver despite this. It stands for a different set of values.

The coarse materialism of Henry Crawford is again shown in his suggestions for improvement at Thornton Lacey, Edmund's future parsonage.

'The farmyard must be cleared away entirely, and planted up to shut out the blacksmith's shop. The house must be turned to front the east instead of the north—the entrance and the principal rooms, I mean, must be on that side, where the view is really very pretty; I am sure it may be done. And *there* must be your approach—through

what is at present the garden. You must make you a new garden at
what is now the back of the house; which will be giving it the best
aspect in the world—sloping to the south-east. The ground seems
precisely formed for it. I rode fifty yards up the lane between the
church and the house in order to look about me; and saw how it might
all be. Nothing can be easier. The meadows beyond what *will be* the
garden, as well as what *now is*, sweeping round from the lane I stood in to
the north-east, that is, to the principal road through the village, must
be all laid together of course; very pretty meadows they are, finely
sprinkled with timber. They belong to the living, I suppose. If not,
you must purchase them. Then the stream—something must be done
with the stream; but I could not quite determine what. I had two or
three ideas.'

'And I have two or three ideas also,' said Edmund, 'and one of
them is, that very little of your plan for Thornton Lacey will ever be
put in practice.'

But Crawford persists in outlining his plan, revealing fully the
contrast between the moral values of Edmund and himself—the
desire for a pleasant parsonage, and the eagerness for the status of a
place. The irony in the writing is a deadly exposure of contemporary
worldly attitudes, expressed in improvement.

'My plan may not be the best possible; I had not many minutes to
form it in; but you must do a good deal. The place deserves it, and
you will find yourself not satisfied with much less than it is capable of.
. . . The air of a gentleman's residence, therefore, you cannot but
give it, if you do anything. But it is capable of much more. . . . By
some improvements as I have suggested, (I do not really require you
to proceed upon my plan, though by the by I doubt anybody's
striking out a better)—you may give it a higher character. You may
raise it into a *place*. From being the mere gentleman's residence, it
becomes, by judicious improvement, the residence of a man of education, taste, modern manners, good connections. All this may be
stamped on it; and that house receive such an air as to make its
owner be set down as the great landowner of the parish, by every
creature travelling the road; especially as there is no real squire's
house to dispute the point; a circumstance between ourselves to
enhance the value of such a situation in point of privilege and indepen-
dence beyond all calculation.'

Edmund will not accept even Mary Crawford's suggestion that her brother should help with the landscaping at Thornton Lacey as at Sotherton. He is content with it as a 'gentleman's residence' and a parsonage house: and it is not to be doubted that he and Fanny lived there after their marriage without improvements. The 're-spectable, elegant, modernized' estate would have been antithetical to the decorum of Edmund and the Picturesque devotions of Fanny. On the other hand, the unscrupulous and coarse Henry Crawford and the asinine James Rushworth are Jane Austen's prototypes for Reptonian improvement.

It is not easy to place the exact location of Mansfield Park.[1] Jane Austen had never been to Northamptonshire, and while writing the novel she inquired of her sister whether she could discover if Northamptonshire was a county of hedgerows.[2] The distance from London (seventy miles) and from Northampton (four miles) of Harlestone makes it a likely identification. But Harlestone adjoined the great Althorp estate of the Spencers, which would presumably have been mentioned in the novel; and it was not so large as Mans-field, which was a 'real park, five miles round'. Yet Mansfield Park was a 'spacious modern-built house so well placed and well screened as to deserve to be in any collection of engravings of gentlemen's seats in the kingdom'. Such an illustration appears in Repton's *Fragments*.

Fragment VII

on

Unity of Character.

In a House entirely new, Character is at the option of the Artistic Proprietor: it may be Gothic or Grecian, whichever best accords with the face of the country; but where a great part of the original structure is to remain, the additions should doubtless partake of the existing character. This we have attempted at Harlestone Park, the seat of Robert Andrew Esq. near Northampton; and as few places have undergone so much alteration both in the House and Grounds, it may serve as a specimen of the combined arts of Landscape Gardening and Architecture, in adapting the improvements to the original Character of the Place.

[1] See correspondence in *The Times Literary Supplement*, 18 March–15 April 1920.
[2] Jane to Cassandra Austen, Friday, 29 January 1813.

The House was formerly approached and entered in the south front, which was encumbered by stables and farm yards: the road came through the village, and there was a large pool in front; this pool has been changed to an apparent river, and the stables have been removed. An ample Garden has been placed behind the house, the centre of the south front has been taken down, and a bow added with pilasters in the style of the house: the entrance is changed from the south to the north side, and some new rooms to the west have been added. Of the useful and modern appendages to this House, the drawing can give little idea: the more essential part of Landscape Gardening is apt to be overlooked in the general attention to the picturesque, which has often little affinity with the more important objects of comfort, convenience, and accommodation.

Had Jane Austen read this, perhaps she might have equated Mansfield Park with Harlestone (Plate XVI), for both had Unity of Character. Certainly, James Rushworth would not have understood it, Sir Thomas Bertram would have disregarded it, and Henry Crawford would have recognized his master. Anyway, Harlestone was demolished in 1940 by a generation that did not appreciate it. *Mansfield Park* lives on, and, intrinsically, Jane Austen's dislike of Reptonian improvers.

Fortunately, other estates by Repton have managed to survive. Like Lancelot Brown's corpus of work, the list is impressive. In many cases it includes places where Brown had started to form a landscape, but in others the typical variety of Repton's work is easily recognizable. One of the last of these was at Ashridge in Hertfordshire. Although little of the detail remains today, the names of the different sections of the garden give an idea of the infinite variety of his imagination: Broad Sanctuary, Holy Wells, Pomarium and Winter Walk, Embroidered Parterre, Grotto, Cabinet de Verdure, Rosarium and Fountain. 'Every estate', he said, 'has qualities which it is the aim of the landscaper to elucidate', and usually these qualities as he saw them were a combination of use and beauty; *in utile dolci* of Switzer in buildings, landscape and horticulture. Among the best are: Antony House, Cornwall; Ashridge, Hertfordshire; Ashton Court, Somerset; Attingham, Shropshire; Bayham Abbey, Kent; Beaudesert, Staffordshire; Blaize

Castle, Gloucestershire; Blickling, Norfolk; Bulstrode, Bucking-hamshire; Burleigh-on-the-Hill, Rutland; Cassiobury, Hertford-shire; Cobham, Kent; Corsham, Wiltshire; Crewe Hall, Cheshire; Harewood, Yorkshire; Harlestone, Northamptonshire; Hatchlands, Surrey; Heathfield Park, Sussex; Holkham, Norfolk; Longleat, Wiltshire; Michelgrove, Sussex; Milton, Northamptonshire; Nune-ham, Oxfordshire; Panshanger, Hertfordshire; Port Eliot, Cornwall; Shardeloes, Buckinghamshire; Sheffield Place, Sussex; Sheringham Hall, Norfolk; Stoke, Hereford; Stoneaston, Somerset; Tatton Park, Cheshire; Thoresby, Nottinghamshire; Tyringham, Buckingham-shire; Uppark, Sussex; Welbeck, Nottinghamshire; Westworth Woodhouse, Yorkshire; West Wycombe Park, Buckinghamshire; Wimpole, Cambridgeshire; Woburn, Bedfordshire.

Many of these great houses and their parks have been lovingly cared for; but a notable exception is the great Whig palace, Went-worth Woodhouse. Its fate has been eloquently told by Miss Dorothy Stroud:[1]

> Repton made the grounds at Wentworth into a splendid setting for a splendid mansion, which for a hundred and fifty years continued to complement each other until the sudden onslaught of opencast mining during the last war. This deplorable mutilation, caused by scratching away the surface of the ground, is spreading towards the house on the one hand and the mausoleum on the other.[2]

It is mistaken to regard such landscapes influenced by Brown and Repton as a small part of the countryside. Apart from the estates mentioned, many clumps of beeches, for example, brushed by gales into giant porcupines, are prominent landmarks on Downs and hills. One such is Chanctonbury Ring above Wiston in Sussex. When Charles Goring, at the age of 16, carried up the beech saplings he cannot have imagined that the clump which he planted would survive salt spray and storm for 175 years. It was an act of faith which has brought about the spread of seeds from these trees along the Downs from Petworth to Arundel. Many people seem to take

---

[1] *Humphry Repton* (London, 1962).
[2] The Coal Board, since this was written, has repaired some of the ravages, though Keppel's 115-foot Column (1778) is now unsafe, and the Mausoleum (1785) uncared for.

such planting for granted, or imagine that a group of trees, which now gives dignity in body and height to an indifferent hill, just 'grow'd' like Topsy. No wonder that after Brown died Horace Walpole remarked that the effect of his genius was 'happiest when he will be least remembered: so closely did he copy nature that his works will be mistaken'.

> With one lost Paradise the name
> Of our first ancestor is stain'd;
> Brown shall enjoy unsullied fame
> For many a Paradise regained.[1]

This might be Repton's epitaph also, yet how much of their work is now Paradise lost? Some has been converted into zoos, playing fields, public parks or golf courses, still more has been built over or mutilated beyond recognition. But a few estates remain to show the sweep of the turf, the reflections in the water and the maturity of the trees. Such are the prospects at Blenheim from the Triumphal Arch to the bright lake; at Chatsworth from the terrace fountains to the peaceful river; and at Longleat from the comforting woods of Heaven's Gate to the great Renaissance house in the valley.

[1] Horace Walpole's epitaph. Letter to William Mason, 10 February 1783.

7

Picturesque Variants

N'avez-vous pas souvent, aux lieux infréquentées,
Rencontré tout-à-coup ces aspects enchantés
Qui suspendent vos pas, dont l'image chérie
Vous jette en une douce et longue rêverie?
JACQUES DELILLE, Les Jardins, ou l'Art d'embellir
les Paysages (1780)

F OR some years the word picturesque had been used to mean a
mixture of historical and pictorial. Richard Steele in *The
Tender Husband* (1705) uses it in this sense:

Niece. I would be drawn like the Amazon *Thelestris* with a Spear in
my hand, and an Helmet on a Table before me. . . .
Clerimont. . . . There shall be a Cupid setting away your Helmet
to shew that Love should have a part in all gallant Actions.
Niece. That Circumstance may be very Picturesque;

In his *Analytical inquiry into the principles of taste* (1808) Richard
Payne Knight says that there is no word of like meaning in ancient
or modern languages, and 'in our own language it has lately been
received into general use; but nevertheless it has not been considered so perfectly naturalized among us, for Samuel Johnson has
not admitted it into his dictionary, though he has received the word
pictorial'. In point of fact, Johnson does use the word in his Dictionary, not alphabetically, but in defining 'graphically' as 'In a
picturesque manner; with a good description or delineation.' And
again, for 'prospect' he writes, 'View delineated; a picturesque

representation of a landscape.' (1772).[1] But there are conceptual overtones in its usage in landscaping which are not listed by Johnson, and it later came to mean much that was in the setting of the Gothic novel. Its basis is a romantic spontaneity visually inspired and sometimes combined with Sublimity as defined by Burke. It was not a new concept, for Denham's 'Cooper's Hill' (1642) had stated, with 'majesty of style', many of the basic features of the Picturesque school:

> While the steepe horrid[2] Roughness of the Wood
> Strives with the gentle Calmness of the Flood.
> Such huge Extremes, when Nature doth unite,
> Wonder from thence results, from thence Delight.

Such sudden contrasts and roughness of texture, through their sublimity, stimulated and delighted the imagination by their visual impact. The dark Grongar hill in South Wales is also described in similar picturesque terms by Dyer in his 'modest Lay',

> Deep are his feet in Towy's flood,
> His sides are cloth'd with waving wood,
> And ancient towers crown his brow,
> That cast an awful look below;
> Whose ragged walls the ivy creeps,

Thus, many of the ingredients of the picturesque—the mossy cells, old castles on cliffs and gloomy pines—add up to a powerful brew, which could drug one with awe and astonishment. This is the sense in which Hannah More uses the term with reference to Cheddar Gorge; having first remarked on her preference for the gentler scenes in Somerset which were 'more delightful to LIVE amongst'. During one of her rides she was able to compare these with the 'lofty cliffs of Cheddar, so stupendously romantic' that her 'imagination was delighted, was confounded, was oppressed, and

---

[1] The term '*genre pittoresque*' had been used by the French Academy in 1732; but this referred to a type of rococo decoration in no way connected with English Picturesque.

[2] 'Horrid' is here used almost as a synonym for 'rough' as in Dryden's 'Horrid with fern, and intricate with thorn, Few paths of human feet or tracks of beasts were worn.'

darted back a thousand years into the days of chivalry and enchantment, at seeing hang over my head, vast ledges of rock exactly resembling mouldered castles and ruined abbeys'. Her delight was so great that she could 'scarcely refrain from crying',[1] especially when she 'sat down upon a fragment of rock and heard one of Gray's odes finely set, and sung with infinite feeling'. However, she thinks that these emotions 'wind up the mind too high' for daily intercourse with society, and are suitable only for poets. Sir William, in replying, tells her that his friend Lord Lyttelton had said that it was because he had a religious turn of mind that he passed from admiration of such scenes to devotion; and had he not inscribed a seat at Hagley with the words: 'These are Thy glorious works, Parent of good'? At almost the same time that Sir William was writing to Hannah More that such feeling terminated in the glory of God and goodwill toward men, Wordsworth was viewing Tintern Abbey for the first time. Five years later he was to write of those same associative feelings

> As have no slight or trivial influence
> On that best portion of a good man's life.
> His little, nameless, unremembered acts
> Of kindness and of love.

In the same summer that Hannah More wrote to Sir William Pepys, Coleridge was on a walking tour in North Wales, where one moonlight night, in the ruins of Denbigh castle, he heard a young man playing a flute, and was much moved. As J. Livingston Lowes has pointed out,[2] the notes of this flute, vibrating in Coleridge's memory for some years, possibly sounds again in:

> And now, 'twas like all instruments,
> Now like a lonely flute;
> And now it is an angel's song,
> That makes the heavens be mute.[3]

Yet Livingston Lowes unaccountably describes the occasion in the moonlit ruins as 'an absurd episode'. To Picturesque writers

---

[1] Hannah More to Sir William Pepys, 1784.
[2] *The Road to Xanadu* (Boston and New York, 1927), pp. 212–13.
[3] 'The Rime of the Ancient Mariner', lines 363–6.

who were endeavouring to reconstruct such natural scenes on their own estates, such moments were far from 'absurd', for they felt that in such places and at such times they might perhaps feel 'a sense sublime' through the impact of certain visual qualities on a mind attuned to an acceptance of these Picturesque concepts.

The first to publish his theory of the Picturesque was William Gilpin, a good-natured schoolmaster-cum-parson who travelled much in his vacations. He was the rare combination of an artist and art critic who could communicate his visual experiences in writing which was both engaging and instructive. So, for example, his readers might look at the detail of mosses, ivy, lichens, liverworts and climbers through his eyes, and see, perhaps for the first time, their variations in tone and texture in different seasons, weathers, and lights. By such means he was able to transmute his theories into practice when on his extensive tours, which, in fact, created a new kind of travel. His three essays, 'On Picturesque Beauty', 'On Picturesque Travel', and 'On Sketching Landscape', were published together in 1792. In the first he distinguishes between the Picturesque and the Beautiful, which although they have certain features as Variety, Contrast and innate Simplicity in common, yet differ. The Beautiful is associated with objects which are smooth and neat, whereas the Picturesque is rough in texture and rugged in delineation. But, above all, the Picturesque is capable of being illustrated in painting, though he did not go so far as later writers in saying that this was fundamental. ·

He declares that the avowed object of his second essay is to find picturesque beauty in different natural scenes, and in this he is perhaps most perceptive, expressing an appreciation of the scenery of vapour, fog, and mists in different atmospheres and lights which is worthy of Turner. Nor is he a pedant who excludes all industrial scenes. Indeed, he admires the activity and bustle of wharfs for coal, and the smoky scenes at iron forges on the banks of the Wye when seen through the morning mist. Nor is he narrowly dogmatic about the Picturesque, as he admires the 'ingenious Mr. Brown' for connecting house and garden so aptly.[1] His sources of pleasure in seeking the Picturesque are threefold: he feels, like Shaftesbury and

---

[1] *Remarks on Forest Scenery* (London, 1791), Section 2, 'Park Scenery'.

Pope, that a follower of picturesque beauty must also be an admirer of the beauty of moral virtue; he senses excitement in the novelty and change which continually take place in the natural scene, and he enjoys sketching it.

Gilpin like Evelyn realizes that the woodland scene is the most perishable, as the 'value of timber is its misfortune'. Yet with buildings, their perishable quality is an advantage, as ruins are among the richest legacies of art, having more picturesqueness in tonal and textural qualities given to them by time, the 'adorner of the ruin',[1] than any other feature in the landscape. And, conceptually, a ruin, ivy-clad and mouldering, displaying the triumph of nature over man's endeavours, is the quintessence of the melancholy appeal of Dyer's

> But transient is the smile of fate!
> A little rule, a little sway,
> A sunbeam in a winter's day,
> Is all the proud and mighty have
> Between the cradle and the grave.[2]

In 1748, Gilpin had written in his first book, *Dialogue upon the gardens . . . at Stow*, 'I think the Ruin a great Addition to the Beauty of the Lake'. Yet unlike Capability Brown, William Mason or Thomas Whately he is not in favour of creating ruins, despite imaginary sketches (Plate XVII). Gilpin has a consistent dislike of opulence, and, in particular, of buildings in park landscapes; so obelisks, Chinese bridges, and even the Palladian bridge at Wilton do not escape his censure. With reference to Houghton, he regrets that no Brown existed when it was landscaped, so that he might have conducted 'the channels of wealth'.[3]

In common with subsequent writers on the Picturesque he prefers the woody vales, sinuous hills, wild rocks and rough waters of Wales to the smooth plains of East Anglia. Had not Gray also thought the banks of the Wye to be 'a succession of nameless

---

[1] Lord Byron, 'Childe Harold', Canto IV, CXXX.

[2] This feeling for ruins was widely felt at the time. Sir Walter Scott, for example, would not remain in his carriage even in wet weather when he approached a ruin. See John G. Lockhart, *Memoirs of the Life of Sir Walter Scott* (Edinburgh, 1837), Vol. IV.

[3] *Observations on . . . Cambridge, Norfolk, Suffolk and Essex* (London, 1769 and 1773).

Ruin illustrated with regard to its general form.

_____ with regard to its parts.

_____ with regard to Decorations.

XVII. Ruin illustrated by William Gilpin.

XVIII. (*a*) Engraving No. 1 by T. Herne from *The Landscape* by Richard Payne Knight.

XVIII. (*b*) Engraving No. 2 by T. Herne from *The Landscape* by Richard Payne Knight.

wonders'?[1] In his *Observations on the River Wye*, Gilpin mentions
Persefield,[2] Valentine Morris's estate near Chepstow, as being
especially romantic in its rocks, woods, and precipices, yet not
essentially picturesque, for it would have been difficult from any
one place in the grounds to have formed the composition of a picture
from such a panoramic scene, embracing the great sweep of the Wye
and Chepstow castle. While there he sees and dislikes the introduction of flowering shrubs, not so much for aesthetic reasons as for
their associations with formality and art. The natural scene between
Monmouth and Chepstow, with its high precipices of bare, rough
crags, towering over abrupt turns taken by the river, was terrify-
ingly awful and sublime; and flowering shrubs, even in a man-made
landscape were not in tune with these diapasons.

The tone soon changes when two scholarly Herefordshire
squires, Richard Payne Knight of Downton, near Ludlow, and
Uvedale Price of Foxley, near Hereford, publish their works. In
1796, Payne Knight brought out 'The Landscape', a so-called didactic poem of over twelve hundred lines in three books, addressed to
Uvedale Price, vigorously attacking all the works of the Brown-
Repton school and outlining his own ideas of the Picturesque, with
practical recommendations for bringing it about. For his opponents,
no punches were too hard, and, as Repton realized and Horace
Walpole deplored, this was no mere sparring. Repton, as we saw,
regarded it as a direct reference to his work, yet parried with a
moderation in his reply which contrasted with the viciousness of
Payne Knight's sharp couplets:

> Hence let us learn, in real scenes, to trace
> The true ingredients of the painter's grace;
> To lop redundant parts, the coarse refine,
> Open the crowded, and the scanty join.
> But, ah! in vain: see yon fantastic band,
> With charts, pedometers, and rules in hand,
> Advance triumphant, and alike lay waste
> The forms of nature, and the works of taste!

[1] Thomas Gray to Thomas Wharton, 24 August 1770.
[2] Today spelt Piercefield (Chepstow racecourse). In 1833 Pugin saw four cathe-
drals and fourteen counties from this spot.

> T' improve, adorn, and polish, they profess;
> But shave the goddess, whom they come to dress,
> Level each broken bank and shaggy mound,
> And fashion all to one unvaried round;
>
> .   .   .   .
>
> Shav'd to the brink, our brooks are taught to flow
> Where no obtruding leaves or branches grow;
> While clumps of shrubs bespot each winding vale,
> Open alike to ev'ry gleam and gale.

Some lines further on there is a more direct onslaught:

> Hence, hence! thou haggard fiend, however call'd,
> Thin, meagre genius of the bare and bald;
> Thy spade and mattock here at length lay down,
> And follow to the tomb thy fav'rite Brown.
> Thy fav'rite Brown, whose innovating hand
> First dealt thy curses o'er this fertile land.

In Book 2 Payne Knight gives practical advice for his ideal landscape, after first lamenting what has been done (Plates XVIII *a* and *b*).

> Oft when I've seen some lonely mansion stand,
> Fresh from th' improver's desolating hand
> 'Midst shaven lawns, that far around it creep
> In one eternal undulating sweep;
> And scatter'd clumps, that nod at one another,
> Each stiffly waving to its formal brother;
> Tir'd with th'extensive scene, so dull and bare,
> To Heav'n devoutly I've addressed my pray'r—
> Again the moss-grown terraces to raise,
> And spread the labyrinth's perplexing maze;
> Replace in even lines the ductile yew,
> And plant again the ancient avenue.
> Some features then, at least, we should obtain,
> To mark this flat, insipid, waving plain;
> Some vary'd tints and forms would intervene,
> To break this uniform, eternal green.

Repton thought that these engravings were caricatures of modern improvement. Both the bridges were absurd: the fantastic Chinese one and the wooden one which was 'perfectly picturesque in its form, and applicable to the steep banks of the Teme, yet in this flat situation looks like the miserable expedient of poverty, or a ridiculous affectation of simplicity'. Brown's clumps and belts of perimeter trees were Payne Knight's most hated features, so he calls for drastic female action to pull down the fences, let the cattle in and restore roughness, sudden variation and irregularity, the three essentials of the picturesque.

> But ah! how diff'rent is the formal lump
> Which the improver plants, and calls a clump!
> Break, break, ye nymphs, the fence that guards it round!
> With browsing cattle, all its forms confound!

The ageing Horace Walpole was quick in his reaction to 'The Landscape' which he described in a letter of 22 March 1796 to William Mason as an 'insolent and self-conceited Poem' by a 'trumpery prosaic poetaster', and he begs Mason to 'dethrone him' with a poetic reply that will defend the memory of Brown.

In his *Analytical Inquiry*, Knight adds Landscape Gardening to six other Arts: Poetry, Eloquence, Music, Painting, Sculpture, and the Stage, all of which are emotive of the pleasures of imagination.[1] He thinks that appreciation of each of these is a question of taste, which is both a distinct faculty and a mode of judgement thereby uniting feeling and reason. Yet taste fluctuates through the influence of prejudice and association, so like Hume before him Payne Knight is sceptical.

On the practical side he joins his friend Uvedale Price in an attack on the 'tyranny of Brown', but in certain features of the distinction between the Picturesque and the Beautiful he parts company with him. Knight thinks that Price's definition of the Picturesque, with its fundamental Variety and Intricacy in the disposition of its objects and its Roughness and Irregularity in the texture of those objects, is chimerical; for he has mistaken facts and allowed his feelings and sympathies to replace external circumstances.

In Part 2 he discusses how organic perceptions of sight with associated ideas lead to a refinement of taste, much as had been

---

[1] cf. Susanne Langer, *Reflections on Art* (Baltimore, 1958), p. 25. '. . . landscaping, an art too often neglected in its importance by aestheticians.'

stated by Archibald Alison before him. Integrally with this, the scene on appealing to a painter's eye will be emotive of memories and a sense of past glory, so the imagination will be pleasurably stimulated. This is much as was also stated by Addison in his 'Essays on the Imagination' in the *Spectator*, and symbolized by Akenside.

> For when the different images of things
> By chance combin'd have struck the attentive soul
> With deeper impulse, or connected long,
> Have drawn her frequent eye; howe'er distinct
> The external scenes, yet oft the ideas gain
> From that conjunction an eternal tie
> And sympathy unbroken.

Even when later Knight is discussing more practical matters concerned with the improvement of grounds, his style of writing is straggling, lacking both terseness or elegance, and sometimes obtusely archaic.[1]

The succinct prose of Uvedale Price's *Dialogue on the distinct characters of the Picturesque and the Beautiful* (1801), is a relief to read after Knight's. Although Price's work was published after Knight's poem, many of his ideas were included, as Knight had seen Price's manuscript. Yet there were differences of emphasis. As with Gilpin, Roughness could be obtained by allowing the action of time and weather to remain on trees and buildings by carefully preserving all mosses, lichens, incrustation and decayed cement, which would give varied tonal qualities in different climatic conditions and lights. The natural patina of time and age must therefore be undisturbed if it was to make its contribution. Irregularity was achieved in skylines pierced by Gothic turrets and pinnacles rather than by straight roofs and regular openings of Palladian architecture. Sudden variation was increased by different colouring in ivy, honeysuckles, or creepers and by abrupt and rugged changes in rock and sandstone formations, such as in Salvator Rosa landscapes. And even in Claude's landscapes the banks with temples mixed with trees are 'perfectly savage' although they have *il riposo*. Neither in Rosa nor

---

[1] e.g. 'the view frowards the house'. Might this be because he received no formal education at school or university?

Claude was there smooth or levelled ground as in Lancelot Brown's landscaping, so there were no 'deep recesses' nor 'bold projections' which might half conceal certain objects, thereby exciting curiosity. The study of pictures is Price's fundamental, for that 'can only produce any real advantage if we use it as a school in which we may learn to enlarge, correct and refine our view of Nature and by that route become good judges of scenery'. It is at this point that Repton answered courteously but clearly in denying that the terms of composition of a picture were the same as those in creating a landscape, which has many points of vision as opposed to one of a picture.

On some points he also parts company with Gilpin. A lake, 'pure, limpid, smooth as the polished mirror', is picturesque to Gilpin, yet Price will not acknowledge that these attributes of Burke's idea of Beauty can also be thought of as Picturesque. Nor, despite his admiration for Claude's radiance, does he consider colour as important as texture and outline; indeed, he extends Gilpin's Roughness to Ruggedness, with sharper and more jagged outlines. Nor is the Picturesque landscaper capable of creating the Sublime, which has titanic qualities 'beyond our contracted powers'. Nor does Price dismiss the signs of opulence near the house, so much scorned by Gilpin. In fact, he is willing to acknowledge staircases and terraces with statues, vases, and urns as no more artificial than the house to which they are adjacent and therefore allowable. Such features appeared in Repton's work and are difficult to equate with Price's Picturesque, for they usually mean regularity and formality. And, as Byron said of Ferrara, 'symmetry is not for solitude',[1] the essence of the Picturesque being reverie or enchantment, those associated ideas, induced by the scene when solitarily viewed; the '*douce et longue rêverie*' of Delille, or Wordsworth at Tintern. It seems equally inconsistent of Price to allow fountains in a garden landscape for the reason that natural geysers do exist; the equation of Villa d'Este with Iceland is remote. Like Repton, he is wise in wishing to preserve the best landscapes of the past even though they do not fit in with his ideas.

After Gilpin's *Tours*, Payne Knight's *Landscape* and Price's *Essays*,

[1] 'Childe Harold', Canto IV, XXXV.

the Picturesque boat runs on a full tide, with efforts by opponents in battling with the current and by exponents in arguing about the course to be taken. William Hazlitt,[1] seeing through a painter's eyes, distinguishes between the picturesque and the 'ideal', the former having some 'striking peculiarity' and surprising us by contrasts, the latter answering to a 'preconceived imagination for beauty' and satisfying us by its 'harmony and continuity'. He regards the landscapes of Rubens as picturesque on account of the extreme quality of some natural feature such as 'rainbows, showers, partial gleams of sunlight, moonlight', whereas Claude exemplifies his 'ideal', having none of these, but in their place a delicate harmony and balanced repose in tonal unity and composition. The rough textures of old stumps of trees, silhouetted rocks, and stubble-fields are all picturesque and should take their place in a painting which should have sharp and vivid points of view. This differs not at all from the qualities of the picturesque of Price; and his 'ideal' differs little from Burke's definition of beauty, its chief characteristic being to please by its peaceful and instinctive harmony.

However, the disagreements of the Picturesque writers were often carried on with strong words, especially from Knight. It is therefore not surprising that Shelley, writing to his friend Peacock, requests him to acknowledge his views of poetry even though they may differ from Peacock's, so that they both might avoid being like Price and Payne Knight, the 'two ill-trained beagles . . . snarling at each other when they could not catch the hare'.[2] And Daniel Malthus, a translator of Girardin, compares the contestants' behaviour to that of Luther and Calvin rather than of 'a couple of West country gentlemen talking of gravel walks and syringas'.[3]

But this was tame talk compared with the wild replies of some of the Repton followers: William Marshall (1745–1818), an apparently respectable rural economist and farmer, reviewed *The Landscape* almost line by line, and Price's *Essay on the Picturesque* chapter by chapter (1795). Marshall's work is both tedious and vituperative. Not content with disagreement with Knight's Picturesque pre-

---

[1] *Table Talk*, Essay XXXII, 'On the Picturesque and the Ideal' (London, 1822).

[2] Percy Bysshe Shelley to Thomas Love Peacock, 21 March 1821.

[3] cf. 'Kent was the Calvin of the reformation of gardens': Francis Coventrie in *The World*, 6 February 1753.

mises and practices, he refers to Knight's other literary work[1] in scurrilous terms by rudely parodying *The Landscape*.

> Thy statue of Colossal size
> In ductile yew, shall nobly rise
> (Think not thy modesty shall 'scape us):
> The God of *Gardens* thou shalt stand
> To fright improvers from the land,
> A huge and terrible *Priapus*.

Another writer, T. J. Mathias, in his satirical poem, 'The Pursuits of Literature', seems equally shocked by this same book of Knight's which he says is a record of

the stews and bordellos of Grecian and Roman antiquity, exhibited for the recreation of antiquaries, and the obscene revellings of Greek scholars in their private studies. . . . The Essays on Landscape Gardening may, I hope, purify the mind.

Some of Knight's best lines in Book III, in which he justifiably wishes for more shade in planning,

> O waft me hence to some neglected vale
> Where shelter'd I may count the western gale;
> And 'midst the gloom which native thickets shed
> Hide from the noontide beams my aching head!

receive only the schoolboy comment from Marshall: 'Oh! for a cold wet towel to wreathe his temples!'

However, Uvedale Price is treated with more respect, perhaps because he is more moderate in his Picturesque requirements, allowing some embellishments near the house—some lawn, gravel walks and ornamental planting, much, in fact, that Repton would have approved of. Yet Marshall's unconstructive critical attitude is summed up by his final remark on Price's work: 'At length, (Thank heavens shall we say?) we reach the last chapter.'

For a brief period the controversy is carried on from Scotland when Sir Henry Steuart in his *Planter's Guide* (1828) attacks the

---

[1] 'An Account of the Remains of the Worship of Priapus lately existing in Isernia; to which is added a Discourse on the Worship of Priapus, and its Connexion with the Mystic Theology of the Ancients, 1786.'

Picturesque followers. The greater part of his book is taken up with a description of his planting at his estate at Allanton, on Clydeside, so much admired by Sir Walter Scott.[1] By means of a machine like a piece of artillery (Plate XIX*a*), originally devised by Lancelot Brown, Steuart was able successfully to transplant trees from twenty to thirty feet high. A large pole was lashed to the tree which was moved at the appropriate moment from a perpendicular to a horizontal position for transportation to its new site. Although Scott admired Steuart's practical work, his grounds at Abbotsford witnessed his love of Price's theories. Even his gamekeeper, Tom Purdie, seems to have absorbed the same ideas, if Lockhart is to be believed, in his account of Purdie's conversion.

When I came here first, I was little better than a beast, and knew nae mair than a cow what was pretty and what was ugly. I was cuif enough to think that the bonniest thing in the country-side was a corn-field enclosed in four stane dykes, but now I ken the difference. . . . See ye there now, the sun glinting on Melrose Abbey? It's no aw bright, nor it's no aw shadows neither, but just a bit screed o'light—and a bit daud o'dark yonder like, and that's what they ca' picturesque; and indeed, it maun be confessed it is unco bonnie to look at.

As time went on Tom Purdie was entrusted with carrying out landscape plans for Sir Walter, who instructed him to make a walk through the woods that was neither straight nor crooked, but just as Tom 'dandered hame of an even'—evidently *via media* between the strongly marked, distinct and regular curves of Brown and Repton, which so disgusted Price, and the obtuse wanderings of the picturesque.

Henry Steuart takes up his stand firmly in favour of Burke. Swelling forms and gentle transitions with smoothness are the most common of all beautiful forms; and the circle, oval and cone are the most elegant forms, especially when they have smooth surfaces. So the clumps of Brown and Repton are beautiful objects needing no elaboration as the Picturesque followers seemed to consider necessary, for they had planted them in 'the shape of pincushions, of

[1] *Quarterly Review*, XXXVII, No. LXXIV (1828).

hatchets, of penny tarts and of breeches displayed at old clothes-men's doors'. To Price the clumps of the Brown school were nothing more than lumps. There was no variety in them, no difference in age and size of the trees, no natural openings and hollows, no intricacy or deep shadow—in fact, mechanical affairs, little deserving the name of art.

The strongest reply to *The Planter's Guide* came from William Sawrey Gilpin (1762–1843), a nephew of the author of the *Tours*. In his *Practical Hints* (1832) he classified scenery into five groups: Grand, which was distinguished by largeness, unity and few bold contrasts yet was fundamentally able to astonish us, as in mountain or lake scenery: Romantic, which is usually on a smaller scale, with great variety and intricacy, though fundamentally tranquil, despite precipitous steeps as in Dovedale: Beautiful, having gentle contrasts with broad, smooth folds of ground as in most park scenery: Picturesque, with smaller and more abrupt folds of rougher texture with mixed woods like parts of Kent in the early nineteenth century: and Rural which was open common with hedgerow tim-ber, well wooded, softening into a rich distance as in the southern counties. Yet whatever the definitions, moderate men saw that the important factor was a right attitude to the three elements of land-scaping, earth, water, and trees—without the jargon. Had not Evelyn expressed Picturesque views in his chapter on 'Sacredness and Use of Standing Groves'? And did not Pope see the beauties of such contrasting landscapes as his own at Twickenham, Lord Digby's at Sherborne or Lord Cobham's at Stowe? For as the Genius of the Place had been consulted in each, was he not able to commu-nicate his particular enchantment? So, not surprisingly, the esoteric pedantry of some of the early nineteenth-century contestants is widely parodied in contemporary writing.

Jane Austen did not, as four of her heroines, though each very different in character, have in common a genuine love of the Picturesque, with a consequent dislike of more formal landscaping. We have seen Fanny Price's predilection at Sotherton for the Pic-turesque combined with a love of Cowper. Marianne Dashwood also loves Cowper and has a knowledge of Picturesque principles; and as she 'could not be happy with a man whose taste did not in every point coincide' with her own, Edward Ferrers was a poor companion, for, on account of his attitude to landscape, he would never have been able to enter into Marianne's feelings. He calls surfaces 'strange and uncouth' which Marianne would have termed 'irregular and rugged', and is incapable of observing 'rocks and promontories, grey moss and brushwood', and what is more, proud of his lack of knowledge of the Picturesque, which justifiably irritates Marianne. In fact, without knowing it, he is grounded in Repton principles of beauty with utility, in preferring 'a troop of tidy, happy villagers' to Rosa *banditti*, and snug farmhouses to watch towers.[1] However, he is a dull fellow who, with Colonel Brandon, represents in the novel the chief opposition to the youthful sensitivity of Marianne. Lines of Cowper which had driven Marianne 'wild', Ferrers could read with only 'impenetrable calmness' and 'dreadful indifference'. Yet Colonel Brandon had most likely never attempted to read Cowper, and all the author's defensive irony—that Marianne was 'born to discover the falsehood of her own opinions'—cannot convince us that she will be happily married to this vacuous formalist with his excessive moral gentility.

Catherine Morland has no knowledge of the Picturesque before she meets Henry Tilney, her future husband. Standing on Beechen Cliff, overlooking Bath, he is easily able to impress her with his knowledge of Picturesque jargon.[2] Although Catherine had declared that she 'would give anything in the world to be able to draw', she did not deserve such a protracted lecture from Henry Tilney on the principles of composition with its detail of 'foregrounds, distances, and second distances; side-screens and perspectives; lights and shades'. So by the time that they reached the top of Beechen Cliff, Catherine was undoubtedly convinced that the Palladian city did not form part of a Picturesque landscape, as well she might be, for contemporary prints show the amphitheatre of hills in which Bath rests to have been open country with sparse planting of young trees. Yet the gentle sensitivity of this conversation and others similar is undoubtedly meant to contrast with the Gothic descriptions from 'the capital pen of a sister author', whom

---

[1] *Sense and Sensibility* (London, 1811), Chap. 18.
[2] *Northanger Abbey* (London, 1818), Chap. 14.

Jane Austen wished to parody. Catherine Morland, having read Mrs. Radcliffe's works with enthralled pleasure, expected, from Henry Tilney's description, that Northanger Abbey would have dark halls, through which the night wind rustled tapestries hiding locked doors leading to vaults in which there were relics of torture or extinguished lamps. But Northanger Abbey turns out to be more credible than any Gothic house in *The Mysteries of Udolpho*; and Catherine, despite her enthusiasm for the ironic and boring Henry Tilney, is more credible than Emily, Mrs. Radcliffe's heroine, who, having had a duel fought over her person after attempted abduction, 'took her instruments for drawing and placed herself at a window to select into a landscape some of the features of the scenery without'. Catherine's taste for drawing was 'not superior', and her houses and hens on bits of paper must have been as different from Emily's sketches as a minuet from a tarantella. Nor was she sure of herself with regard to the Picturesque, for when at Northanger Abbey she felt the need of Henry Tilney to tell her 'what was picturesque when she saw it'. But Picturesque it undoubtedly was.

The whole building enclosed a large court, and two sides of the quadrangle, rich in Gothic ornament, stood forward for admiration. The remainder was shut off by knolls of old trees, or luxuriant plantations, and the steep woody hills rising behind to give it shelter were beautiful even in the leafless month of March. Catherine had seen nothing to compare with it.

And later she walks by a gloomy, 'winding path through a thick grove of old Scotch firs', which inspired a 'delightful melancholy'. Although the author may be parodying the Gothic novel, her heroine will presumably one day live in this Picturesque setting.

Elizabeth Bennet, more mature, complex and acute in judgement than any of the other heroines, was delighted with Mr. Darcy's Pemberley in the Peak District, for it satisfied her Picturesque awareness.[1] On turning in at the lodge gates she saw that

The park was very large, and contained great variety of ground. They entered it in one of its lowest points, and drove for some time through a beautiful wood stretching over a wide extent.

[1] *Pride and Prejudice* (London, 1813), Chap. 43.

Elizabeth's mind was too full for conversation, but she saw and admired every remarkable spot and point of view. They gradually ascended for half-a-mile, and then found themselves at the top of a considerable eminence, where the wood ceased, and the eye was instantly caught by Pemberley House, situated on the opposite side of a valley, into which the road with some abruptness wound. It was a large, handsome stone building, standing well on rising ground, and backed by a ridge of high woody hills; and in front, a stream of some natural importance was swelled into greater, but without any artificial appearance. Its banks were neither formal nor falsely adorned. Elizabeth was delighted. She had never seen a place for which nature had done more, or where natural beauty had been so little counteracted by an awkward taste.

And from the windows of the house,

The hill, crowned with wood, which they had descended, receiving increased abruptness from the distance, was a beautiful object. Every disposition of the ground was good; and she looked on the whole scene, the river, the trees scattered on its banks and the winding of the valley, as far as she could trace it, with delight. As they passed into other rooms these objects were taking different positions; but from every window there were beauties to be seen.

During the circuit of the grounds, after she had recovered from the unexpected appearance of Mr. Darcy, she noticed further Picturesque features when crossing

a simple bridge, in character with the general air of the scene; it was a spot less adorned than any they had yet visited; and the valley, here contracted into a glen, allowed room only for the stream, and a narrow walk amidst the rough coppice-wood which bordered it. Elizabeth longed to explore its windings;

In this setting with its deep woodland clothing steep ground above the stream in its narrow glen, she muses ironically that 'to be mistress of Pemberley might be something!' Of the four heroines she most deserves to live in such a landscape with which she is obviously so much in sympathy, and she chooses a husband who owns it.

The Picturesque also enters *The Monk*, the bloodiest and most sinful of the Gothic novels; in which there is no other description of a natural scene comparable to the one at the point at which the Abbot starts on his downward path. In the setting of a romantic hermitage he meets, by chance, Rosario, the young woman disguised as a monk, and from then until his frightful death we watch with horror as he becomes ravisher, double-murderer and seller of his soul to the devil.

In the bosom of this little grove stood a rustic grotto, formed in imitation of an hermitage. The walls were constructed of roots of trees, and the interstices filled up with moss and ivy. Seats of turf were placed on either side, and a natural cascade fell from the rock above. Buried in himself, the monk approached the spot. The universal calm had communicated itself to his bosom, and a voluptuous tranquillity spread languor through his soul.[1]

Except for the sensual epithet qualifying tranquillity, this is a scene that Lyttelton might have created at Hagley, or Wesley rested in with moral impunity. So it is reasonable to think that the author uses it as a symbol of monastic purity from which the Abbot declines, for the scene strongly contrasts with subsequent ruined abbeys, earthquakes, seductions, matricide, black magic, poison, vaults, rape in tombs, instruments of torture and mutilation.

Of all contemporary fiction, Peacock's satire of the suspect whims and fashions of the landscape controversy was the most successful. In Chapter VI of *Headlong Hall* we saw Mr. Milestone outlining his plans for improvement of Lord Littlebrain's estate. Here[2] he is endeavouring to convince the earthy Squire Headlong that *his* estate needs cleaning up in the Repton manner; whilst Sir Patrick O'Prism, the dilettante painter (Uvedale Price) represents the case for the Picturesque, condemning all the works of Brown or Repton. Unfortunately, after a query from Mr. Milestone, he fails to make a clear distinction between the Picturesque and the Beautiful, so Mr. Gall, the chief of the corps of critics, endeavours to introduce a further characteristic—that of surprise or unexpectedness, as in Payne Knight. He receives the inevitable snub from Mr. Milestone.

[1] Matthew G. Lewis, *The Monk* (London, 1796), Chap. 2.   [2] Chap. IV.

'I perceive' said Mr. Milestone, after they had walked a few paces, 'these grounds have never been touched by the finger of taste.'

'The place is quite a wilderness,' said Squire Headlong 'for during the latter part of my father's life, while I was *finishing* my *education*, he troubled himself about nothing but the cellar, and suffered everything else to go to rack and ruin. A mere wilderness, as you see, even now in December; but in summer a complete nursery of briers, a forest of thistles, a plantation of nettles, without any livestock but goats, that have eaten up all the bark of the trees. Here you see is the pedestal of a statue, with only half a leg and four toes remaining; there were many here once. When I was a boy I used to sit on the shoulders of Hercules; what became of *him* I have never been able to ascertain. Neptune has been lying these seven years in the dust-hole; Atlas had his head knocked off to fit him for propping a shed; and only the day before yesterday we fished Bacchus out of the horse-pond.'

'My dear sir', said Mr. Milestone, 'accord me your permission to wave the wand of enchantment over your grounds. The rocks shall be blown up, the trees shall be cut down, the wilderness and all its goats shall vanish like mist. Pagodas and Chinese bridges, gravel walks and shrubberies, bowling-greens, canals, and clumps of larch, shall rise upon its ruins. One age, sir, has brought to light the treasures of ancient learning; a second has penetrated into the depths of metaphysics; a third has brought to perfection the science of astronomy; but it was reserved for the exclusive genius of the present times to invent the noble art of picturesque gardening, which has given, as it were, a new outline to the physiognomy of the universe!'

'Give me leave', said Sir Patrick O'Prism, 'to take exception to that same. Your system of levelling, and trimming, and clipping, and docking, and clumping, and polishing, and cropping, and shaving, destroys all the beautiful intricacies of natural luxuriance, and all the graduated harmonies of light and shade, melting into one another, as you see them on that rock over yonder. I never saw one of your improved places, as you call them, and which are nothing but big bowling-greens, like sheets of green paper, with a parcel of round clumps scattered over them, like so many spots of ink, flicked at random out of a pen, and a solitary animal here and there looking as if it were lost, that I did not think it was for all the world like Hounslow Heath, thinly sprinkled over with bushes and highwaymen.'

'Sir,' said Mr. Milestone, 'you will have the goodness to make a distinction between the picturesque and the beautiful.'

'Will I?' said Sir Patrick, 'och! but I won't. For what is beautiful? That what pleases the eye. And what pleases the eye? Tints variously broken and blended. Now, tints variously broken and blended constitute the picturesque.'

'Allow me,' said Mr. Gall. 'I distinguish the picturesque and the beautiful, and I add to them, in the laying out of grounds, a third and distinct character, which I call *unexpectedness*.'

'Pray sir,' said Mr. Milestone, 'by what name do you distinguish this character, when a person walks round the grounds for the second time?'

Mr. Gall bit his lips, and inwardly vowed to revenge himself on Milestone, by cutting up his next publication.

There is a further satiric passage in Chapter VIII, concerned with making the tower at Llanberis ruinous. The action is reminiscent of Cowper's description of the fine ruins that the late Lord Holland had at great expense improved by rebuilding them after they had fallen: yet, says Cowper, 'it is hardly possible to put stones together with that air of wild and magnificent disorder which they are sure to acquire by falling of their own accord'.[1] In this case the ruined tower on the Headlong estate excites Milestone's admiration; but the ivy needs trimming, spruce firs (Knight's *bête noire*) should be planted and the rugged ascent converted into a smooth, turfed slope by blowing up part of the rock. The athletic and vigorous squire fetches labourers with pickaxes and gunpowder, and servants with lunch and Madeira: but at the crucial moment Mr. Cranium and Mr. Panscope appear at the top of the tower, engaged in pseudo-scientific conversation. The explosion sends Cranium bouncing from a bush to the waters, and after the smoke clears Panscope can be seen majestic but solus. Lunch and drinks all round satisfactorily conclude the operation.

There is no better parody in verse of the excesses of William Gilpin's followers than William Combe's best-selling poem, 'Dr. Syntax in Search of the Picturesque'. It was published in 1810 in magazine form, then with Rowlandson's prints and Ackermann plates quickly went through eight editions, becoming so much the rage that Syntax hats, wigs and coats were a passing fashion. Dr.

[1] William Cowper to the Rev. William Unwin, July 1779.

Syntax was a parson-schoolmaster, modelled on William Gilpin, who left his wife in his vacations and toured the countryside on his mare, Grizzle, stopping to sketch at inns or friends' houses. Rowlandson's prints are some of his best satirical work, and later the poem was continued in two further volumes of adventures. Combe knew the Picturesque writers well. Here is Dr. Syntax pausing on his journey, and citing reasons for the subject-matter and the method of his sketching, exactly in the manner of William Gilpin.

> But as my time shall not be lost
> I'll make a drawing of the post;
> And though a flimsy taste may flout it,
> There's something picturesque about it:
> 'Tis rude and rough, without a gloss,
> And is well cover'd o'er with moss;
> And I've a right—(who dares deny it?)—
> To place yon group of asses by it.
> Aye! this will do; and now I'm thinking,
> That self-same pond where Grizzle's drinking,
> If hither brought would better seem
> And faith I'll turn it to a stream.
>
> .　　.　　.　　.　　.　　.
>
> What man of taste my right will doubt
> To put things in, or leave them out?
> 'Tis more a right, it is a duty,
> If we consider landscape beauty:
> He ne'er will as an artist shine,
> Who copies Nature line by line:
> Whoe'er from Nature takes a view,
> Must copy and improve it too,
> To heighten every work or art,
> Fancy should take an active part:
> Thus I (which few I think can boast)
> Have made a Landscape of a Post!

And later, in Canto XIII, he satirizes picturesque references to the human face: comparing his own smooth face to that of a lean curate.

> With curious eye and active scent,
> I on the picturesque am bent;

XIX. (*a*) Moving a Tree: from *The Planter's Guide* by Sir Henry Steuart.

XIX. (*b*) Dr. Syntax: plate 11, drawn by Thomas Rowlandson, from William Combe's *Tour of Dr. Syntax*, 1712.

XX. Fonthill Abbey from the American Plantation: drawn and engraved
by James Storer, 1812.

This is my game, I must pursue it,
And make it where I cannot view it,
Though in good truth, do not flout me,
I bear the self-same thing about me,
If in man's form you wish to see
The picturesque, pray look at me;
I am myself without a flaw,
The very picturesque I draw.
A Rector, on whose face so sleek
In vain for a wrinkle seek;
In whose fair form, so fat and round,
No obtuse angle's to be found;
On such a shape no man of taste
Would his fine tints or canvas waste;
But take a curate who's so thin
His bones seem peeping through his skin,
Make him to stand, or walk, or sit,
In any posture you think fit,
And, with all these points about him,
No well-taught painter e'er would scout him:
For with his air, and look, and mien,
He'd give effect to any scene.
In my poor beast, as well as me,
A fine example you may see:
She's so abrupt in all her parts—
O what fine subjects for the arts!

His mare would have appeared 'abrupt' as, after her theft, she had had her ears cut back by robbers in order to escape recognition.[1] Syntax had managed to reclaim her. Even this is a direct reference to Gilpin's writing, for in his '*Remarks on Forest Scenery*', Section X, he digresses to discuss the offensive customs of docking horses' tails and clipping their ears, for apart from the cruelty involved, both tails and ears are picturesque objects. In Canto XIV, a final satirical reference is made to Payne Knight's 'But shave the Goddess whom they come to dress', as well perhaps as Pope's 'Nor overdress, nor leave her wholly bare'.

---

[1] As can be seen in Plate XIXb, where she watches as her owner loses hat and wig through choosing a picturesque but dangerous viewpoint to sketch.

E.L.L.—M

> Nature, dear Nature is my goddess,
> Whether arrayed in rustic bodice,
> Or when the nicest touch of Art
> Doth to her charms new charms impart:
> But still I somehow love her best,
> When she's in ruder mantle drest:
> I do not mean in shape grotesque,
> But when she's truly picturesque.

The extent of descriptive writing in fiction or essays, and the satires in poetry and prose may give the impression that the influence of the Picturesque landscapers was more widespread than it was in practice. Because few of the great houses of England are set in wild terrain, or because Victorian taste later came to be governed by a class of new rich who were visually untrained,[1] not many picturesque landscapes were made, and of those only a handful remain.

In the autumn of 1810, Wordsworth had been on a pleasant tour, including the Leasowes at Hagley, and ending with Price at Foxley, near Hereford, which he thought a 'melancholy spot',[2] having neither rock nor water and lacking variety. He went again in 1828 when Price was in his eighty-first year, yet still 'active in ranging his woods like a setter-dog'. The house survived until the 1950s. The distant view to the Malverns still delights, but the grounds are threatened, making Mrs. Browning's gentle epitaph the more poignant.

> My thoughts are far. I think upon the time
> When Foxley's purple hills and woods sublime
> Were thrilling at thy step; when thou didst throw
> Thy burning spirit on the Vale below,
> To bathe its sense in beauty. Lovely ground!
> There, never more shall step of thine resound![3]

[1] And it could easily degenerate. Poe's ideal landscape, not intentionally nightmarish, in 'Landor's Cottage' (1845), is an inchoate jumble of disparate elements which he describes in exact detail: these include a serpentine path, a ledge of granite, a foaming rivulet (3 ft. to 8 ft. wide), a light birch canoe, a small crystal-clear, irregular lake, a 100 ft. precipice, a neat stone wall (no fences), some sheep and three tamed deer; hydrangeas and geraniums buried in pots.

[2] Letter to Sir George Beaumont, 28 August 1811.

[3] 'To the Memory of Sir Uvedale Price, Bart.' *Poetical Works* (London, 1904).

And today the Downton estate bears little resemblance to the Downton Payne Knight created. The Castle with its garden has been added to in late Victorian times, the surrounding hills planted in spruce and fir (his most unloved trees), the delicate Castle bridge is crumbling, and the hermit's cave, in the gorge of the Teme, is too ruinous even for a hermit. The irregular castellated Castle, the prototype, except for Strawberry Hill, of the Picturesque, still dominates the scene from its terraced ridge—no Brownian lawns to the front door—but all the foreground is bare and bald to the river below. All is too exposed and open, except in the woods of the river gorge. The iron which covers his grandfather's grave in the near-by church has entered the soul of this landscape, not industrially as at Hagley, but through economic agricultural necessity.

Until the 1950s, Guy's Cliffe, near Warwick, was a romantic, wooded spot in which the stone house on a cliff overhung the Avon, which at this point formed a natural pool. A remarkable succession of antiquarians and travellers have sung its praises. 'A place fit for the Muses,' wrote John Leland (1506–52), 'there is sylence; a praty wood; *antra in vivo saxo* (grottoes in the living rock), the river rolling over the stones with a praty noise.' William Camden (1551–1623), who was usually scant of praise, spoke of

a shady little wood, cleere and cristal springs, mossie bottoms and caves, medowes alwaies fresh and greene, the river rumbling heere and there among the stones with his streame making a milde noise and gentle whispering, and besides all this solitary and still quietness, things most grateful to the Muses.

The eccentric Thomas Fuller (1608–61) praised the 'steep rock, full of caves in the bowels thereof, washed at the bottom with a christall river, besides many clear springs in the sides thereof, all overshadowed by a stately grove. This pleasant spot, with its thousand pleasant memories, is the scene of the last days of the fabled Saxon hero, Guy, Earl of Warwick.' Sir William Dugdale, the author of *Antiquities of Warwickshire*, echoes the others: 'a place of so great delight in respect of the river gliding below the rocks, the dry and wholesome situation, and the fair grove of lofty elms overshadowing it, that to one who desires a retired life either for devotion or study the like is hardly to be found'. And that stern critic, Gray, when taken over it by Samuel Greatheed, the young owner who had just bought it and was endeavouring to 'improve' it, writes:

It was naturally a very agreeable rock, whose cliffs covered with large trees hung beetling over the Avon, which twists twenty ways in sight of it; there was the cell of Guy, Earl of Warwick, cut in the living stone where he died a hermit (as you may see in a penny history, that hangs upon the rails in Moorfields) there were his fountains bubbling out of the cliff;—there was a chantry founded to his memory in Henry VI's time. But behold the trees are cut down to make way for flowering shrubs, the rock is cut up, till it is smooth and as sleek as satin; the river has a gravel walk by its side; the cell is a grotto with cockle-shells and looking-glass; the fountains have an iron gate before them, and the chantry is a barn, or a little house. Even the poorest bits of nature, that remain, are daily threatened, for he says (and I am sure, when the Greatheads are set upon a thing, they will do it) he is determined, it shall be ALL NEW. These were his words, and they are fate.[1]

In the two hundred years after Gray's visit Nature was largely allowed to take command and it again became true Picturesque—a riot of deep wood, caves, water and lawn. Then fate decreed a declension; first to an hotel, then to demolition. And what are grounds without a house which is lived in and an owner to care for them?

As Strawberry Hill was to *The Castle of Otranto*, so Fonthill was to *Vathek*. After social ostracism, the eccentric William Beckford desired solitude amongst hills 'blackened with fir', rising from 'gloomy circles' of deep lakes; and this was the origin of the Gothic creation, from 1794 to 1822, of Fonthill Abbey and its surrounding landscape on the Wiltshire-Dorset border. It was Promethean Picturesque, yet influenced by Price's 'Essay on the Picturesque' and his modest creation at Foxley. As one approached the Abbey along a straight mile-long avenue of irregularly planted trees Wyatt's great Octagon Tower always remained in sight whether the road dipped or rose; and on either side stretched great woods of Scotch pine, larch and birch, rising steeply to the south above the

---

[1] Thomas Gray to Thomas Wharton, 18 September 1754.

dark Bitham Lake. The whole estate, largely of declivitous wood-land, was a fitting setting for the 'first Gothic building to create sentiments of amazement, of shock and even of awe'.[1] In all direc-tions vast panoramas spread out; from the terrace, running for nine miles along the top of a wooded ridge, over the country northwards across the Wiltshire plains; from Stop Beacon's seven hundred feet to the south past Wardour Castle, and westwards to the woods of Stourhead. In Beckford's opinion these rough trees created anima-tion. No smooth pastures and repose found a place in his hectic life at Fonthill, and he rightly refused to allow Repton to have a hand in its landscaping.

His father had already spent a quarter of a million pounds on the estate, and William Beckford brought the work to fruition on an even larger scale. With his devoted gardener, Vincent, and his three hundred workers he converted a quarry into an Alpine garden; formed the Norwegian Lawn and its romantic wooden Norwegian buildings; planted an Arboretum with American trees and shrubs, from which Wyatt's Octagon Tower dominated the scene (Plate XX). It was seeds of these American oaks, hickories, and walnuts that William Cobbett asked for in his letter to William Beckford from Newgate prison in September 1811. Beckford was able to gallop, or drive his four-horse phaeton, along twenty-seven miles of rides, interlaced with woods and carpeted in close-cropped turf. It was a terrain which must constantly have reminded him of his tours through the mountains of Switzerland, France, and Portugal, where Nature had been 'liberal'. As he disliked blood-sports, the whole estate was enclosed by a twelve-foot wall with locked gates to keep sportsmen out, so creating an exceptional sanctuary for wild life.

It had a brief life. Beckford ran into debt, sold the estate in 1823, and two years later Wyatt's tower fell to the ground. For the last twenty-one years of his life Beckford lived in Bath, where he con-structed another, very different tower on the brow of Lansdown. From his house in Lansdown Crescent he used daily to walk up another carpeted ride made by Vincent and his workers, through

---

[1] Nikolaus Pevsner, Foreword to H. A. N. Brockman, *The Caliph of Fonthill* (London, 1956).

woods and gardens, past pools and grottoes, to this Graeco-Roman tower in stone, designed by the young architect, H. E. Goodridge. The third stage of this, a 'very original adaptation of the Choragic Monument of Lysicrates, carried out in wood with a fluted column of iron at each angle, was originally finished with colour and gilding'.[1] And from this belvedere Beckford could view the Welsh mountains, the Severn Estuary, the Wiltshire Downs and the Mendips. There, after a hectic life, he found peace, and his body lies in a great granite sarcophagus. The 130-foot tower, though now incongruously mated to an adjacent concrete water-tower, is still a fine eye-catcher from all the western approaches to the city of Bath.

Samuel Johnson did not like contemporary park landscapes, yet was extremely sensitive to feelings animated by certain features of the Picturesque. His description of a visit to Hawkstone in Shropshire is the quintessence of one aspect of what Picturesque exponents sought for in reactions to scenes inspiring awe and terror. No other landscaping which Johnson saw on his journey into north Wales in 1774, even at Chatsworth, Kedleston, Hagley or the Leasowes, is dealt with by him in such detail as this at Hawkstone. Obviously the scene much impressed him, for he writes with even more emotion than when in the Highlands of Scotland. In fact, there is no prose passage in English which so reaches the sublime soul of the Picturesque.

We saw Hawkestone, the seat of Sir Rowland Hill, and were conducted by Miss Hill over a large tract of rocks and wood; a region abounding with striking scenes of terrifick grandeur. We were always on the brink of a precipice or at the foot of a lofty rock; but the steeps were seldom naked; in many places, oaks of uncommon magnitude shot up from the crannies of stone; and where there were not tall trees, there were underwoods and bushes. Round the rocks is a narrow path, cut upon the stone, which is frequently hewn into steps; but art has proceeded no further than to make the succession of wonders safely accessible. The whole circuit is somewhat laborious;[2] it is terminated by a grotto cut in the rock to a great extent with many windings and supported by pillars, not hewn into regularity,

---

[1] Walter Ison, *The Georgian Buildings of Bath* (London, 1948), p. 186.
[2] S. J., aged 64, was carrying much weight, and the weather was hot.

but such as imitate the sports of nature, by asperities and protuberances.

The place is not without any dampness and would afford a habitation not uncomfortable. There were from space to space, seats in the rock. Though it wants water it excels Dovedale, by the extent of its prospects, the awfulness of its shades, the horror of its precipices, the verdure of its hollows and the loftiness of its rocks. The Ideas which it forces upon the mind are the sublime, the dreadful and the vast. Above is inaccessible altitude, below is horrible profundity. But it excels the Garden of Ilam only in extent.

This refers to Ilam, on the Staffordshire side of Dovedale, a spot much beloved by Johnson; less wild than Hawkstone and therefore, according to Johnson, typified by Parnell's verse, rather than Milton's. It seems strange of him to compare two landscapes of obviously equal merit with two poets who are of unequal stature. Yet the gentle lyricism of Parnell, expressed in ingenious cadential variations of trochee and iamb, is a relief after much of the regularity of the typical couplets of his time. Although the melancholy of 'The Night-Piece on Death' and the horror of 'The Hermit' may be better known, 'The Hymn to Contentment' has a May-time, daylight serenity of which Johnson may have been thinking, and which is typical of much of Parnell's small output.

> Lovely, lasting peace, appear!
> This world itself, if thou art there,
> Is once again with Eden blest,
> And man contains it in his breast.
>
> 'Twas thus, as under shade I stood,
> I sung my wishes to the wood
> And lost in thought, no more perceiv'd
> The branches whisper as they wav'd:
> It seem'd as all the quiet place
> Confess'd the presence of the Grace.
>
> .   .   .   .   .
>
> Oh! by yonder mossy seat,
> In my hours of sweet retreat
> Might I thus my soul employ,
> With sense of solitude and joy.

Boswell describes Ilam,[1] as a

romantick scene . . . I recollect a very fine amphi-theatre surrounded with hills covered with wood and walks neatly formed along
the side of a rocky steep, on the quarter next the house with recesses
under projections of rock, overshadowed with trees in one of which
recesses, we were told, Congreve wrote his *Old Bachelor*.[2]

Johnson continues the comparison between this and Hawkstone:

Ilam has grandeur tempered with softness, the walker congratu-
lates his own arrival at the place, and is grieved to think that he must
ever leave it. As he looks up to the rocks his thoughts are elevated, as
he turns his eyes on the vallies he is composed and soothed.

He that mounts the precipices at Hawkestone, wonders how he
came hither and doubts how he shall return. His walk is an adventure,
and his departure an escape. He has not the tranquillity but the
horrour of solitude, a kind of turbulent pleasure between fright and
admiration.

Ilam is the fit abode of pastoral virtue and might properly diffuse
its shades over nymphs and swains. Hawkestone can have no fitter
inhabitants than giants of mighty bone and bold emprise,[3] men of
lawless courage and heroic violence. Hawkestone should be described
by Milton and Ilam by Parnell.

Miss Hill showed the whole succession of wonders with great
civility. The house was magnificent compared with the rank of the
owner.

The Hill family left Hawkestone in 1906. Since then the statue of
their ancestor, the first Protestant Lord Mayor of London, has
fallen from his 112-foot Tuscan column, presumably still holding
Magna Carta, which he had in his hand. He has not been replaced,
though his virtues were 'like the Prospect before us, East, West,
North and South, far surpassing all bounds'. The shell grotto is

---

[1] Boswell's *Life of Johnson*, Monday, 22 September 1777.

[2] 'Three places laid claim to the writing of "The Old Bachelor", but none has
sufficient evidence to support it.' Daniel Crane Taylor, *William Congreve* (London,
1931), p. 28.

[3] 'Giants of mightie Bone, and bould emprise.' 'Paradise Lost', Book XI, line 642,
is not entirely appropriate, as Archangel Michael points out to Adam that these
giants are the products of the 'ill-mated marriages', of a previous passage.

ruined and all its stained glass broken, though its opalescence remained until 1949. Yet the originator of the Penny Postage might still view with pleasure, from his Elysian Hill, the ruins of the impregnable Red Castle hewn from the sandstone crags, and the octagonal crenellated gazebo.

Whatever else the Picturesque movement achieved it certainly re-stressed visual qualities, with emotive associationist ideas; and, as Christopher Hussey in his great book has said, 'it was necessary in order to enable the imagination to form the habit of feeling through the eyes'. Thus the imagination of Coleridge in his nocturnal wandering in the ruins of Denbigh Castle or Wordsworth gazing over the water to the 'rugged pile of Niedpath' was stimulated by scenes such as the Picturesque landscapers reproduced in their own grounds. Their squabbles over aesthetic or philosophic details may now seem trifling, yet they were the culmination of a movement in landscaping which from the Restoration on had literally put on the ground the ideas of Shaftesbury, Pope, and Burke, by taking English landscaping nearer to Nature in the fundamental treatment of earth, water, and trees.

Wordsworth's frantic question: 'Is there no nook of English ground secure From rash assault?' is more relevant today than in 1803. Soon it may be impossible to visualize many of those scenes created by a great succession of landscapers from Switzer to Price; scenes which have inspired, from 1660 to 1840, some of the best of English poetry and prose. And despite many variations of the theme, the philosophy and aesthetics from which these scenes are derived are the ground-base of a very special English contribution to the art of living, played by the 'three new graces, Poetry, Painting and Gardening'.

Bibliography

Addison, Rt. Hon. Joseph, *Remarks on several parts of Italy. 1701–3*, London, 1705.

Akenside, Mark, *The Pleasures of Imagination*, London, 1744.

Alison, the Rev. Archibald, *Essays on the Nature and Principles of Taste*, Edinburgh, 1790.

Amherst, the Hon. Alicia, *A History of Gardening in England*, London, 1895.

Attiret, le Frère Jean Denis, *A Particular Account of the Emperor of China's Gardens near Pekin*, trans. Sir Harry Beaumont, London, 1752.

Austen, Jane, *The Novels*, ed. R. W. Chapman, Oxford, 1923.

Bacon, Francis, Viscount St. Albans, *Of Gardens*, London, 1625.

Badeslade, Thomas, *Thirty-six Views of Noblemen's and Gentlemen's Seats*, London, 1720.

Baillie, John, *An Essay on the Sublime*, London, 1747.

Bate, W. J., *From Classic to Romantic: Premises of Taste*, Harvard, 1946.

Beeverele, James, *Les Délices de la Grande Bretagne*, Leiden, 1707.

Bickley, Francis L., *Life of Matthew Prior*, London, 1914.

Blair, Dr. Hugh, *Lectures on Rhetoric and Belles Lettres*, London, 1783.

Blair, the Rev. Robert, *The Grave*, London, 1743.

Boileau-Despreaux, Nicholas, *Le Lutrin*, Lyons, 1862.

Boswell, James, *Life of Johnson*, Oxford, 1940.

Bradley, Richard, *New Improvements of Planting and Gardening*, London, 1717.

Brayley, Edward, and Britton, John, *Beauties of England and Wales*, London, 1801–15.

Britton, John, *The Beauties of Wiltshire*, London, 1801.

Brockman, H. A. N., *The Caliph of Fonthill*, London, 1956.

Browne, Sir Thomas, *The Garden of Cyrus*, London, 1658.

Burke, Rt. Hon. Edmund, *A Philosophical Enquiry into the Origin of our Ideas of the Sublime and Beautiful*, London, 1757.

Byng, John Viscount Torrington, *The Torrington Diaries*, ed. C. B. Andrewes, London, 1934–8.

Cambridge, Richard Owen, *Works*, London, 1803.

Campbell, Colen, *Vitruvius Britannicus*, London, 1717–25.

Chambers, Sir William, *Designs of Chinese Buildings, Furniture, Dresses, Machines, and Utensils. Engraved by the best hands, from the originals drawn in China. . . . To which is annexed, a Description of their temples, houses, gardens etc.*, London, 1757.
A Dissertation on Oriental Gardening, London, 1772.

Charageat, Marguerite, *L'Art des Jardins*, Paris, 1933.

Chase, Isabel W., *Horace Walpole: Gardenist*, Princeton, 1943.

Clark, H. Frank, *The English Landscape Garden*, London, 1948.

Clark, Sir Kenneth, *Landscape into Art*, London, 1946.

Cobbett, the Rev. Richard, *Memorials of Twickenham*, London, 1872.

Cobbett, William, *Rural Rides*, ed. G. D. H. Cole and M. Cole, London, 1930.

Colman, George the elder, and Garrick, David, *The Clandestine Marriage*, London, 1766.

Combe, William, *The Tours of Doctor Syntax*, London, 1812–21.

Cowper, William, *Poems*, ed. H. S. Milford, Oxford, 1934.

Craig, William M., *Essay on the Study of Nature in drawing Landscape*, London, 1793.

Dallaway, the Rev. James, *Anecdotes of the Arts in England*, London, 1800.

de Caus, Isaac, *New and rare Inventions of Water-works*, trans. John Leake, London, 1659.

Defoe, Daniel, *A Tour thro' the Whole Island of Great Britain*, ed. G. D. H. Cole, London, 1927.

Delany, Mrs. Mary, *The Autobiography and Correspondence*, ed. Lady Llanover, London, 1862.

de La Quintinie, *The Compleat Gard'ner*, abridged by George London and Henry Wise, London, 1699.

de La Rochefoucauld, François, *Mélanges sur l'Angleterre*, trans. S. C. Roberts, Cambridge, 1933.

Delille, Jacques, *Les Jardins*, Paris, 1782.

Denham, Sir John, *Cooper's Hill*, London, 1642.

Dennis, John, *The Critical Works*, ed. E. N. Hooker, Baltimore, 1939.

Derrick, Samuel, *Letters written from Leverpole, Chester, Corke etc.*, Dublin, 1767.

Dézallier d'Argenville, A. J., *La Théorie et la practique de jardinage*, trans. John James, London, 1712.

Dobson, Austin, *At Prior Park & other papers*, London, 1912.

Dodington, Bubb, Lord Melcombe, *Diary*, ed. H. P. L. Wyndham, London, 1784.

Dodsley, Robert & James, *London and its Environs described*, London, 1761.

Dudden, F. Homes, *Henry Fielding*, Oxford, 1952.

Dyer, John, *Grongar Hill*, ed. R. C. Boys, Baltimore, 1941.

Evelyn, John, *Diary*, ed. E. S. de Beer, Oxford, 1955.

Sylva, London, 1664.

Farington, Joseph, *Diary*, ed. James Grieg, London, 1928.

Felton, Samuel, *Gleanings on Gardens*, London, 1829.

Fiennes, Celia, *The Journeys of Celia Fiennes*, ed. Christopher Morris, London, 1949.

Fouquier, Marcel, *De l'Art des jardins*, Paris, 1911.

Gerard, Alexander, *An Essay on Taste*, Edinburgh, 1759.

Gibson, John, *Several Gardens near London*, London, 1691.

Gilbert, Katherine, and Kuhn, Helmut, *A History of Esthetics*, New York, 1939.

Anon [Gilpin, William], *A Dialogue upon the Gardens . . . at Stow*, London, 1748.

Gilpin, William, *Three Essays: On Picturesque Beauty, On Picturesque Travel, On Sketching Landscape*, London, 1792.

Observations on the river Wye and several parts of South Wales, London, 1782.

Observations on the Western parts of England, London, 1798.

Remarks on Forest Scenery, London, 1791.

Gilpin, William Sawrey, *Practical Hints upon Landscape Gardening*, London, 1832.

Girardin, René-Louis, marquis de, *De la composition des paysages*, Paris, 1777.

Goldsmith, Oliver, *History of a Poet's Garden*, *Westminster Magazine*, London, 1773.

The Citizen of the World, London, 1773.

Gothein, Marie Luise, *A History of Garden Art*, trans. Mrs. Archer-Hind, London, 1928.

Granger, James, *A Biographical History of England*, London, 1806.

Graves, The Rev. Richard, *The Spiritual Quixote*, London, 1773.

Columella, London, 1779.

Recollections of some particulars in the life of the late William Shenstone, London, 1788.

Gray, Thomas, *Correspondence*, ed. Paget Toynbee and Leonard Whibley, Oxford, 1935.

Green, David B., *Gardener to Queen Anne*, London, 1956.
  Blenheim Palace, London, 1951.
Green, Matthew, *The Grotto*, London, 1732.
  The Spleen, London, 1737.
Grosley, Pierre J., *Londres et les Anglais*, Paris, 1770.
Hadfield, Miles, *Pioneers in Gardening*, London, 1955.
  Gardening in Britain, London, 1960.
Halfpenny, William and John, *The Country Gentleman's pocket companion*,
  London, 1753.
  New designs for Chinese temples, London, 1750.
Hanmer, Sir Thomas, *The Garden Book*, ed. E. S. Rohde, London, 1933.
Hartley, David, *Observations on Man*, London, 1749.
Hazlitt, William, *Table Talk*, London, 1822.
Hazlitt, William Carew, *Gleanings in Old Garden Literature*, London,
  1887.
Heely, Joseph, *Letters on the Beauties of Hagley, Envil and the Leasowes*,
  London, 1777.
Henn, Thomas R., *Longinus and English Criticism*, Cambridge, 1934.
Herring, Dr. Thomas, *Letters to William Duncombe, 1728-57*, London,
  1777.
Hipple, Walter, *The Beautiful, the Sublime and the Picturesque, in 18th
  century British Aesthetic Theory*, New York, 1957.
Hirschfeld, Christian, *Theorie der Gartenkunst*, Leipzig, 1775.
Hogarth, William, *The Analysis of Beauty*, London, 1753.
Home, Henry, (Lord Kames), *Elements of Criticism*, Edinburgh, 1762.
Huet, Pierre, *The Weakness of Human Understanding*, trans. E. Combe,
  London, 1725.
Hume, David, *Essays, Moral and Political*, London, 1741.
Hurd, the Rev. Richard, *Moral and Political Dialogues*, London, 1759.
Hussey, Christopher, *The Picturesque*, London, 1927.
Hutcheson, Francis, *An Inquiry into the Original of our Ideas of Beauty
  and Virtue*, London, 1726.
Hutchinson, William, *An Excursion to the Lakes*, London, 1774.
Ibbetson, Julius C., *A picturesque guide to Bath, Bristol*, London, 1793.
Ireland, Samuel, *Picturesque views on the River Thames*, London, 1792.
James, John, *The Theory and Practice of Gardening* (trans. Le Blond),
  1728.
Jellicoe, George A., *Gardens of Europe*, London, 1937.
Johnson, George W., *A History of English Gardening*, London, 1829.
Johnson, Samuel, *Works*, London, 1787.

Jourdain, Margaret, *The Work of William Kent*, London, 1948.

Kalm, Pehr, *Account of his visit to England in 1748*, trans. Joseph Lucas, London, 1892.

Kennedy, Ruth W., *The Renaissance Painter's Garden*, New York, 1938.

Kimball, Sidney Fiske, *The Creation of the Rococo*, Pennsylvania, 1943.

Knight, Richard Payne, *The Landscape*, London, 1794.

× 　*An analytical inquiry into the principles of taste*, London, 1805.

Knyff, Leonard, and Kip, Jan, *Britannia Illustrata*, 1708–20.

Langley, Batty, *New Principles of Gardening*, London, 1728.×

⇒ Langley, Batty and Thomas, *Gothic Architecture*, London, 1747.

Lassels, Richard, *The Voyage of Italy*, Paris, 1670.

Leland, John, *The Itinerary*, Oxford, 1710–12.

Le Rouge, George Louis, *Détails de nouveaux Jardins à la mode*, Paris, 1776–87.

× Lewis, Matthew G., *The Monk*, London, 1796.

London, George, and Wise, Henry, *The Retir'd Gard'ner* (abridgement from Louis Liger), London, 1706.

Longinus, *On the Sublime*, trans. William Hamilton Fyfe, London, 1927.

Loudon, John C., *Observations on the formation and management of useful and ornamental plantations*, Edinburgh, 1804.

　A Treatise on forming, improving, and managing Country Residences, London, 1806.

Loveday, John, *Diary of a Tour in 1732*, London, 1890.

Lysons, Daniel, *The Environs of London*, London, 1792–96.

Macky, John, *A Journey through England*, London, 1714.

McKillop, Alan D., *The Background of Thomson's Seasons*, Minneapolis, 1942.

Manwaring, Elizabeth, *Italian Landscape in Eighteenth Century England*, New York, 1925.

Marshall, William, *Review of an Essay on the Picturesque*, 1795.

Martyn, Thomas, *The English Connoisseur*, London, 1766.

Mason, George, *An Essay on Design in Gardening*, London, 1768.

Mason, William, *The English Garden*, London, 1772–79.

　An Heroic Epistle to Sir William Chambers, 1757, ed. Paget Toynbee, London, 1926.

Mathias, Thomas J., *The Pursuits of Literature*, London, 1794.

Mead, William E., *The Grand Tour in the Eighteenth Century*, New York, 1914.

Meager, Leonard, *The New Art of Gardening*, London, 1697.

Meissonier, J. A., *Livre d'Ornements en 30 pièces*, Paris, 1734.

Miller, Hugh, *First Impressions of England and her People*, London, 1847.

Miller, Philip, *The Gardener's Dictionary*, London, 1731–39.

Milne, James Lees-, *Earls of Creation*, London, 1962.

Milner, Henry E., *The Art and Practice of Landscape Gardening*, London, 1890.

Milton, John, *Works*, New York, 1931.

Mollet, André, *Le Jardin de Plaisir*, Stockholm, 1651.

Monk, Samuel Holt, *The Sublime*, New York, 1935.

Montagu, Elizabeth, *Her Correspondence*, ed. E. J. Climenson, London, 1906.

More, Hannah, *Letters*, Selected by R. B. Johnson, London, 1925.

Morris, Richard, *Essays on Landscape Gardening*, London, 1825.

Neale, John P., *Views of the Seats of Noblemen and Gentlemen*, London, 1824.

Nussey, Helen G., *London Gardens of the Past*, London, 1939.

Ogden, Henry and Margaret, *English Taste in Landscape in the Seventeenth Century*, Michigan, 1955.

Opie, John, *Lectures on Painting*, London, 1809.

Page, Russell, *The Education of a Gardener*, London, 1962.

Patching, Resta, *Four Topographical Letters*, Newcastle upon Tyne, 1757.

Peacock, Thomas Love, *Headlong Hall*, London, 1816.

Pepys, Samuel, *Diary*, ed. Guy Pococke, London, 1948.

Plaw, John, *Ferme Ornée*, London, 1795.

Pococke, the Rev. Richard, *Travels thro' England*, ed. J. J. Cartwright, London, 1888.

Poe, Edgar A., *The Domain of Arnheim, Poems, Essays*, London, 1955.

Pomfret, John, *The Choice or Wish*, Edinburgh, 1699.

Pontey, William, *The Rural Improver*, London, 1822.

Pope, Alexander, *Poetical Works*, ed. John Butt, London, 1963.

Powys, Mrs. Philip Lybbe, (Caroline), *Passages from the Diaries*, ed. E. J. Climenson, London, 1899.

Price, Sir Uvedale, *An Essay on the Picturesque*, London, 1794–98.
  A Dialogue on the distinct characters of the Picturesque and the Beautiful, Hereford, 1801.

Prior, Matthew, *Poetical Works*, ed. R. B. Johnson, London, 1907.

Pückler-Muskau, Prince Hermann, *Andeutungen über der Landschaftsgärtnerei*, Stuttgart, 1834.

Radcliffe, Mrs. Ann, *The Mysteries of Udolpho*, London, 1794.

Rapin, René, *Of Gardens*, trans. John Evelyn, London, 1673.

Ray, John, *Catalogus Plantarum Angliae*, Londini, 1670.

Redding, Cyrus, *Memoirs of William Beckford*, London, 1859.

Repton, Humphry, *Sketches and Hints on Landscape Gardening*, London, 1794.
> *Observations on the theory and practice of Landscape Gardening*, London, 1803.
> *An Enquiry into the changes of taste in Landscape Gardening*, London, 1806.

Riat, Georges, *L'Art des Jardins*, Paris, 1900.

Robinson, William, *Garden Design and Architects' Gardens*, London, 1892.

Rousseau, Jean Jacques, *La Nouvelle Héloise*, Paris, 1759.

Salmon, Dr. William, *Polygraphice*, London, 1681.

Sands, Mollie, *The Gardens of Hampton Court*, London, 1950.

Scott, Sir Walter, *Quentin Durward*, Edinburgh, 1823.
> *The Quarterly Review*, Vol. 21. 1828, On Landscape Gardening.

Serle, John, *A Plan of Mr. Pope's Garden*, London, 1745.

Shaftesbury, Ashley Cooper, 3rd Earl of, *Characteristicks*, London, 1711.

Shebbeare, John, *Letters to the People of England*, London, 1756.

Shenstone, William, *Unconnected Thoughts on Gardening*, London, 1765.
> *Shenstone's Miscellany, 1759–63*, ed. I. A. Gordon, Oxford, 1952.

Sieveking, Forbes A., *The Praise of Gardens*, London, 1885.

Siren, Osvald, *China and the Gardens of Europe of the Eighteenth Century*, New York, 1950.

Sitwell, Edith, *Alexander Pope*, London, 1930.

Sitwell, Sir George, *Essay on the Making of Gardens*, London, 1909.

Smith, John Thomas, *Remarks on rural scenery*, London, 1797.

Somerville, William, *The Chace*, London, 1735.

Spence, Joseph, *Anecdotes, observations and characters of books and men, collected from the conversation of Mr. Pope and other eminent persons of his time*, London, 1820.

Steegman, John, *The Rule of Taste from George I to George IV*, London, 1934.

Steuart, Sir Henry, *The Planter's Guide*, Edinburgh, 1828.

Storer, James S., *A Description of Fonthill Abbey*, 1812.

Stroud, Dorothy, *Capability Brown*, London, 1950.
> *Humphry Repton*, London, 1962.

Stukeley, William, *Itinerarium curiosum*, London, 1724.

Switzer, Stephen, *Ichnographia*, London, 1718.

Temple, Sir William, *Works*, London, 1720.

Templeman, William D., *The Life and Work of William Gilpin, 1724–1804,* Illinois, 1939.

Thomson, James, *Poetical Works,* ed. J. L. Robertson, Oxford, 1951.

Thrale, Mrs. Hester, *Thraliana,* ed. K. G. Balderston, Oxford, 1942.

Dr. Johnson's Tour in Wales, ed. A. M. Broadley, London, 1910.

Autobiography, Letters, ed. A. Hayward, London, 1861.

Tinker, Chauncey B., *Painter and Poet,* Cambridge, Mass., 1938.

Vanbrugh, Sir John, *Complete Works,* ed. Geoffrey F. Webb, London, 1927.

Van der Groen, Jan, *Den Nederlantsten Hovenier,* Amsterdam, 1688.

Von Erdberg, Eleanor, *Chinese Influence on European Garden Structures,* ed. B. W. Pond, Cambridge, Mass., 1936.

Walpole, Horace, *Letters,* ed. Mrs. P. Toynbee, Oxford, 1903–25.

Essay on Modern Gardening, London, 1785.

The Castle of Otranto, London, 1765.

Journals of Visits to Country Seats, The Walpole Society, Vol. 16, 1928.

Warton, Joseph, *An Essay on the Writing and Genius of Pope,* London, 1756.

The Enthusiast; or the Lover of Nature, London, 1744.

Odes on various subjects, London, 1746.

Warner, the Rev. Richard, *Excursions from Bath,* Bath, 1801.

Watelet, Claude, *Essai sur les jardins,* Paris, 1774.

Whately, Thomas, *Observations on Modern Gardening,* 1770.

Whistler, Laurence, *Sir John Vanbrugh,* London, 1938.

Wilkinson, John G., *On colour and on the necessity for a general diffusion of taste among all classes. With general remarks on laying out . . . geometrical gardens,* London, 1858.

Withers, William, *A Letter to Sir Walter Scott, Bart.,* London, 1828.

Wordsworth, William, *The Letters of William and Dorothy Wordsworth,* ed. Ernest de Selincourt, Oxford, 1935.

Worlidge, John, *Systema horticulturae,* London, 1677.

Wren, Christopher (jun.), *Parentalia,* London, 1750.

Wrighte, William, *Grotesque Architecture,* London, 1767.

Young, Arthur, *Six Weeks' Tour through the Southern Counties,* London, 1768.

Six Months' Tour through the North of England, London, 1770.

Young, Edward, *The Complaint, or Night Thoughts,* London, 1742.

Index